Foreword

Mary Davis

For decades, psychoanalysts have understood that working with the mother-infant dyad can have profound effects on the long-term psychological health of the developing child. Selma Fraiberg and her colleagues helped us to understand the ways in which the parents' internal psychic world affects the child's developing internal psychic world, as the "ghosts in the nursery" shape parental interactions with the child and thus shape the child's developing representations of those significant others.

In more recent years, there has been an increasing focus on the specific nature of the parent-child relationship, and the ways in which the nature of that relationship can either help or hinder the child's overall psychological and emotional development. Attachment theory has offered the concept of a secure attachment (and various categories of insecure attachments). Secure attachments, we know, promote the formation as the child grows of a more integrated internal world, with enhanced capacities to relate to others and to function effectively in the external interpersonal world. Children with insecure attachments are more likely to be diagnosed with behavioral disorders such as oppositional defiant disorder or conduct disorder; they are more likely to have significant difficulties with affect regulation (Feeney); and they may have problems with attention and cognitive functioning (Gillath). In her individual case histories in this book, Ann Smolen clearly illustrates both the ways in which insecure attachment interferes with development, and the ways in which fostering a more secure attachment with mother and others can help the child developmentally.

In a previous volume in this Vulnerable Child Series, Regina Pally and her colleagues reported on their own work in "reflective parenting," and the enormous value of helping parents to learn to "mentalize" and to understand the internal emotional world of their children (Etezady & Davis, 2012). Psychoanalytic observations and theories about mentalization and attachment, and the ways in which the developing ego uses the early attachments, have influenced our current work with children at risk for later behavioral or psychological problems.

Homeless parents have particular challenges in providing a stable, secure environment for their children that can foster a secure attachment with all its implications for later life. These parents themselves almost always have a chaotic life, filled with trauma and dislocation, and themselves often had insecure attachments as children. They may be suffering from the effects of severe trauma, may have problems with affect regulation, and often have difficulties with attachment and interpersonal intimacy. The struggles to provide for the physical needs of their children, in the absence of a stable home, complicate their efforts to provide for the emotional needs of their children, when their own physical and emotional needs are not being met.

When she reported her research at the Vulnerable Child Discussion Group at the American Psychoanalytic Association, Dr. Smolen provided a moving description of her work with five of these mothers, and her efforts to study patterns of attachment in this population. In this book she expands that discussion, and also shares with us how she came to be interested in these questions, through her work individually with residents of a homeless shelter. She suggests that what was originally designed as a research study failed to achieve clear results. But she succeeded in providing a clear description of what these mothers struggle with, and examples of ways to work with these mothers which can be profoundly helpful. As she worked to help these women imagine what their babies might be thinking or feeling—to "mentalize"—she also helped them to reflect on their own inner world, their past histories of trauma, and the ways in which their own histories affected their ways of functioning in the world. As they were able to think about themselves, rather than acting out their conflict-filled feelings about the children, they began to be able to react differently, and to provide more effective "holding environments" for their children. This in turn helped the children to learn to manage their own affective lives in more appropriate and positive ways, and to use the parent-child relationship for their psychological and emotional growth.

As Dr. Smolen tells us, there is an enormous lack of appropriate and helpful programs for these parents. Children who live in chaotic environments, without the opportunity to develop secure attachments and all the later psychological developments which depend on secure attachments, are at enormous risk for developmental distortions, delays, and arrests, and for later psychopathology. Children of the homeless are the most vulnerable of vulnerable children in our society.

Parenting work with parents who can come to clinics, and who can find funding for work in clinic-based programs, is of course important. But parents who cannot come to clinics because they have no transportation, or do not know about the resources for help, or have no way to pay for the help, are too often lost to our efforts. Psychoanalytic insights, and the changes they can make in daily functioning, offer a way to move out of the snares of poverty and dysfunction, and to break the cycle of trauma, chaos, and homelessness. We know that psychoanalytic insights can be helpful for individuals and for groups. Dr. Smolen, in her work here, offers us a way to think about how society can use psychoanalytic insights with families, to help the poverty-stricken and homeless children who so often become poverty-stricken and homeless adults. As we help these children to be less vulnerable, they have opportunities to thrive and to eventually offer homes and secure attachments in turn for their own children. Intergenerational patterns of dysfunction can be interrupted and redirected, and Dr. Smolen's work offers one way to approach that goal.

REFERENCES

Etezady, M. H., & Davis, M. (Eds.). (2012). *Keeping your child's mind in mind: Perspectives on reflective parenting.* Lanham, MD: Jason Aronson.

Feeney, J. A. (2000). Implications of attachment style for patterns of health and illness. *Child: Care, Health and Development, 26*(4), 277–288.

Fraiberg, S., Adelson, E., and Shapiro, V. (1975). Ghosts in the nursery: A psychoanalytic approach to the problems of impaired infant-mother relationships. *Journal of the American Academy of Child Psychiatry, 14,* 387–421.

Gillath, O., Giesbrecht, B., and Shaver, P. R. (2009). Attachment, attention, and cognitive control: Attachment style and performance on general attention tasks. *Journal of Experimental Social Psychology, 45*(4), 647–654.

Introduction

Mothers with young children are the fastest growing segment of the homeless population. When there is chronic stress as a result of extreme poverty and racism, how do families stay functional and cope? What happens when family structure breaks down, leaving young, single mothers alone to care for these children? What happens to parenting skills when the mother is poor, homeless, and isolated from family and community support? The combined stress of extreme poverty and homelessness can greatly impair the ability of single mothers to parent their children effectively. A history of poor attachments and abusive relationships added to the chronic stress of poverty and homelessness may cause the mother to feel powerless and inadequate.

It has been documented that infants whose mothers are unable to provide comfort and protection, and who do not foster an interest in the world, form insecure attachments and are often unable to self-regulate. Greenspan states that these babies show increased tendencies toward muscle rigidity, gaze aversion, and disorganized sleep and eating patterns (Greenspan, 1990). Moreover, the homeless mother is preoccupied with daily, and sometimes hourly, survival. The homeless infant may be overwhelmed, and sleep, as a primitive defense, brings peace from an overstimulating and abusive environment (Koplow, 1996).

The mother without a home is unable to provide an intimate environment wherein the infant may experience her as provider and protector. This mother often feels helpless and inadequate in her ability to care for her child in terms of the most basic provision of shelter. Because she herself is totally dependent on others for survival she may defensively detach from her child's dependency needs (Koplow, 1996). Opening herself to her infant's emotional needs would require her to become reacquainted with painful experiences in the present and the past. If her experience was one of rejection and neglect it is much too painful and dangerous to *feel* in the absence of family and home. Karen states: "when one becomes a parent, unresolved pain is shaken loose, the defensive wall is breached and new defensive efforts are required" (Karen, 1998, p. 374). When a homeless mother gazes at her child, her own pain and sadness is mirrored back. Unable to bear her own painful feelings, the mother is also unable to feel empathy for her child's plight. Her new defense is to distance herself from her child. The mother's own depression and powerlessness become overwhelming.

This book tells the story of how psychoanalytic psychotherapy and psychoanalysis, and psychoanalytically informed research, may promote the understanding of attachment behaviors and their meanings. This allows us to help homeless mothers and children form healthier relationships, with the goal of confronting trauma and beginning the healing process. Many of the stories told here about these families are profoundly sad and difficult to read and some do not have happy endings, while others are more successful. All of the life stories demonstrate the inner lives of homeless mothers and their children as they struggle to cope with complicated and problematic external realities as well as internal conflicts and traumatic memoires.

The first half of this book consists of five case studies of individual psychoanalytic psychotherapy; four are work with very young children, the fifth is with a teen mother. I undertook this work early in my professional career. These profound experiences propelled me to return to the homeless shelter years later to conduct a research study focusing on the use of psychoanalytic interventions to understand attachment behaviors in homeless mothers and children. It was this early work that convinced me of the need to work with the mother/infant dyad and to give *voice* to silenced and marginalized women. The second half of this book describes the research project.

Chapter One

Sara

Sara spent her first four years of life in homelessness. Her mother (Esther) spent the first two years of motherhood pushing Sara in a stroller by day in search of a warm, safe place to sleep at night. Esther's own history is one of severe poverty, physical abuse, domestic violence, neglect and ultimately abandonment. Her mother was neglectful of her as a child, and then was murdered when Esther was a young teenager. In Esther's narrative, she is called *stupid* and *retarded* as far back as she can remember. She carries the labels *Developmentally Delayed* and *Cognitively Limited*. Esther tells of physical abuse at the hands of her father and was literally thrown out of her father's house by his girlfriend when Sara was one month old. As Esther sat in my office telling me "facts" about her past, without visible emotion, she experienced a vivid memory. She became agitated and recalled: "It was January, I remember. It was January and cold [she shivers]. She put me and the baby out. I was standing on the porch with no place to go. It was night too and really cold." Esther looked at me (one of the few moments where she was able to maintain eye contact) in disbelief.

It was easy to imagine Esther taking off down the city streets with Sara in tow, walking quickly and with purpose. I imagine she is trying her best simultaneously to walk away from her abusive past and painful memories and walk toward a better, safer place. For two years Esther and Sara lived on the street. There was a kindly old grandfather, who offered his couch many a night, but he died; then there was nobody. When Sara was two, Esther had another baby girl. Esther was no longer able to survive on the streets with two babies. Only then did this young family enter the shelter system. I first met this young family when Sara was 27 months old, as they had come to live at our shelter.

Sara was recommended for individual therapy because the daycare and clinical staff were concerned that the mother/child relationship was poor. Staff members observed that Esther seemed not to "see" her daughter and was unaware of the child's emotional needs.

During our first session I was struck by Sara's profound sadness. Though painfully shy, she left her daycare room with me easily. It is important to note that I was a complete stranger to Sara, and she left her daycare with me without any visible anxiety or emotion. When children have not been able to develop a secure attachment in infancy they often feel little or no distress or anxiety when separation or loss of love is threatened (Freud, 1965, p. 122).

Sara presented developmentally as a 12-to-18-month-old baby. Her vocabulary consisted of fewer than 20 words. She seemed unaware of her own body in space; her movements were stiff and awkward. She did not notice obstacles and would trip over small toys. She stiffened when touched, and it was reported by daycare staff that she would not allow other children to touch her. She cried and fought staff when they changed her diaper. For the most part, her affect was flat and she did not make eye contact.

My first goal with Sara was to foster her ability to form an attachment and connect with me. I began to see her three times per week. Thus the most exhausting, heart-wrenching, yet beautiful and rewarding relationship began to develop between Sara and myself.

Our work began on the most primitive, preverbal level. I slowly began to connect with her through body movements, facial gestures, and responses and shared posture. For example, Sara discovered the sink in my office and began to pour the water in and out of a baby bottle. As she did this she made noises and I joined her, using similar inflections in my voice, as I mirrored her facial expressions. This was the first time she made eye contact with me.

In another early session Sara found the baby lotion on my shelf and gestured for me to help pour some on her hands. She took the lotion and gingerly rubbed it into my cheek while maintaining deep eye contact. I asked her if I could put some lotion on her and began to rub some on her arm. Her affect changed from serious exploration to deep sadness and she became immobilized. I said to her in a very sad voice: "You are feeling so sad." She nodded her head "yes" and two tears rolled down her cheek. Through this interaction I was able to validate Sara's feelings and at the same time allow her to view herself. Winnicott relates a vignette about a little girl who sat on his knee, bit his knuckles, cried, and played a game of throwing spatulas. He explained that while playing a game of throwing spatulas from his lap she was able to express hostile aggression and great sadness (Winnicott, 1996). Just as Winnicott's little patient was able to express her sadness through play with spatulas, Sara was able to express her sadness while playing with the baby lotion.

Our play with the baby lotion touched a very deep place in Sara. Her longing to be touched was immeasurable. Her lack of physical and emotional proximity with her mother was overwhelming, causing her to feel profound sadness.

Sara's play was mechanical and joyless and possessed an emptiness, which kept others at a distance. However, she included me in her play, and it was through her play that I was able to engage Sara on an affective level. In these early sessions she would feed a baby doll a bottle, empty out the dollhouse and hand me all of the objects, or hold on to one end of a Slinky and place the other end in my hand. She played in silence and I provided the narrative. "You are feeding your baby milk in her bottle" or "You want me to hold all of the people in this dollhouse" or "You want me to play Slinky with you."

Over the next several weeks she began to mimic me, verbally stringing together three to five words together in sentences. Her sense of her own body seemed to improve. She no longer lost her balance as easily and was better able to navigate her surroundings. She began to laugh and sustain short periods of eye contact without experiencing overwhelming anxiety. Perhaps most important, but painful, Sara began to feel deeply. She now was capable of expressing both hostile aggression and great sadness. In her play with dollhouse figures she began to act out aggressively toward the mother doll, hitting her on the head with the little girl doll, and finally stomping on the mother doll's head. She played a similar game with a stuffed squirrel family, always attacking the mother figure.

In one particular session I elicited a game of peekaboo that fascinated Sara and captivated her attention as she maintained deep eye contact, but this game also caused her to feel intensely sad. At first I found it extremely difficult to maintain the engagement when the therapy elicited these affects. For example, if Sara became profoundly sad in a session, I felt the need to make it all better for her, to make the bad feelings go away. I needed to be able to "hold" Sara in whatever she was feeling in the moment. It was my job to validate her feelings and show her that both she and I could survive them.

The following vignette illustrates the importance of play in the therapeutic relationship and how Sara was able to use play to communicate with me while fighting a deep depression. This vignette also illustrates the strength and meaning of attachment. This session was pivotal in our work and demonstrates how after a weekend absence, Sara felt abandoned and rejected by me.

When I went to daycare to retrieve Sara for our session I found her in a dissociated state. Daycare staff reported that she had been in this condition when her mother brought her in. She was mute, unable to walk, and did not respond when spoken to. When I picked her up to carry her to my office her body was stiff, but she offered no resistance. Once in my office she made an attempt to play by feeding a bottle to the baby doll but was unable to do this as the bottle fell from her hand. I felt at a loss and did not know what to do. I instinctively picked her up and began to pace and sing to her as if she were an infant. Slowly her body began to relax and she molded to my body and fell asleep. I sat down in my chair and, as she slept, I wondered what had happened to this little girl and how I possibly could help her. We sat still for 30 minutes. I hoped she had a high fever, for that would explain the behavior, but I knew that she was not physically ill. However my need to make her well was very powerful, so I covered her with my coat and headed back outside, across the street, and back to daycare to take her temperature. Her teacher inserted the thermometer under her arm as she slept in my arms, and of course it registered normal. As I spoke with her teachers, trying to discern if there had been some abuse of some sort, she awoke. I did not realize she was awake because she remained motionless; her teachers informed me that her eyes were open. We decided that perhaps she would want to lie on her cot, so her teacher got out her cot and I sat on the floor with Sara still motionless in my arms. She was unable to move from me. I began to talk to her very slowly and quietly, telling her how sad she was and how hard it is to feel so sad. I held her in my arms and we rocked together as I sang a lullaby. At this point the teacher came over and asked Sara if she would like to join her class in a project. Her barely audible "no" let me know she was beginning to feel safe enough to come back. I asked her if she would like to return to my office and she nodded her head "yes."

Once back in my office I continued to sing and speak softly to her. She lay in my arms like an infant at the breast and began to explore my face. She gazed into my eyes as her fingers explored my lips. I responded to her as if she were an infant. As I continued to verbalize her sadness she slowly became able to move from me physically and began to communicate with me through her play. She handed me the toy phone. When I asked with whom I should speak, her answer was unintelligible, so I asked her if she wanted me to call her. She nodded her head "yes." I began: "Hello Sara, you were so sad this morning that you couldn't even talk, and you couldn't even walk. But now you are beginning to feel better and we are having a safe time together."

She returned to her continuing drama using the squirrel family. This time the mommy squirrel held the baby and did not hold the big sister. The sister became very angry and began to hit the mommy on the head. She gathered up the whole family; the mommy, baby, and sister, and threw them into my lap. I responded: "You are throwing them all at me and now I have the whole family and I can hold them in my arms." Sara had communicated how rejected she felt by my weekend absence, and her sibling rivalry. After this conversation she came very close to me where I was sitting on the floor and she took my hair and covered my face. I said: "Where did I go? I have disappeared!" I could see her face through my hair and she became very frightened. I moved my hair away from my face and exclaimed that I was back, but that I could see how sad she had become when she thought I had gone away. She was then able to repeat this several times—both covering me up and bringing me back. As she did this she maintained eye contact. This interaction was not a happy, funny peekaboo game, but rather a very serious use of play.

This session lasted just under three hours. Just as we were leaving my office, Sara deliberately plucked a handful of tissues from a box near my desk. As we walked back to daycare she was able to talk with me and notice her environment. She opened her daycare door and looked back over her shoulder at me as if to give me one last look before I left her again. I watched her from the window as she rejoined her class, seated around a table to paste and paint Thanksgiving turkeys. She clutched the tissues tightly in her hand as she sat among the other children, struggling not to dissociate once again. I was shaken. I had never experienced such profound sadness in another human being.

That afternoon I met with Esther in an effort to discover some hidden abuse or mysterious illness that would cause Sara to dissociate. When I began my session with Esther I was aware of my anger toward her for not protecting her child from such intolerable pain. These feelings quickly vanished as I felt that Esther, too, was like a small child crying out for connection and love. It was obvious that Esther did not abuse her daughter; she was even unaware that Sara was in this state. Her lack of empathy for Sara was startling. Sara seemed invisible to her.

For the next several sessions I helped Sara to internalize my image by providing her with Polaroid pictures and making little transitional objects during her session that she could keep with her the rest of the day. I pretended to take her picture with an imaginary camera and told her I was taking her picture to keep in my head so I could think of her. I then suggested that she take my picture to put in her head.

Sara continued to make progress in her ability to form attachments and in so doing began to rapidly catch up in her development. Every session I made sure a Polaroid snapshot of Sara was on my desk. Each session she would pick it up and I would ask her who it is. She always answered "Mommy." I made a joke out of it, and while we laughed I would tell her that it is not her mommy and she would laugh but continue to tell me that it was a picture of her mom. Six months into our work together she picked up the picture and proudly said her own name. Around the same time she began to use pronouns in her speech. Sara also began to use the word *no* a lot. She seemed to feel power in that little word and it was wonderful to see her begin to gain autonomy. A few months later she became interested in toilet training and we spent session after session making clay "poop," exclaiming how glorious it was, and pretend-flushing it down the toilet. A few weeks after the interest in toilet training began, Sara began to test limits, something she had never done before. She was playing in my sink pouring water when all of a sudden I found myself soaked because she had deliberately poured a whole bottle of water on me. She thought this was hilarious and laughed a long and hard belly laugh. However, I was not pleased. I acknowledged that it made her laugh and that it seemed funny to her but that I did not want to get wet and I could not allow her to do that. We made a rule that the water stays in the sink. She immediately tried to pour water on me again. This time I was ready for her and intercepted the bottle. She took it and dumped it all over my floor. I turned off the water and she became very angry and we both tolerated her anger.

Shortly after the toilet training interest and limit testing began Sara began to "play" baby. She was aware that this play was pretend and she was in control. Over the next several weeks "Sara-baby" grew, slowly proceeding through phases of development. For example, the first several times she played the game she was a newborn infant. She made crying sounds and lay in my arms demanding that I hold her bottle and feed her and soothe her cries. This continued for several sessions. At times she could not be calmed and her cries were piercing and sounded real as if she had become that infant who could not be comforted. It was obvious that she relished her new game of pretend and told me when I picked her up at daycare for her session that we were going to play "baby." Eventually she held the bottle and fed herself. She also added eating cookies and asking to be burped while sitting in my lap.

I was taking a two-month leave and began to prepare Sara for this long absence. Sara was unable to play after this news. She disengaged from me by regressing to repetitive water play for the rest of the hour. In her next session Sara once again played "baby." She began to throw the bottle and demand that I retrieve it. Sara's play of throwing the baby bottle across the room for me to retrieve had multiple meanings. For example, this play may illustrate cognitive development. At this stage of development the child gains object permanence where she begins to understand that if an object is hidden it has not disappeared but is still there, just waiting to be found. It could be postulated that this play constituted a stage of cognitive development that was lagging in Sara. It is likely that Sara and her mother never engaged in a game of throw and retrieve. This play may symbolize my leaving and coming back. Sara was working through separation and loss. Sara's rage was directed at me as a real object who leaves and returns but within the transference I was Sara's mother who is often unable to meet Sara's emotional needs.

In the following sessions Sara began to crawl and retrieve her own bottle after she threw it. After this session I was away for one week. Upon my return Sara ignored me and refused to come to her session and climbed into the lap of an unknown volunteer. This was unusual behavior for Sara. She is not indiscriminate with her attention. She was telling me: "This is how it feels to be left!" However, she was also showing me that she was now capable of seeking out other adults to help her cope with difficult feelings.

Shortly after my weeklong absence, Sara, within her pretend game of "baby," began to climb to the top of my couch and fling herself off. She did this with such force that, had I not caught her, she would have hurt herself. This continued for several sessions and seeped into her other play with puppets and dollhouse figures as she showed me over and over how it feels to be dropped.

During my two-month hiatus Sara's teacher provided her with postcards that I had prepared, and she made a small section of wall in the classroom available for Sara to display pictures and notes from me. When I returned, at first sight of me, Sara burst into tears and, while sobbing, exclaimed: "I don't want to come to your office with you" as she held her arms to be picked up and carried. Her play gradually changed as she began to play baby with a doll and she became the mommy. She would spend many sessions nurturing and singing to her baby. At this point Sara rarely played the infant. However, when her mother was going through a difficult time, Sara used the "baby" game to let me know she was feeling vulnerable.

As Sara approached her fourth birthday her speech was clearer and age appropriate, she was completely toilet trained, her gait remained somewhat stiff as if she needed to be very careful to keep her balance and keep her place safe in her world, but she was able to smoothly navigate her surroundings. She communicated verbally when she was scared or angry and sought out adults for comfort. Most striking was Sara's ability to play. Her play evolved to where she made up complicated scenarios using animal figures. Using symbolic play she continued to work through feelings of being dropped and uncared for, but she also exhibited age-appropriate conflicts. With a lion family she played out oedipal fantasies and wishes, anger toward her mother, sibling jealousies, and separation conflicts.

CONNECTING MOTHER AND DAUGHTER

Early on in my relationship with this family I was struck by Esther's indifference to her daughter. There were many times that Sara and I would pass Esther in the lobby as we made our way to and from daycare. In these chance meetings there would be no interaction; neither mother nor child would acknowledge the other. Every time this would occur I would give Sara a voice and supply the needed words. I would say: "Hi Mom, I am going to Miss Ann's office now. I will see you after my nap." After this occurred several times I pushed further and said: "Hi Mom. I sure could use a morning Mommy hug," and I would help Esther hug her daughter.

In the beginning it was difficult to get Esther to keep appointments with me. She seemed petrified, as if she expected to be scolded by me. I found myself "mother chasing." When I would see her leave the building, I would run out to catch a few words with her on the sidewalk before she quickly took off into the depths of the city streets or into the elevator as she ran from me. When she finally came for an appointment I realized that this mother longed to play as she eyed my toys and touched items with longing. So we played. We made calendars that she colored with glitter and a mommy/baby animal book that she could give to Sara for Christmas. What was most appreciated was a photo book that we made together of her little family, a book that took months to construct. As I nurtured Esther she slowly became more able to nurture Sara.

We began weekly family sessions to which Esther brought both her daughters, and we sang nursery rhymes and made a nursery rhyme book that she could read to her children at home. Slowly Esther began to play with Sara. And then it happened! Sara and I met Esther on our way to my office and Sara ran to her mom shouting: "Hi Mom! I need a morning hug. [Esther smiled and gave her a hug.] I'm going with Ann now. See you later." It became a regular interaction and there were several incidents where Esther initiated the "morning hug" and began to take my words as her own: "I will see you later after your nap!" There were setbacks where Esther was physically abusive and she lashed out at Sara verbally when her own life was not going well. But the improvement in the relationship was striking.

ESTHER STAYS ATTACHED

Esther and her children concluded their time at the shelter and graduated from the program. They had been given extended time in the shelter but could no longer stay. To Esther's credit she continued to bring both of her children to daycare and Sara was able to continue her therapy. Esther was helped to find housing and moved from her protected "holding" environment back out into the world, where she experienced grave difficulties keeping her children safe. It was becoming increasingly apparent that Sara was being exposed to some type of sexual behavior. Her play became more driven and there was an underlying anxiety. The manifest content of the play continued to be ambiguous as she played out dramas between Mom and Dad and both daughters. These play/dramas mostly consisted of Mom and Dad kissing and the children becoming aggressive and scared. Sara ended these sessions needing physical contact. She let me know this either by regressing into her "baby" game or asking to be carried back to daycare. I felt that Sara was witnessing sexual behavior between her mother and father, who had secretly moved in with the family although it was against housing rules.

Sara's younger sister, Nancy, (two years old) began to present with disturbing symptoms. It is important to note that this child had been developing normally. She also benefited from being her mother's adored child. The daycare staff alerted me to their concerns, stating that she had stopped talking, was unhappy most of the time, and seemed to *disappear* and not hear them when they spoke to her. With my urging, Esther took Nancy to the doctor, who reported that she had been sexually molested. The proper authorities were notified and Esther was terrified that her daughters would be taken from her. The sexual abuse charge was never founded and the case was closed, but the tragedy had occurred. I began to see Nancy in therapy, as no other therapist was available.

In Esther's mind I had failed her. By allowing her to leave our agency and once again venture unprotected into the world, she thought it was me who had not kept her children safe. She let me know this with intense anger toward me. It took weeks for her to begin to speak with me again. Slowly, as I built up her self-esteem and self-worth as a mother, she began to trust me again. It was my hope that Esther would join me in working with both of her daughters so they too could feel safe and protected by their mother.

Sara continued working on difficult issues. She began to act out her sister's abuse and she demonstrated how unsafe she herself felt. Two weeks after I began to see Nancy in therapy, Sara refused to come with me for her session. At first I used persuasion such as quietly reminding her how important our time was together, so important it could not be missed, but that only worked once. Next I resorted to my creative powers and that helped as she pretended to be a bus driver and drive me to my office. This role-play was also useful, as she often refused to pick me up and take me to McDonald's, but at the last minute, she would leave me stranded. However, this too lost its appeal as her feelings of loss became overpowering. Eventually I resorted to picking her up and carrying her screaming all the way to my office. She would calm down as soon as we entered my office but would walk around touching things and asking: "Who did this? Who touched that?" Her play regressed to infancy, as she became the "dropped" infant. She would cry pitifully and could not be comforted. When she was not the anxious and apprehensive baby, she attempted to fling herself off the top of my couch. For weeks, this continued. As I carried her to my office from daycare her chant became "Leave me alone!" I began to hear it as: "You have left me. I am so alone."

I addressed her feelings of loss, anger, sadness, and abandonment. I began to tell her a story about "a little girl who loved her mommy so much that she thought that her mommy would never need or desire another child. One day her mommy had a new baby and the new baby was always in Mommy's arms. It made the little girl feel very sad and very angry because she wanted Mommy all for herself." Sara listened intently and it seemed to help calm her and enable her to work in her session. These were painful weeks for both of us as I attempted to help Sara work through her loss of me as the "good mother" who loves only her. She reexperienced her feelings of loss from the time when her little sister was born and her mother rejected her even more forcefully than when she was an infant. The following vignette is from Sara's last session before an unexpected and abrupt break in our work. In retrospect it is apparent that Sara was fearful that she was about to lose me.

As soon as I entered her classroom, Sara began to wail and moan. She grabbed hold of the child nearest to her and begged him to protect her from me. He came to her aid and blocked me with his body as she hung onto his back. Sara's teacher was visibly upset as I explained to the little boy that I was not going to hurt Sara, but that it was important for her to have her special time with me. He understood this, as he too has a "special time" with a beloved therapist. As I carried Sara kicking and screaming, "Leave me alone," she began to try to hit me in the face. I retold her the "little girl story" that had come to be known as just "the story." As usual she was calmed by the story but she remained angry. She picked up the two old phones, handed one to me, and called me. "Ring ring!" I answered and she said: "Did you take Nancy?" I said: "You are thinking about how I take your sister and it makes you feel very angry with me and so very sad because you want me all for yourself." Sara slammed the phone down in its cradle. She called me several times, and each time I answered she slammed down the phone and refused to speak. This play caused her to experience overwhelming anxiety, and she did something that she had not done for almost two years: she began to open and slam my desk drawer. The large bang caused her to laugh hysterically. I said: "Remember when you were little, so little you wore diapers and you would come here and when you felt bad feelings inside you would bang this drawer? I think you are feeling that now." Sara smiled. She then began a game of leaving me behind. She enacted this with little Fisher-Price figures; she was the mom who came to pick me, the child, up and before I could get into the car she would race off. It was torture. Her message was evident when she picked up the little house, all the little people, and their car and threw it all into my garbage. She sat back and began to cry like an infant. I asked her if she wanted to play baby and held out my arms to her. She shook her head yes and climbed into my arms. I fed her cookies and a bottle and sang her a special lullaby that was all about how she was feeling. She accepted this nurturing and quickly settled down and was once again able to play. It was time to end the session so I suggested that the house and all the people did not always feel so bad and that maybe we could rescue them from the garbage. She agreed to this and locked up all the people safely inside the house. However, before locking it all up, she attempted to put her own head into the little house. I said: "You just want to be locked up all safe with me." She began a game of "knock, knock," a word game she always enjoyed, but this time when it was my turn and I said "it's Miss Ann," she corrected me and said: "No, you are Miss Ann Williams!" She insisted that her last name was mine.

CONCLUSION

Sara quickly learned that her world was cold and unfriendly, and she withdrew to a safer place. Her pain must have reached intolerable limits. Fraiberg suggests that when the infant withdraws into herself it is a primitive defense, which serves to obliterate the intolerable pain (Fraiberg, 1982). Slade adds that when a mother grossly misinterprets, misreads, or ignores her child's needs the child develops inadequate methods of communicating those needs to the parent (Slade, 1998). Winnicott tells us that when an infant is left too long without human contact the child's experience can only be described by "such words as: going to pieces; falling for ever; dying and dying and dying" (Winnicott, 1987, p. 86). When Sara became distressed she just went to sleep. Bowlby suggests that when children experience neglect they form numerous and intrinsically conflicting representations of the same reality (Bowlby, 1988). As Sara grew, her primitive defenses helped her to keep unwanted feelings from her consciousness. Sara dissociated from her feelings.

Fraiberg, Adelson, and Shapiro, in their famous article "Ghosts in the Nursery," ask the question "Why doesn't this mother hear her baby's cries?" (Fraiberg, Adelson, & Shapiro, 1975, p. 344). We saw that Sara had taken on her mother's affective life. Esther's sadness was mirrored in Sara's whole being. In a healthy relationship between mother and infant the mother reflects back to her infant the infant's affect. Thus, when the child gazes into her mother's face she sees herself (Winnicott, 1987; Beebe, Lachmann, & Jaffe, 1997). Esther was unable to mirror Sara's own feeling states; instead Sara looked into her mother's face and what was reflected back was a misrepresentation of her emerging self. She took on as her core representation of herself her mother's "distorted and barren picture of the child" (Fonagy & Target, 1998, p. 95). Sara's early attempts to engage her mother had failed, so she found a "way-of-being-with-mother" (Stern, 1995, p. 101) by identifying and mirroring her mother's depression. Esther's own history of rejection, neglect, and abandonment was now being reenacted with her daughter. Sara's emotional needs were too threatening for Esther to bear. Her own defense was to deny similar feelings pertaining to her own early relationships. Sara's yearning to be held and loved, coupled with her fears and anger, caused Esther to feel and remember her own intolerable memories (Slade, 1998). Esther's own infant cries were probably rarely comforted. Her pain needed to be acknowledged and her story needed to be told and witnessed. "When this mother's own cries are heard, she will hear her child's cries" (Fraiberg, Adelson, & Shapiro, 1975, p. 395). But meanwhile Sara was suffering and could not wait for her mother, so treatment began.

Sara and I created a "transitional space" (Winnicott, 1971), and I accepted her stipulations of engagement. Through use of attunement, mirroring, and empathy, Sara slowly began to engage. The therapy provided a holding function wherein Sara was able to feel safe and contained and experienced pleasure. However she was in control as I respected her necessary defenses against painful affects (King, 1993). My office became a safe environment where she could regress to infancy, act out in rage against her mother, safely test limits, and enact many other emotions that would be too dangerous for her mother or other adults in her life to tolerate.

Because Sara had endured profound neglect I imagine that she had few experiences of physical comfort and affection. The social environment of this family was intrusive and fragmented. Esther's own inner life must have been one of chaos. She was unable to respond to her infant's signals; perhaps she ignored them or misread them. Her own profound depression and life circumstances caused her to be preoccupied and unavailable to Sara. One only had to spend a few minutes with this mother to understand that she was hungry and starving in her own way. Esther was unable to provide her infant daughter with attunement that is necessary for secure attachment (Greenspan, 1990; Hughes, 1997; Karen, 1998).

In the normal mother/infant relationship affect regulation occurs through attunement, mirroring, and empathy. In the beginning of our work together, whenever Sara expressed an emotion I mirrored it for her. In this way she had the opportunity to learn to regulate and integrate her feeling states so that she could begin to develop a sense of herself as different from others. It is through this mechanism that the core origin of self begins to emerge (Shore, 1994). In a healthy relationship the mirroring that occurs between a mother and child is not just a mere reflection of behavior but rather is more like a "magical mirror" (Coates, 1998, p. 122). The mother reflects back to her infant her potential, thus creating the space for the infant to experience herself. Coates states "the mother's ability to see the potential in the infant is what allows the infant to find it for himself or herself, in the face of the mother" (Coates 1998, p. 122). It is this type of mirroring that I attempted to achieve with Sara. If all goes well for an infant and an affective, pleasurable relationship has been formed, "then with growing maturational abilities the infant develops complex patterns of communication in the context of this primary relationship" (Greenspan, 1990, p. 154). Sara had learned that her attempts to communicate elicited very little or no response. Therefore her sensory and motor skills, so vital to engagement, did not develop. Because of this disruption in the attachment process, Sara did not learn "to appreciate causal relationships between people and to experience compassionate and intimate feelings" (Greenspan, 1990, p. 154). Early in my work with Sara she withdrew from my touch and her "play" was mechanical and repetitive. She had learned that little value was placed on communication, and thus she did not have the ability to "facilitate the recognition and expression of thoughts and ideas" (Hughes, 1997, p. 25).

When life is good and things go well, the human relationship grows as the infant develops. As the mother provides protection, comfort, and regularity, an emotional attachment is formed. In this way the parent facilitates her baby's developmental growth (Greenspan, 1990). My job with Sara was to form a connected relationship. I did this by deeply engaging her on an affective level. Sara responded and quickly began to catch up in her development.

The day after Sara dissociated I questioned that perhaps Sara might have been physically ill, even autistic. Upon reflection I realized Sara had formed an attachment to me and my absence, just over a weekend, struck a deep, primitive wound in her. It became unbearable for her to feel the loss and she probably experienced an anaclitic depression. In our early weeks of work together I played with Sara as a mother plays with her infant. She experienced what it is to be played with and to be playful. My absence brought on feelings of annihilation. Sara might have lost "all vestige of hope of the renewal of contacts" (Winnicott, 1987, p. 86). She had not reached object constancy in her development and was unable to internalize my image. When we were apart she experienced it as desertion. I incorporated in our play the use of a Polaroid camera. Photographs, along with other homemade transitional objects, became essential in our work.

When I took Sara's younger sister as a patient I had let Sara down and hurt her terribly. Sara was both furious with me and fearful that she had lost me. On another level Sara was able to bring into her therapy the experience of losing what little attention and love she received from her mother when her sibling was born. Esther was open about her bias toward Nancy. Nancy was the preferred and loved child while Sara was pushed further back in her mother's mind and continued to experience rejection. Esther often expressed the idea that Sara embarrassed her and openly displayed disgust toward her daughter.

As noted in the clinical material, Sara regressed back to infancy where she could not be comforted. Her cries were those of a tiny infant screaming in anguish. When she attempted to fling herself from the top of my couch, it could be interpreted as falling forever because she felt unloved and worthless. When a child feels this, "it leaves the child alone with the devastating thought that it is better not to be alive than not being loved" (Lussier, 1999, p. 155).

Winnicott speaks of "the gradual failure that has to be experienced by the child when the parents are not available" (Winnicott, 1987, p. 21). Perhaps Sara's ego was not yet strong enough to tolerate my *realness* and she could not permit frustration. She had not had sufficient experiences of omnipotence and had yet to develop a sense of self. Winnicott reminds us that the growing sense of self through time is reinforced by the mother's empathic responses. It is this mother/infant dance that strengthens the child's sense of her own omnipotence (Winnicott, 1978). My reactions were felt by Sara as being insensitive to her ego needs, and this led to her feeling disintegration, withdrawal and a feeling of annihilation.

As difficult as these months were it was an opportunity for me to help Sara realize that no matter how hard she tried to destroy me I would survive and be there for her. Her reexperiencing the loss of her mother's love when her little sister was born also gave me the opportunity to help Sara learn new and more adaptive ways of coping.

Fonagy argues that a major role of the therapist is to help children learn to think reflectively or to be able to mentalize. I feel I did this as I assisted Sara in labeling and thus understanding her emotional states. This is seen very early on in our work when Sara became extremely sad when I rubbed lotion on her arm. By helping her to view herself as feeling sadness she began "to understand both the conscious and the unconscious relationships between [her] behavior and internal states" (Fonagy & Target, 1998, p. 105). Sara's emotions and affects changed quickly within a session and by staying with her in the moment, I taught her how others see and know her. She took on my perceptions of her inner states as her own self-perceptions and this facilitated the emergence of her core self (Fonagy & Target, 1998; Stern, 1985). Through our therapeutic relationship, Sara found a way of thinking about and coping with her feelings. Just as she learned as a newborn that the only way to be with her mother was to take on her depressive and flat affective qualities, she now learned a *new way of being* with another person. She was able to take her *new way of being* and offer it to her mother. Luckily, Esther responded, due in part to feeling nurtured and held by me, and Sara and Esther began to relate in a healthier, growth-promoting fashion.

Giving Sara words: "Hi Mom, I need a morning hug!" and helping Esther to see and hear her child gradually over the months transformed Esther's understanding of her daughter. She began to be able to see Sara as a separate individual. Esther's projections and distortions became fewer, which was an essential contribution to Sara's growth (Slade, 1998). On Sara's end of the interaction, she had learned to "avoid placing an attachment demand upon a parent who would not tolerate it and who might react by creating greater distance between them" (Stern, 1995, p. 106). Over time and with many repetitions, Esther became more of a secure base for her child as Sara became able to verbally ask her mother for a "morning hug" and Esther responded with genuine joy.

It has been documented that securely attached children are more capable of making use of symbolic play. Therapists often use symbolic play as a means of assessing the child's ability to be self-reflective (Karen, 1998; Fonagy & Target, 1998). As Sara formed an attachment to me and then was able to transfer what she learned from our relationship to her relationship with her mother her play changed. Sara gradually was able to play symbolically, as evidenced in her play with animal families and in her "baby" game. Sara had entered the world of imagination and make-believe and her life became much more enjoyable and bearable.

In conclusion, when Sara entered therapy she had limited capacity to play. Her play was stilted, mechanical, repetitive, and joyless. Her affect was constricted and she had few resources for coping. Her development had been severely compromised. As our relationship developed, I helped her to imagine and create through the use of both words and play, and she began to symbolize. In her play she was gradually able to express profound sadness and tremendous rage. As I labeled her affects they were given meaning and brought into understanding. This enabled Sara to begin to understand her world, including both inner fantasies and reality. As she began to make meaning of her own inner world she also developed the ability to understand and relate to others. Sara began to experience herself as "known" and therefore as a separate individual with a sense of self. Sara's body began to regulate, as her toilet training illustrated, and her affective expression changed. Her dejection and joyless behavior gave way to a delightful sense of humor and an enjoyment of the world. What was most helpful in Sara's growth was Esther's ability to begin to imagine her child's experience. As successful as I was in meeting Sara's inner mental state, it was Esther's own growth and healing that was most beneficial. Crucial to Sara's growth was the act of giving voice through symbolic play to Sara's inner world. As Sara felt safe enough to form an attachment she began to learn to think reflectively, and as a result she has attained a more differentiated and integrated sense of self (Mahler et al., 1975). Sara's ability to form attachments and make meaning of her inner thoughts and feelings had given her a newfound resiliency that enabled her to seek out new attachment figures. Most important, Sara was able to make contact with her mother at a time when Esther was unable to reach out to her.

Had Sara not entered intensive psychoanalytic psychotherapy when she did it is possible that she would have been diagnosed as autistic or severely mentally retarded and eventually been institutionalized. Sara now has a chance for a life where she will become a functional member of society. Sara's story illustrates the need for combined attachment work to be done with the mother and her children. The tragedy that befell this family also demonstrates, albeit painfully, the need for housing for cognitively limited women who wish to keep their families safe and together.

Sara has given me a great deal and I have learned a tremendous amount from this small vulnerable child. My initial emphasis was on helping her to form an attachment. Sara's story clearly demonstrates that attachment is an innate drive needed for survival. Her treatment made it possible for her to continue to develop, which in turn enabled an attachment relationship to grow and thrive. In addition, this case emphasizes the importance of working with the mother in order to nurture the attachment between the mother and her child.

Chapter Two

Three Cases

BETTY FORGIVES HER MOTHER

I began working with Betty just before her third birthday after she had experienced a terrifying night walking the streets of the inner city alone and afraid. She was discovered by the police and put in a temporary children's home until her family could be located. She spent two days in the temporary shelter as red tape was being unraveled so her grandparents could obtain custody of her. In her daycare room Betty was conspicuous as she was the solitary blond, blue-eyed child among a class of darker skinned children, mostly African American. She was also noticeable by her somewhat oddly shaped head and her timid comportment.

Betty began life at risk. Her mother suffered from bipolar disorder, as did several family members, and was drug and alcohol addicted during her pregnancy. Betty was born with a major medical problem and at three months old underwent major surgery to her skull. Betty's mother (Linda) came to live at the shelter while pregnant and Betty was born at the shelter. Linda made good progress and moved out after one year into housing, but had subsequent relapses of her addictions and her mental illness was difficult to control. Betty developed normally, with an above-average intelligence, and continued in our daycare program. She lived with her grandparents but spent many days at a time with her mother. Her mother had legal custody of Betty, but needed her family's help in caring for her. Luckily the grandparents were more than willing to help. In contrast to many of the shelter families, Betty had a stable extended family with lots of love and support.

On a cold March night when Betty was two and a half years old her mother relapsed while Betty was with her. Linda left Betty with a prostitute to babysit her, while she left to get high. Linda never returned for her daughter and somehow Betty ended up wandering the streets of the inner city alone and terrified. Linda went into long-term, inpatient rehab and Betty's grandparents obtained a lawyer and were granted full custody of Betty. When Betty returned to daycare after this traumatic experience we began intensive therapy. I saw Betty three times per week and met with the grandparents monthly. When Linda recovered I also met monthly with her.

When we began our individual therapy Betty was already familiar with me as she was a member of a small group (three children total) that I met with weekly. However, she was terrified to come with me alone. For her first individual session I had to walk two blocks to a playground where her class was playing. When the three children saw me they came running, thinking I was taking them for our group time. When I explained to the children that this was Betty's time alone the other two began to cry. Betty left with me easily but refused to speak to me as her bottom lip protruded further and further as we navigated around the broken glass on the sidewalk. Once in my office she was difficult to engage. She put grandparent figures and a child figure into a car as I told her I had met with her grandparents right here in this office. This did not impress her. She asked me to read a book to her and chose one but once I began to read she turned her back on me and dumped the rest of the books off the shelf. She found the doctor's kit and asked what each instrument was for. She took a baby doll and told me this doll had a hurt head and put a bandage on its head. I wondered if she worried about her own head and she said: "I was scared and I cried." She put a bandage on her own head and then one on my forehead. I commented that bandages are very helpful and make us feel better. When it was time to end she dumped a box of blocks and insisted that we build the picture on the box. I explained we could do that in her next session the next day. Her mood remained sullen and angry throughout this first session.

The next day when she saw me approach the playground she ran away crying and screaming "no!" After trying to talk with her for about ten minutes she began to wail for her Grandpop. I explained that I could see how sacred she was and how Grandpop did not want her to feel so scared all the time. I explained that I help children with worries and with scared feelings and Grandpop asked me to help her with her scared feelings. I picked her up and carried her crying the three blocks from the playground to my office. She stopped crying as soon as we entered my office and she drank heartily from my sink. She accidentally sprayed me with water and I thanked her since we were both very hot from our long walk. She laughed a deep hearty laugh and said: "You are all sweaty and I fixed your sweaty!" She found my collection of bandages, told me she had many, many boo-boos and got busy sticking bandages up her entire arm. She then told me she was the doctor and I was not to be scared and she applied six bandages to both of my arms. She remembered she wanted to build with the blocks and built her mommy's house, her daddy's house, and her nana's house. It is important to note that her father with whom she had contact, had recently died. She said: "My daddy is dead, an angel came and took him to heaven. He is in heaven now and I will see him when I get to heaven." She got a mom and a dad doll from the dollhouse and put them both facedown in front of the houses. "Mommy and Daddy are dead. My mommy is coming home today." Betty understood that her mother had been in the hospital as she had visited and spoke with her on the phone; perhaps this play showed her confusion over what it is to die, or perhaps she was demonstrating her anger with her mother for leaving her both on that terrifying night and long term with her grandparents.

For the next month Betty cried as soon as she saw me coming to take her for her sessions, and stopped crying as soon as we entered my office and spent most of our sessions covering her arms and legs with bandages telling me she has so many boo-boos. Then she surprised me and seemed happy to see me and came with me easily. In this particular session she described her father's funeral. She called her father up on the phone and told him she did not miss him and asked him if he was scared when he saw all the people in church crying. I said it can be very scary to see grown-ups cry. "My mommy didn't cry. People cried. I don't feel scared."

Betty was happy to come to her sessions for the next two weeks and then began to once again look very sad and worried when she saw me approach. She had begun to act aggressively toward other children and there had been another death in her family. Her grandmother's mother who lived next door to them had died and Betty had attended another funeral. She showed aggression toward me by throwing toys at me and dumping toys off of shelves in my office. She was extremely anxious and began to wet herself both in school and in her sessions. This unhappy, anxious behavior continued for another month.

Several weeks later she began as usual, unhappy and worried about coming with me. She wet herself and used the bathroom three times and then lay down on the floor and asked me to lie next to her. She began to kick her feet and wanted me to imitate her. I kicked my feet. She did some strange contortions with her body and wanted me to repeat her actions. I told her I was unable to do those movements and she seemed pleased that she could do something that I was unwilling to try. She smiled and said, "I stopped crying." A: "Yes you did. But you were very scared. I wonder what makes you feel so scared." B: "You Miss Ann. Miss Ann is scary!" A: "Oh I scare you." B: "No, monsters scare me." Betty sits up and in a serious voice states, "Nobody else can come in here when I'm here with you." A: "That's right

Betty. This is a special time just for us." She asked for crackers and helped clean up and sang and skipped all the way back to daycare.

By calling me a monster and telling me I scared her she had succeeded in making me the bad guy, her abuser. I realized that I had begun to feel like the mean lady who made her cry three times every week. I no longer felt like the mean guy and told Betty that I was proud of her for coming with me. I talked about how she cries every time she sees me and I was wondering about that. I continued that sometimes I think she is worried and sometimes I think maybe she is scared and sometimes I think perhaps she feels sad but I wondered if maybe she also felt very angry. Her mood lifted immediately and she seemed less anxious. She included me in her play and was engaged making up dramas about families and bad guys who turn good. At the end of the session she sat on my couch to eat cookies and I start the conversation. A: "I missed you on Monday. I came to get you and you weren't there. Your teacher told me you had to go to a funeral." B: "I go to lots of funerals." A: "It is sad when people die." B: "My daddy died and my mommy is in the hospital." A: "Your daddy went away to heaven and your mommy went away to the hospital." B: "My mommy is angry." A: "Who is your mommy angry with?" B: "Me, that's why she went to the hospital." A: "Mommy is sick but I bet that makes you very angry with Mommy." She did not respond verbally but she smiled. She ended her session smiling asking if I was coming for her the next day.

For the first six months of our work together Betty would cry or be sullen and refuse to speak to me or look at me until we got to my office. Once in the office she would play and began very slowly to work through her traumas: her terrifying abandonment that one dark, cold night; her early surgery as an infant; and her chronic trauma of having a very depressed and drug-addicted mother. Betty's mother finally graduated from her inpatient program and was back living in her apartment. She called me to set up an appointment to meet me although she was worried I would blame her and think of her as a bad mother. That day Betty once again greeted me with tears. I told her that her mother had called me and that we were going to see each other next week; she immediately stopped crying. She began to pile books on the floor and I began: "Betty, every time I come to get you, you cry very angry tears. I went away a couple of weeks ago and I was gone for a whole week and did not come to get you. Sometimes when people you care about go away it hurts inside and gives you bad and angry and sad feelings." She did not respond and continued to pile books but she was listening. Later in the session she drew a picture of her mom and said, "My mom is always mad. When I take a bath my mommy gets mad." At the end of the session she was making Christmas cards and writing her name on them. She asked me to write my name then crossed it out and said "You made me go away!"

From the time I began to meet with Linda, Betty stopped crying and began to show positive feelings for me. After months of covering herself and me in bandages and telling me not to be scared of the doctor and not to cry if it hurt, she began to work on her nighttime terrors and her abandonment. She built houses out of my couch, taking apart the cushions to make walls and a roof. We were neighbors. It was nighttime and we had to go to sleep. She covered me with a blanket and then herself and told me not to have bad dreams. "Be good and don't have bad dreams because I don't want to hear that in the middle of the night!" A: "What shall I do if I do have a bad dream?" She got up and got a superhero for herself and for me and said they would protect us from the bad dreams. She moved her pillow and herself next to me and said a bad man had moved next to her. She suddenly had to make a bowel movement and we went down the hall to the bathroom. She invited me in with her but I told her it is best if she has privacy but I would stand right outside the door. She demanded that I stay right there and not move. Once back in my office she said it was time to go back to sleep and have good dreams and dropped her pants. I told her that I could see that she was very excited and wanted to take off her clothes but in here we keep our clothes on and we can talk about what it feels like to want to take our clothes off. She ended her session by calling her Grandpop on the phone: "Hello Grandpop. Well we played house and went to sleep and if you want to come here you can just come here and talk but you can't come with me 'cause that is just for me and Miss Ann but you can come talk and see all the good stuff."

It was close to the one-year anniversary of Betty's abandonment trauma. We were making cards for people in her family and she asked me to make a card for her mommy and told me about how she likes to go to her mother's apartment. I reminded her that when she was little she lived with her mom in that apartment. B: "My mom got lost and I looked for her and my Grandmom and Grandpop saved me!" A: "That must have been very scary." She ended the verbal exchange but continued the conversation by hiding stones in the sand for me to find. A month later she was playing with a baby doll and told me it was crying. A: "Why is this poor baby crying so hard?" B: "That's not a baby it's a mom." A: "Oh a crying mommy." B: "She wants her daughter." As we ended the session and we were walking back to daycare, Betty said: "My mommy says God bless Miss Ann every night."

In this particular session I arrived to retrieve Betty for her session after I had gotten a haircut. The first thing she told me was that my hair was very ugly. Once in my office she called me on the phone and said: "Miss Ann your hair is very ugly but don't worry you are still beautiful." She hung up the phone and began a series of "My dress is ugly, no it's pretty, my hair is ugly, no it's pretty, my face is ugly, no it's beautiful." A: "This is reminding me of how we talk about all the bad guys and how some of the bad guys can have good in them too. Maybe you are practicing having two feelings at the same time. You can think my hair is ugly and pretty all at the same time."

We had been working intensively for over a year when Betty began to work through her trauma, which had produced a symptom of not being able to sleep in the dark. She had to have a light on at all times. Her grandmother reported that she would turn the light off after Betty had been asleep and she would awaken every time in a fright. Betty discovered that the lamp in my office had a dimmer. She began a game of going to bed at night. The game had many variations. Sometimes I was the mom and she was the child, sometimes we were best friends, sometimes sisters. But it always involved making my office very dark, going to sleep, and waking up in the morning. She would gradually dim the light and then gradually make it light again. In some sessions there were monsters and bad guys who would frighten us in the night and the light had to come on. In some sessions we had nightmares and had to be comforted. This play was continuous session after session for eight months. One session she did not play this but instead she began a new game of packing up and moving. I found out from a meeting with the grandparents that Betty no longer needed the light on at night and her night terrors had stopped. I also was told they had sold their home and were moving to a better neighborhood where Betty would begin kindergarten in the fall. Her packing and moving aided Betty in dealing with moving to a new home and also in preparing her for termination, which we had begun. Betty's last appointment was in late August before she went on a family vacation. She was given a good-bye party in the daycare class. She had been born in the shelter and had spent her whole life in the daycare. Many of the teachers and staff had known Betty from birth and had sad feelings about her leaving but were also thrilled with her development. I stayed in touch with Linda for another six months. Betty adjusted very well to her new school and her new neighborhood; she was making friends and doing well academically.

Betty's story is heartwarming as I can look back and know our work together helped her to work through her multiple traumas and she was able to get back on the path of normal development and move forward. She was fortunate as she had a mother who, although ill, loved her very much and wanted to help her, and grandparents who were also invested in her well-being. Even though Betty was born in a homeless shelter, she had secure attachment relationships with her mother and her grandparents, which benefited her greatly in her ability to face her trauma and work through it. Both the mother and the grandparents attended regular meetings with me and developed a strong bond and a positive working alliance with me; thus as Betty and I worked through her traumas her home environment was stable and supportive as the adults eagerly took my advice. It is clear that only when I began meeting regularly with Betty's mother was Betty able to begin to trust me and begin the work of healing.

MELINDA GROWS UP

I first met Melinda when I did her entrance evaluation for my agency. I found myself sitting across from a strikingly beautiful 19-year-old cradling her six-day-old infant in her arms. She became homeless when her pregnancy began to show and her family could no longer offer her a place to live. She lived in several poorly staffed shelters until coming to us. Melinda desperately wanted to be admitted to our program and presented as an intelligent, articulate, motivated young woman with a remarkable capacity for insight. It was also immediately apparent that she possessed a wonderful sense of humor and we connected instantly.

Melinda is the second oldest of four children. She and one of her brothers have the same biological father. Her oldest sister and youngest brother have different fathers. Melinda and her sister and brother (the youngest brother was not yet born and is 15 years younger than Melinda) were neglected, and physically and emotionally abused, by their mother. The mother has in recent years been diagnosed as schizophrenic and is an active drug and alcohol addict. Her mother remains homeless to the present day.

When Melinda was five years old her maternal grandmother found her with an open head wound and called the Department of Human Services (DHS). The grandmother was granted custody and Melinda lived with her grandmother until she was 12 years old, at which time her grandmother died from cancer. At this time Melinda was placed into the foster care system. Melinda found her foster care families lacking and was never able to relate to any of them (she had several). Her solution was to run away to a family member, but she was always given up to authorities and placed back into the system. At age 15, desperate to be given back to her biological mother, Melinda attempted suicide by taking pills. This desperate act was successful and DHS granted custody back to the ill, abusive biological mother. After the suicide attempt, Melinda received psychotherapy and was prescribed an anti-depressant. She saw this therapist for six months and never took the medication. She lived in homeless shelters with her mother until becoming pregnant at age 18; then she found herself on her own. She entered our shelter three weeks after her baby was born and asked to begin treatment with me. She had successfully completed high school.

For the first six months of our work together, Melinda showed up early for every appointment with her baby in arms. I was impressed with her mothering capabilities and witnessed many beautiful interactions of attunement and mirroring. It was a joy to watch a secure attachment develop between this teen mother and her baby.

Six months into our relationship changes began to occur. One day we met on the street as I was leaving for the day, when Melinda ran up to my car yelling my name out. She approached and asked if I could write a note to her teacher to get her out of class (she had entered community college). She stated she needed to go food shopping for her baby. I explained that I could not do that but I understood that she really wanted me to. This was the first of several requests that I could not grant her. They included requests for babysitting; requests for some money; requests to take her on errands in my car, and writing to SSI and lying about her diagnosis so she could receive disability. It was also at this time that she began to miss her appointments. More puzzling was the fact that she continued to see me but would show up at odd times at my office. It just so happened that at those times she appeared I was free to see her. After each such occurrence we would schedule an appointment that she would not keep. After several weeks of this she asked me to walk her to the elevator after her session. As we were walking down the hall we passed the staff kitchen. She observed that there were cookies on the table and asked if I would get her a cookie. I granted this request and she was elated.

In her following session a noticeable movement in therapy occurred by accident. My cell phone rang and as I reached to turn the power off she saw that the phone said *call from home.* For the rest of the hour she harangued me about my mothering, stating that I was a bad mother. She went on and on making up all types of fantasies of why my child would be calling me. Her final fantasy was that my teenage daughter was now going to have sex with a boyfriend because I was not there to protect her. This gave me lots of openings, not only about her own relationship with her mother but also about how she felt toward me.

Nine months into our work together Melinda became pregnant again and was devastated. She wrote me a frantic note and slipped it under my door the day she found out. This was the first time that she came to a session without her baby. She begged me to make her decision for her. She said: "If it were you what would you do?" and other similar statements. She left my office angry with me declaring that I was "worthless, and no help at all, a lousy therapist!"

Melinda had the abortion and became depressed and angry. This led us into her feelings about the man currently in her life, her past relationship with her baby's father, and her relationship with her own father. As we dove deeper into her relationship with her father and mother, she had vivid memories of multiple abuses she suffered as a very young child. These involved emotional torture (chased with a knife by her mom until she hid under the sofa, where the mom would jab her with the knife in her bottom), physical beatings, physical neglect (days without food and being left with her siblings alone in the house), and witnessing abuse to her baby brother and her father's finger being cut off by her mother. She also remembered being left on her father's doorstep by her mom. Her mother would ring the bell and run, leaving her for a week at a time. One day her father became wise and as the mother left Melinda on the doorstep and began to run away the father shot the mother in the arm. Melinda was about four years old when this incident took place. She was relieved that she was finally able to verbalize these memories but was also quite distraught, and she missed more and more appointments. Also, to add to her anger, it so happened that at the times she chose to come to my office unannounced, I was with other patients. We went four weeks without seeing each other.

After our month-long hiatus Melinda once again began to come promptly to her scheduled appointments. She began to identify why she has trouble with intimacy and trust and has stated that she would like this to change. Melinda became more self-reflective and identified deep feelings. She began to give jumbled, painful memories words and meaning. She also became much less depressed and was able to experience her daily life with increased amounts of joy.

After one year Melinda graduated from the shelter program and moved out into an apartment in a lovely tree-lined street with many young children on the block. She continued to work and go to college. She expressed the desire to continue our work together, but travel and finances made it difficult. I left the door open, trusting her to come if and when she needed to. She continued to call to touch base for the next year.

Melinda reenacted her chaotic life experiences and relationships within our relationship. I understood her unreasonable demands on me as I became the much-desired, needed, and sought-after mother within the transference. Melinda's demands demonstrated that she was desperately searching for a loving attachment to a mother who could love her in return. When I allowed her to appear any old time for her sessions I must have seemed like the always-available fantasy mother of infancy. When I was unable to see her on demand the frustration was intolerable for her but it also helped her to internalize the fact that no mother, not even the good-enough mother, is always available.

Melinda's ability to finally have me bear witness to her painfully abusive childhood memories showed her capacity to begin to trust me. Within the therapeutic space that we co-created, she reenacted what it felt like to be the infant who needed to be fed, and when that was no longer needed she enacted the demanding rapprochement-phase toddler. Melinda would have benefited from continued therapy and I felt sad that she moved and was unable to continue. However, she was resilient and possessed many strengths. It is my belief that bringing her infant to her sessions not only helped her to be a proud, attentive mother as she shared her baby with me, but she was able to nurture herself as she cared for her infant. My work was primarily with Melinda, but the attachment that formed between the two of us clearly facilitated her infant daughter's development. It was remarkable to witness.

ISABEL: A FAILED THERAPY

Isabel's story is a sad one to tell. I saw her in intensive psychoanalytic psychotherapy for only ten months when she was taken from her mother and placed in foster care. I facilitated this event, which was an excruciating process. This was a difficult and heart-wrenching experience but an action which I felt I had no other choice but to make and follow through with.

When Isabel and her mother (Christy) moved into our shelter she was two years, nine months old. Christy was in her eighth month of pregnancy. Christy had lost custody of Isabel when she was 23 months old and they had just been reunited before being accepted by our agency. During the ten months that Isabel was in foster care Christy visited her seven times.

Isabel was born to a young 16-year-old mom still in high school and the pregnancy was difficult. At 33 weeks' gestation Isabel went into fetal distress and was delivered by emergency cesarean section. Isabel developed asthma before her first birthday and often had difficulty breathing. My first impression of Isabel was that she was a chubby child with a wide, expressionless face. In the short time she had been in our daycare she had already developed the reputation of being a "handful." I observed her with her mother in the lobby running from her, crawling on the floor making noises, and turning a deaf ear to her mother's harsh demands. I found her to be an awkward child, unaware of her own body in space and seemingly oblivious to what was going on around her.

In our first contact she was unable to make eye contact and was highly anxious. She was extremely worried about her mother's whereabouts. Isabel was difficult to understand as she jumbled her many words together in a rush. She showed delight in discovering my toys and exploring my office but it was as if I was not in the room. She completely ignored me, made no eye contact, and never included me in any of her play. I felt very disconnected from this little girl. I wondered if she felt this way with her mom. Her experience had been one of great loss when she was placed in foster care before her second birthday.

Christy came to meet with me with her infant son in her arms. She was a very tall, mature-looking girl. I had to keep reminding myself that she was only 18 years old. She was an imposing angry young woman. She told me how her own mother called the authorities to have Isabel removed from the home and how she herself was kicked out of her mother's home. I found her to be intelligent and articulate yet her rage and hate were frightening. Later that day, I realized she had stolen from my office, a valued tiny baby figure that I kept on my desk that she had asked to look at and hold. I felt intruded upon as a prized possession of mine had been taken. I wondered why she needed to take this tiny doll? What was the meaning to her?

Isabel's play was wild, confused, disconnected and frantic. She would try to attack my body and often attempted to pull up my shirt. It was difficult to understand her speech and I had trouble getting her to look at me. I had cookies in a cabinet and she ate the whole box with a ravenousness that it seemed could not be satisfied. However as she stuffed cookies and crackers into her mouth I would sit with her and speak quietly to her or read to her. This activity, over time, had a calming effect and became a ritual in our work. Isabel's eating was a metaphor: she was showing me how emotionally hungry she was and I attempted to feed her with understanding and being with her.

Weeks went by as I saw Isabel three times per week and she remained scattered, wild, and disconnected except when consuming cookies. Then one session at the very end as we were cleaning up, which I did as she refused to help, she began to make up a game with the dollhouse people. The white mom was me. She put Miss Ann and Isabel into the car and sat on top of it. I: "I want a kiss and a hug from the Miss Ann doll." She showed me how much our relationship meant to her by displacing her feelings onto the doll. This was a safe way of expressing her affection for me. She was telling me that she wanted me to return her love and she would sit on top of me to make sure I did not escape her affection or be taken away from her. She began to put words to our hunger metaphor and as soon as she saw me she would ask to be picked up and say: "Feed Me!"

She began to reenact her abandonment trauma. Her play was all about babies looking for their mommies. However, this play caused her overwhelming anxiety and she would become wild, try to hit me and attempt to run away on the inner-city streets on our walk back to daycare. In one particular session she began to play in the sand but was unable to follow my rule of not throwing sand. I had to physically remove her from the sand area and she tried to kick me and slap me in the face. I was able to intercept these attacks by physically restraining her, simultaneously telling her that I would not allow her to hurt me. She screamed at me to shut up! A: "Isabel you are feeling very angry feelings for me right now but I can't let you hurt me just like I won't let anyone hurt you." She turned her back to me, disengaged, and quietly talked to herself as she played with the dollhouse people. She asked to be carried back to daycare and as we walked across the street I reminded her of how angry she was with me today. She put her head down on my shoulder and gently patted my back. This was a tender moment not to be repeated for many months. Her sessions were extremely difficult and I found myself dreading them. I was always protecting myself from getting physically hurt and she was all demands and rage. Her sadness was too painful, too intolerable to surface. Her fury and hate were her only protection from a terrible, harsh world.

Four months later, her father, who had been incarcerated since before her birth, came into her life. She was to spend two weeks with him. When she came back from this visit she acted out with the dollhouse people many violent, sexual interactions with narration such as: "My daddy bites men. He bites men on the tummy and kicks them in the head." Then she would have the mom and dad doll kiss and hug and put the mom, dad, and baby brother in one bed and put herself in a separate bed. When it was time to clean up Isabel became violent and attempted to break toys. As I carried her back to daycare I spoke to her about all of her angry feelings and how we can still have our special time together even when she is so angry. She put her head down and I could feel her tense body relax as she molded to my body.

A month later daycare teachers were making daily complaints about Isabel's hygiene. Her mother was not keeping her clean and her bottom was raw from caked-on feces. After many warnings and attempts at helping Christy to take proper care of her daughter a call was made to Childline for neglect, but it was considered unfounded. The downward cycle had begun. Christy was avoiding me, standing me up for all appointments as she became angrier and more enraged with all who tried to help her. She tested positive for drugs, was unable to keep her unit clean, had not paid her rent, and was observed hitting Isabel on the front steps of the shelter. The list of mishaps and problems went on and on. Isabel's play in her sessions demonstrated harsh mothering. All of her dollhouse dramas included children being punished in closets and being hit and left. She played out this abuse with flat affect. As her life at home became more chaotic she played that Mommy is a monster: "The Mommy is a monster." A: "Sometimes when moms get very angry they seem like monsters." She shook her yes with wide eyes as if being understood for the first time. I: "I'm scared of mommy monsters who put girls in closets and hit girls." A: "Yes that is very scary for a little girl to be put in a dark closet and be hit by a mommy monster." She goes to the dollhouse and takes only mom dolls. She gives them time-out and tells them to "shut your face!" She finally yells: "go to bed you monster!"

I had begun seeing Isabel in June, and in the first week of November I was away for a week. When I returned I learned that due to noncompliance, Christy and her children had been dismissed from the shelter, given one month to find a place to live. When I went to Isabel's daycare classroom to get her for her first session since my vacation I found her sitting at a table, head down, looking very sad. I knelt down beside her and softly told her that I missed her when I was away. She took my hand and we began to walk to my office when she said: "Please pick me up, I don't want to walk. I need you to carry me." In the past she demanded to have her needs met by making use of hostility and rage. She was now allowing me to see her vulnerability, her profound sadness. In her session she ate and drank greedily, gave me many shots but put a bandage on each one and comforted me. She made dinner and fed me pretend food. I spoke to her about moving and going to a new daycare and not seeing me anymore, but she did not respond. On the way back to daycare she said: "I need you to carry me. If I walk I might fall down." An hour later I had to retrieve another child I was seeing from her class. Isabel came up behind me and put her back to my back and stood there motionless in silence. It seemed as if she could only approach me backward, and her only way of getting comfort from me was to stand back to back. I felt very bad that this family was being put back out on the streets. What would become of Isabel and her infant brother?

The next week when I went to pick up Isabel for her session, Christy was in the daycare classroom. Isabel saw me enter her classroom and came over to me and took my hand. Her mother said: "You can't go with Miss Ann because you didn't ask me." It was obvious that Christy was teasing her daughter but Isabel seemed unsure and stood frozen holding my hand with a half-smile which showed her anxiety. Christy came across the room and made Isabel repeat after her word for word "Can-I-go-with-Miss-Ann?" Christy walked with us across the street holding Isabel by the armpits "playing" with her. At first Isabel seemed to enjoy this rough physical play but it quickly became painful and overstimulating and she began to yell out "Stop it!" Christy did not heed her child's cries and continued. When Isabel's expression changed from anxiety to anguish I spoke up and told Christy that I thought perhaps Isabel was no longer enjoying their play and really meant it when she asked her mom to stop. Christy continued for a few more seconds perhaps in an effort to ward off humiliation as I had clearly observed her being inappropriate with her child. When we got to the lobby Christy demanded a kiss and Isabel stood frozen and anxious once again. Her mother grabbed her and kissed her forcefully and long on the mouth. Once in my office Isabel was fearful that her mother would enter our safe play space and had me look out in the hall as she hid behind the door. She drew Mommy and Daddy and monster. I was not sure just who the monster represented. Was it Mom? Or was it Isabel herself or both? For the first time I was aware of Isabel's unclean odor: she clearly had not been bathed properly and smelled of feces.

For the next several days Isabel was away staying with her father again. When she returned she told me a monster had hit and kicked her mother and knocked her down. As we walked across the street she pointed to an African American man and yelled out: "There's the monster, there's the monster!" We ran into Christy in the lobby drinking a bottle of juice. Isabel asked for a drink and Christy let her take a little sip but insisted she say thank you several times. She played cooking, ordering me to eat and not to eat in a very controlling manner. She ate cookies in a frantic way and was unable to focus when she asked me to read to her. Isabel enacted sexual intercourse with the dollhouse people and wanted to kiss me on the mouth as her mother had kissed her. It was a very difficult session.

In her next session she played out "killing the monster." I was the monster whom she shot over and over. I began to feel abused and vulnerable and told her that it was not a good feeling to be killed over and over. She became agitated and extremely overstimulated by the aggression that she was unable to modulate. I did my best to help her calm down but she became frantic as she attempted to kick, bite, and slap me. I was forced to end this session early in order to help Isabel regulate her hostile aggression. She asked to be carried back to daycare, which was the only way she could be calmed.

Her next several sessions were extremely difficult. Isabel was overwrought, as she screamed, hit, bit, and attempted to destroy my office by hurling and dumping everything in sight. No intervention proved effective and many sessions were ended early.

Christy took her children and disappeared for several days, reappearing but refusing to speak to anyone. Isabel was thrilled to see me and sat listening to "Cinderella" and "Snow White" for almost her entire session. She interacted with the stories, focused well, and sat close to me leaning heavily against me. When her session ended she asked to be carried and relaxed, molding her body against mine. This behavior was short-lived. When I went to get her the next day she spit at me as I was helping her on with her coat. She was dirty, loud and demanding. She showed extreme anxiety as she paced my office touching things, demanding food, screaming, and attacking me physically. The next day she was better able to play and made pretend phone calls. I [looks scared]: "Hi mom. Mommy is mean she's a monster. Mommy isn't a monster Mommy is a dear." A: "Sometimes when Mommy gets angry she seems to be like a monster and you get very scared. But you are also telling me that sometimes Mommy can be nice and you love your mommy." I: "Hi Mom will you be nice?" She became agitated and went to the dollhouse, putting the mom and dad together acting out intercourse. I: "Don't touch my butt! Don't touch my butt! Don't touch my daughter!" I verbalized her fear and anger at being touched inappropriately. She became angry, attacking me as I became the *monster*!*

Christy and her children were given a reprieve by the shelter and they stayed on. However, I saw very little of Isabel for several weeks due to vacation over the Christmas holidays. Christy had also begun to leave Isabel with different people for several days at a time. Christy was still hostile to all staff and maintained her silence, refusing all appointments and not responding when spoken to.

When Isabel returned to the shelter I called Christy and asked if I could have a session with Isabel. Christy was eager for me to take her and met me at the elevator with Isabel in hand. Isabel continued with Monster stories and sexual dramas in the dollhouse. When I returned her to her unit her mother played a cruel and heartless game. Isabel knocked loudly on the door calling out for Mommy, telling her she was home. Her mother called through the door to go away. Isabel knocked again. This time Christy opens the door a crack and said: "You don't live here anymore," and closed the door. Isabel's expression was one of terror. Luckily Christy did not continue the game and opened the door again, but just enough so Isabel could squeeze through. The door was shut quickly in my face.

By February I noticed that Christy was practically nonfunctional. Isabel was kept in the unit for the most part and would come to sessions in a sleeper, dirty and smelly. The unit was a disaster and the baby was not looking like he was thriving. Christy was being secretive and it was difficult to get a look at the baby but when I was able to see him he seemed tiny and lethargic. I continued to voice my concerns at team meetings and to Christy that I was worried about both of her children. Isabel appeared to be hungry and devoured any food she could find. The shelter was successful in getting Christy to put both of her children back in daycare where they could be monitored. After two weeks the baby had gained three pounds and seemed more active although he was delayed in development. Daycare had begun to weigh him weekly and keep a record. The baby's failure to thrive was reported to Christy's DHS caseworker by me, which made Christy furious. She screamed at me for over 30 minutes and was unable to listen to anything I had to offer. In sessions Isabel continued to communicate through her play the many abuses she suffered at the hands of her mother. She told me the monster grabs the throat and squeezes. In another session using the dollhouse figures she

---

* It should be noted that numerous calls were made to Childline and DHS, all unfounded.

acted out her hunger. "Mommy Mommy I'm hungry! Go away I'm busy! I'm hungry Mommy! Leave me alone go shut your face in the closet." She locked the doll in a closet.

As a team we struggled long and hard with this fragile family. Everything was done to try to help keep them together, to help Christy be a good-enough mother and to keep the children safe. In April another resident witnessed and reported that she saw Christy punch Isabel in the face and made her nose bleed. DHS was called once again. After an investigation DHS decided to place both of the children in foster care. I spoke with Isabel about leaving and going with a foster mom. She asked for a bottle and a pacifier and lay on my couch for the remainder of her session. I was not sure how much she understood.

Isabel and I had a difficult good-bye. In the end Christy gave her children over to foster care willingly in order to try to get her life together. I helped Isabel act out the leaving with the dollhouse figures. She screamed and hit the foster mom and yelled that she was staying with her mom. She screamed at me to never touch her and ran away from me down the hallway. It was a very sad ending.

It seems quite clear that Isabel's difficulties in regulating her affects was related to her extremely insecure and disorganized attachment to her mother. One year later, as I was driving home from the shelter, I saw Christy. She had her children back. Isabel looked taller and thinner, more mature. Christy was holding the baby and was far along in a third pregnancy. Later I heard they were still homeless, living in another shelter. When I think about this young girl and her children I feel sad and wonder what could I have done different. Where did I fail Isabel and her mom? Isabel's therapy gave her a safe place to be with another person who cared. There just was not enough time to make a difference.

Chapter Three

Cathy: Giving the
Child Back to Her Mother

When I first met Cathy she was two and a half years old. She is African American, quite small for her age, but strikingly beautiful. She lived with her mother and sisters in a small one-bedroom unit in the main building of the shelter. Cathy was recommended for treatment for loss of appetite, weight loss, selective mutism, and withdrawal from relationships. Cathy was unable to relate to the other children in her daycare class and isolated herself to the perimeter of the room where she sat staring off into space. She had been previously toilet trained but had regressed and was now back in diapers. At the onset of treatment, Cathy's mother (Carina) was unstable. She had recently moved into the shelter and was having difficulty following shelter rules. In addition she was experiencing difficulty in appropriately caring for her children. The Department of Human Services (DHS) had told her and the shelter that this was her last chance to keep her children. Hence my initial meeting with Carina was difficult and unsettling, although she was grateful for my involvement in her life, and I sensed her relief.

Carina had lived with her own drug-addicted mother until she was abandoned at seven years of age. Her memories of these early years are few, but she does remember being treated very badly by her mother. She was called names and was physically abused by her mother. She never knew her father. She was sent to live with an uncle who sexually abused her. At age nine she was put into foster care, where her foster father sexually abused her for the next six years. She began to use alcohol at age 11. At 15 she ran away and lived in an emergency shelter for two months until she was placed in a drug and alcohol rehabilitation facility. She remained in this facility for 11 months. For the next 13 months she lived in a children's home. At age 17 she reconnected with her mother and moved in with her. Their relationship was poor

33

and this arrangement was doomed to failure. Months into our relationship Carina was able to tell me about her years spent as a prostitute.

Carina's relationships with the fathers of her children were abusive. She was beaten and forced to prostitute herself. Cathy witnessed domestic violence from birth until three months of age when Carina's paramour called DHS and had Cathy and her one-year-old sister removed from the home, alleging neglect and abandonment by their mother. Both babies were placed in separate foster homes. Carina pleaded with the court to allow her frequent visitation with her infant daughter in order to continue breastfeeding, but the request was denied. Carina, feeling completely demoralized and defeated, visited her infant only twice in the eight months they were apart.

Carina was reunited with her two babies around Cathy's first birthday. Carina was now seven months pregnant with her third child. She was reunited with her children because she was living in a shelter. She lived with her three babies in several ill-equipped and unsafe shelters until they arrived at our shelter when Cathy was two years, five months old.

Cathy did not thrive in her foster care environment. At 12 months old she was not yet sitting unassisted (she sat slumped over), was not crawling, and she did not smile or vocalize. From this history it appears that Cathy was suffering from anaclitic depression (Spitz, 1946). Carina cannot remember if Cathy had a social smile before she was removed to foster care. She stated that she was "born serious and quiet." Reunification was very difficult. Cathy did not know her mother and was very unhappy, as was her older sibling who was also not speaking and was head-banging. Carina reported that after Cathy got to know her again she began to develop quickly. She was walking and talking by 16 months and was toilet trained by 22 months.

During the year and a half of going from shelter to shelter Carina continued to get involved in abusive relationships and continued to prostitute herself. It is very possible that Cathy witnessed sexual activity and violent abuse during these months. As stated earlier, when this family moved into our shelter, DHS had threatened that this was Carina's last chance to keep her family together. Carina (age 21) did not know how to keep her children clean, properly feed them, or protect them from danger. She herself had never been cared for, loved or properly parented.

I began to see Cathy in a three times per week, intensive psychoanalytic psychotherapy. I observed Cathy in her classroom and sensed that this little girl was fading away. She was like a small flickering flame on a melting candle. However her need to connect and attach (Bowlby, 1969) came through, as I found out the first time I sat next to her against the wall in a corner of her daycare room.

At first she seemed to ignore me or perhaps not even notice I was sitting near her. I took a small car and began to drive it from me to her, making very quiet car noises. After several minutes she took the car from my hand and drove it back to me. She made eye contact as we continued this play for several minutes. She left her classroom with me easily and explored my office but did not play. She was completely silent but seemed to listen to me as I quietly spoke. At the end of our first week she gestured to be carried to my office and when it was time to end she had a violent silent tantrum. She threw herself backward, hitting the floor hard, her body heaving in silent sobs. At the end of our first month she began to speak. Her voice was almost a whisper but her speech was clear and she spoke in full sentences. She also began to speak in daycare and to her mother.

Eight months into our work she began to spend many of her sessions asleep in my arms. She would crawl onto my lap, put her head down on my chest, and ask me to sing to her. In many sessions she slept the whole time, in other sessions she would sleep for part of the time, awaken, and be able to play. I was not sure what to make of her disappearance into sleep.

At this time I was a first-year candidate in both the child and adult programs in my psychoanalytic institute, and I was given permission to begin an analysis with Cathy. I was now forced to look into the concept of analyzability and all of its many facets. I began to ponder practical and philosophical matters concerning the course of treatment that would most benefit my young patient. Therapeutic benefit of the treatment is an essential component that cannot be properly evaluated until treatment has been ongoing for a considerable length of time. Erle and Goldberg state that "[t]he fullest assessment of a patient's analyzability can be made only after continuing evaluation of the patient and the treatment process throughout the entire course to termination" (Erle & Goldberg, 1984, p. 716). However, Cathy's progress to this point could be evaluated.

Cathy was literally ripped from her mother's breast at three months of age and given to a stranger to care for her. As stated earlier, her history of delayed development while in foster care points to an anaclitic depression. I felt this was compounded by once again losing her primary caretaker (this time, the foster mother). Carina was unable to provide sufficiently for Cathy's physical and emotional needs and the anaclitic depression continued. My decision to embark on the analysis was partly based on the fact that Cathy responded to her intensive psychotherapy by exhibiting changes in her functioning. Her attachment to me and her ability to find pleasure in our relationship could be described as improved object-relatedness. The disappearance of her selective mutism was an indication that her defenses were changing to perhaps more productive and adaptive defenses. And her increased ability to play with other children and begin to learn her daycare curriculum showed additional growth of ego functioning. Cathy remained depressed, but was making developmental gains. She demonstrated growth in autonomy and self-regulation as she once again became toilet trained and began to make her needs known. All of these advances were indications that Cathy would benefit from an analysis.

Carina made a commitment to her daughter's therapy and was capable of allowing her child to cultivate a close relationship with her analyst without feeling threatened. Carina was also able to form a positive alliance with me. She used me for support and as an educational guide in mothering skills, but also made use of me as a developmental object for herself. The young child's internal and external worlds are not yet firmly separated and new object experiences may therefore have more impact on his intrapsychic world. Conversely the young child is more vulnerable to pathological input, and we need to be more concerned about how analytic gains can be consolidated and sustained in the face of massive pathological parental influence. "Work with parents then becomes an essential part of the young child's treatment and will represent another set of intermediary aims and aims of outcome that the child analyst has to take into account" (Kennedy & Moran, 1991, p. 190). Carina was able to understand that I needed her help in helping her daughter and she was willing to participate in the analysis. Carina formed an attachment to me, and a positive transference developed. I became the mother she longed for as I helped her to mother her own little girl.

Cathy, although extremely depressed, appeared to be bright and above average in intelligence. She had several strengths, such as being able to focus and concentrate on a difficult task for long periods of time. She was able to make use of symbols and metaphor in her play and demonstrated the ability to attach and make good use of me as both a developmental object and a transference object. Her academic performance in her daycare program was age appropriate and she had begun to play with other children.

There is never a guarantee that any analysand will remain in treatment long enough for analytic goals to be reached. However, Carina and her children had a full year remaining in our agency and it was my hope that Carina would come to highly value our relationship so that when she was able to move into her own home she would choose a place that was geographically close enough to be able to continue our work. In hindsight this was wishful thinking on my part and not realistic.

I realized that there were risks in beginning an analysis with Cathy. It was possible that Carina would not form a strong enough attachment to me to support the work and that environmental reality would get in the way. Both Carina and her children had suffered lifelong abuses and abject poverty. Carina was unable to provide a safe home for her children and at times was unable to provide enough food to nourish them. Many analytic scholars would argue that the extreme conditions of this family's life would be counterproductive and outweigh any gains that an analysis may bring. However, as long ago as 1954 Stone remarked that "[h]opeless or grave situations, lack of talent or ability (usually regarded as 'inhibition'), lack of an adequate philosophy of life, and almost any chronic physical illness may be brought to psychoanalysis for cure" (Stone, 1954, p. 568). In making the decision to get under way with the analysis, I relied on the fact that Carina responded positively to the holding environment that the shelter provided.

Carina began her own individual therapy with another therapist and she developed a close trusting relationship with her case manager. Cathy's older sister also entered her own individual therapy. As Cathy and I embarked on our analytic journey, Carina verbalized her support of the work and began her own process of growth and healing. It was crucial to the work that Carina be involved in the analysis. To exclude her would be "akin to a neglect of the child's developmental needs" (Harley, 1986, p. 141). However, I also realized that the shelter held this young family together, and it was the shelter that also supported and held the analysis.

Certainly Cathy is far from the "ideal" analytic patient but I was steadfast in my belief that an analysis was the most beneficial treatment for her. In the end, it was not Cathy's analyzability I was so concerned about but my own limitations as an analyst that loomed ahead. "Analyzability as a characteristic of the patient has lost ground while increased weight has been given to the limitations of the analyst, especially insufficient empathy, attunement, and so on" (Castelnuovo-Tedesco, 1994, p. 162). Carina was unable to bear Cathy's profound sadness. I worried about my own capabilities to bear such despair.

THE ANALYSIS

I will focus on three segments of the analysis. First I will show the growth of Cathy's sense of self and the development of her healthy primary narcissism. Second I will speak about her gender identity development and confusion, and the beginning of her oedipal conflict. Last, I will demonstrate how mother and child reconnected and developed a new and healthier relationship.

Developing Sense of Self

It is well understood and accepted that trauma jeopardizes emerging ego functions in the infant. Cathy began life in a chaotic environment that was not conducive to the sensitive needs of a newborn and she was further traumatized when she was taken from her mother at three months of age and placed in foster care for the next eight months, where we know she did not develop well. As Cathy developed trust in our relationship she was able to form an attachment to me and make use of me as a developmental object. As this took place an odd symptom developed; she began to fall asleep in her sessions. As I would sit on my couch with this sleeping child in my arms, many thoughts would go through my mind. From *She must be sick!* to *Is this therapy?* to, finally, *Why? What is she getting from this?* I came to understand her sleeping on several levels. Carina's inner life was one of chaos and thus she was unable to set limits or develop rituals for her children. There were no nighttime rituals in this house. Carina's inner chaos was reflected in the messiness/ dirtiness of their living unit and in Carina's inability to put her children to bed at night. There were no bedtime rituals and her little girls often ran wild, through the hallways of the shelter until the middle of the night. Cathy was often just simply tired and would fall asleep in my arms. But on other days when she had received adequate sleep her desire and need to sleep in my arms needed another explanation. I began to understand it as an effort to return to infancy and make use of me as the mother who was taken from her so early. Her sleeping for all or part of her sessions became a replacement for the other symptoms that communicated her striving for attachment and connection.

On still another level Cathy's sleepiness can also be understood as a defense against unbearable feelings. Perhaps sleep was a way of dissociating. At the time I wondered if she was aware of my uncertainty and concerns about my own ability to help her with her overwhelming depression. Coen states: "To bear the unbearable, patients need to gain the confidence that painful affects no longer will be overwhelming as they once seemed" (Coen, 1996, p. 1186). Finally, Cathy's use of me as mother could be understood as transference hunger. Her wish to be one with me felt "insistent, impatient, urgent, and demanding" (Coen, 1996, p. 1187). Simultaneously, my work with Carina was moving forward as I helped her to observe and understand Cathy's need and desire to be held. Carina was receptive and began to see Cathy as a separate person with thoughts, feelings, and needs of her own. She also began to view Cathy's behaviors as developmental needs as opposed to being "spoiled" or acting "like a baby." Slowly, as the months wore on, Cathy slept less and less until this symptom/defense disappeared.

I have described how Cathy was anaclitically depressed. It was almost as if she was attempting to become an infant once again as she lost weight, went back into diapers, and was unable to speak. She stopped interacting with her environment and withdrew into herself. In the first weeks of her therapy she would often spend the entire session sitting on my couch, as I would try to engage her with puppets or other toys. One day as we sat side by side in silence I placed a mirror in front of her and observed that she was unable to gaze upon herself. She looked right past her reflection as if she was invisible or did not exist at all. Periodically I would show her the mirror and found it painful that she was unable to acknowledge herself. As our relationship developed and an attachment began to form, she began to enjoy viewing herself in the mirror. Simultaneously, Carina was beginning to form strong relationships with her own therapist and with me. As mentioned above, it was crucial that Carina see her child as a separate individual. As Cathy began to gain a sense of self she would gaze into the mirror and declare with flat affect and a barely audible monotone voice that it was herself. As she developed a firmer sense of self she began to enjoy primping in front of the mirror, making faces and labeling affects and especially being a monster in the mirror, as she felt safe enough to begin to acknowledge and express her anger. In one of our last sessions she demanded that I follow her around my office with the mirror so it would be available for her to see her reflection. I understood this as an indication that she was developing a necessary dose of healthy narcissism. This is the result of a good enough oral stage of development where the infant's physiological and emotional needs are met, and marks the beginnings of a basic ability to trust (Erikson, 1950) and the "achievement of healthy narcissism, comfort in bodily functioning, and the beginnings of cathexis of the environment-the taste of milk, the feel of warm enfolding arms, the acceptance of mothering persons" (Murphy, Mintzer & Lipsitt, 1989, p. 608). Cathy was unable to acquire "healthy narcissism" as a young infant when it was developmentally appropriate to do so. I imagine that her living conditions were chaotic and hostile as her mother was involved in abusive relationships, prostituted herself, and disappeared for sometimes days on end. Cathy was "unable to develop stable expectations of gratification" (Murphy, Mintzer & Lipsitt, 1989, p. 609).

As Cathy was developing a newfound healthy narcissism through her relationship with me and through the holding environment I was providing for both Cathy and her mother, I too was developing a healthy narcissism as a new analyst within the holding environment that my supervisor provided for me. My training provided me with the foundation to begin the work; theory gave me background and substance, but it was within supervision that I learned the most. My supervisor helped me not to run away from my patient's pain. Week after week she helped me, patiently and with compassion, to understand what Cathy was trying to communicate through her silence, her sleeping and with her joy in discovering her own image in the mirror. As I mirrored Cathy and became attuned to her emotional needs my supervisor became my mirror as I began to view myself as an analyst.

One year after Carina and her children came to live at the shelter and only four months into our work, this vulnerable family was given housing by the city. This meant they would not be staying for their second year and would move as soon as suitable housing could be found. It became painfully apparent to me that Carina would not be capable of bringing her child to her sessions once they moved. However I was not able to face this fact until I forced myself to look at the reality of the situation. Morning after morning I would knock on their door and find them all completely naked, sprawled out, legs intertwined on the pullout single bed in the living room of their one bedroom unit. I was able to be flexible with my schedule and would see another child first as Carina would get her children up and ready for their day. But there were days she was unable to do even this and they would sleep until afternoon. If Carina couldn't bring her child down three flights of stairs to my office she would never be able to cross the city by public transportation.

The goals of Cathy's analysis changed to focus on helping Cathy leave her analysis and me with the least amount of pain and damage. I did not want the analysis to become a reenactment of her early abandonment by her mother and then again by her foster mother. As part of this work I began to make a book for Cathy to take with her. I brought my camera to my office and took many pictures of Cathy in her sessions and included pictures of Cathy and Carina in sessions together. In the last several weeks Cathy and I would look at this book together and she was able to identify how she felt in each picture. I was amazed as she pointed to the photographs and stated: "I am sad there. I was angry with you that day. I was sick that day. I wanted my mommy." In one particular photograph Cathy had an expression of longing mixed with anger and sadness, as she held a baby doll in one hand and reached toward me with the other. In one of our last sessions she pointed to that picture and said: "I wanted you to pick me up and you didn't!" I realized at that moment that I was so intent on taking pictures for her book that I forgot about Cathy's needs. She wanted to be held, needed at that moment to be held, and I missed it. The fact that she was able to view these photographs and explain to me what she was feeling at the time was amazing. These interactions exemplify her developing sense of self and her newfound ability to identify and communicate her affective states and in turn have her emotional needs met. Fonagy states that a major role of the child analyst is to help the child learn to mentalize or think reflectively. Cathy demonstrated her ability to begin to do this as she was able "to understand both the conscious and the unconscious relationships between behavior and internal states" (Fonagy & Target, 1998, p. 105).

Gender Identity and Sexual Development

When we began the analysis Cathy was three years, five months old. In many of her sessions her play included a puppet turtle that would bite off my finger or her own and she would repair this damage by applying bandages to the injured party. This play went on day after day for several weeks. Then one session she wanted me to draw her mother. As I attempted to do this she dictated exactly how this picture should look. I did pretty well until she stated that she wanted her mother to have a "boy-leg." I unfortunately was not as quick minded as my little patient would have liked and I did not know what to do. She became enraged, threw the picture to the floor, had a temper tantrum, and was angry with me for the remainder of her session. As so often happens the opportunity arose a few sessions later to repair my mistake. She was playing with dollhouse figures and told me that the Grandmom doll had a "boy-leg." This time I was prepared. I suggested that perhaps Cathy herself wished that she too could have a penis. She looked at me and said: "Yes! I want a penis." The tone in which she expressed this wish communicated: *You idiot! That is what I have been telling you!*

For the next three months she argued with me over who has a penis and who has a vagina. I attempted to educate her explaining that girls have vaginas and boys have penises but she would have none of my common sense, constantly bestowing girls with both genitalia and insisting that is how it is. During this period of time Carina became involved with another female resident in a sexual relationship. It came to my attention that both women would lock their collective children (nine total) in one room while they had sex in the other room. It became apparent that Cathy witnessed sexual behavior between her mother and her lover. This compounded her gender confusion and helped explain the difficulty she was experiencing as her sexual identity developed. Subsequently, when Carina ended her relationship with this woman Cathy became less sexually stimulated and her gender confusion waned. Her dollhouse figures now possessed the correct genitalia.

As her analysis was coming to an end, Cathy entered her oedipal phase of development. She played out many dramas where she would tape the father doll to her chest and wear him for her entire session. In other play she would have the little girl drive off with her father and live at his house. She would then reintroduce the father and mother who would kiss and hug. She ended her play with the little girl going to sleep in Grandma's bed.

I include clinical material of Cathy's psychosexual growth to demonstrate her use of her treatment and how her relationship with me helped her to work through gender confusion and development, and demonstrate how she was then able to begin her oedipal phase of development.

Reconnection of the Mother/Child Dyad

The first time I saw Carina and her children was just a week or so after they moved into my agency. I watched as Carina walked across the street to deliver her children to daycare. Carina pushed the baby in the stroller while Cathy's older sibling held tight to her mother's skirt. Cathy was 20 feet behind walking with her head down. As they crossed the street Carina never looked behind her to see if her middle child was even following along. This was symbolic of the relationships in this family. The baby was held, carried or pushed, the older sister seemed to instinctively know to grab hold of her mother and not let go. Cathy was left to her own devices. She was left behind.

A goal of the analysis was to help Cathy hold on to her mom. I attempted to do this in the play. As Cathy would play with a mom and girl dollhouse figures I would add: *I think the little girl wants to hold her mommy's hand* and in this way show Cathy that she too could hold onto her mother. However, she was not ready to accept this. As a result of this premature interpretation she became enraged with me and threw the figures to the floor, ending the game.

After her session I would carry Cathy back across the street to her daycare class. We would often meet Carina and her other children in the lobby as they too were going to daycare. I would try to hand Cathy over to her mother but she would refuse to leave my arms and I would walk next to Carina carrying her child. I felt awkward and uncomfortable. It did not feel good to have Cathy choose me over her mother. I would say: *Cathy really wants to be carried and I am available to be the carry lady.* Carina did not seem to mind and in fact appeared relieved that she did not have to deal with dragging her unhappy daughter across the street.

Two months into her analysis, when I went to their living unit to pick up Cathy for her session, she was sick with a very high fever. Carina seemed unconcerned and in fact became angry that her child would interfere with her plans for the day. She planned to take her to daycare and hoped they would not notice she was sick. I touched her and felt her burning skin and suggested that Carina take her temperature. Carina stated matter-of-factly that she lost the thermometer or perhaps lent it out. I inquired if she had given her medication for the fever. She was out of Tylenol. I took over and instead of helping Carina care for her child I did it. I took her to the shelter clinic and reported back to Carina that her child had a high fever, needed to be seen by a doctor, and she needed to stay home and take care of her. Carina became angry and began to throw things around the apartment, fearful that she would be fired from her job and angry that her child needed her.

I did not handle that very well, giving the message to Carina that I was the good mother and she was the bad mother. I knew how to love and care for her child . . . she did not. Carina calmed down and was able to empathize with her child. She stayed home with her and cared for her. The next day she felt proud. Carina may have learned that her first responsibility is to her child and was able to take pleasure in that responsibility. This interaction showed me that it was essential that I revisit and deepen my understanding of my own needs. I was able to face that I took over when Cathy became ill because I felt I could do it better. However there was a deeper driving force that was operating from deep inside me. I was unaware that because of an earlier personal trauma involving a young child of my own I was unconsciously attempting to redo my own ordeal. In other words, in my unthinking quick attempt to make Cathy better (to save her), I was reenacting and attempting to undo the loss of my own child. By saving Cathy's life, perhaps I was trying to go back and fix or somehow erase the illness and subsequent death of my own child. This revelation and deeper understanding of myself allowed me to set new limits and boundaries and allowed me to be better able to bear the unbearable, which in turn permitted me to help Carina reconnect with her child. Stanley Coen states that in order to analyze patients who have experienced trauma "we need to be capable of bearing for the patient, the overwhelming affects from which these patients have needed to wall themselves off" (Coen, 2001, p. 13). As a result of my affective identification with Cathy she was able to tolerate intense affects that before her treatment, had caused her to develop maladaptive defenses such as anorexia, selective mutism, and depression.

Six weeks later Cathy became ill again. This time when I entered the apartment Carina asked me if I would help her out by taking her other children across the street to daycare so she could take Cathy to the doctor. She took the initiative to be the "good enough" mother, I stepped back and was able to be the "good enough" analyst.

My confrontation of my own narcissism and revisiting my own trauma and mourning not only allowed me to include Carina more in the work, bringing her closer to her child but I was now better able to stay with Cathy's most difficult affects without experiencing an overwhelming desire to "fix" them or to make them disappear. Coen asks the question: "So, how much do we analysts need to feel?" (Coen, 2001, p. 20). He answers: "Whatever it takes to help our patients to be able to feel what they cannot bear to feel . . . the analyst needs to feel intensely painful feelings, wishes, and needs" (Coen, 2001, p. 20). Carina did not have the capacity to contain her daughter's distressing affects. Carina had difficulty in containing her own emotions and often became dysregulated. It is the analyst's job to act as the container of often-unbearable affects. But it is also the therapist's obligation to help the mother become better able to take over that job. The following clinical vignette exemplifies this newfound strength in myself as a therapist and the consequences that occurred between mother and child.

Carina began a new job where she had to leave the shelter at 6 a.m. She made arrangements with another resident on her floor to watch her children and take them to daycare. She dressed them while they slept and left them with the door slightly ajar. When Cathy awoke and found her mother gone she was distraught. When her sisters went across the hall to the babysitter Cathy closed the door and locked herself in the apartment, refusing to come out. After two hours her older sister finally persuaded her to open the door and they were taken to daycare where I retrieved her for her session.

In her session she told me what had occurred and said, "I'm mad at my mommy!" She took a stuffed bear that she loved and always treated in a gentle manner and became rough with him. She tossed him into the air, allowing him to drop heavily to the ground. She left the bear in a heap on the floor and got her favorite baby doll. She made a bath for her but instead of washing and powdering and dressing the baby she became angry with her and left her facedown in the water. Cathy spent the remainder of her session on the phone speaking the following dialogue: "Don't you hurt me no more. I told you to listen to me. I'm very mad with you." She called her two grandmothers holding a phone to each ear and said: "Don't hurt Cathy. I said to listen to me! I'm mad with her!" She ends this play by calling her mother: "I'm mad with you. I love you, Mommy." She kisses into the phone. She had a very difficult time ending her session. She exhibited anger toward me and then sadness as she seemed to give up, and withdrawal as she went limp in my arms. As we walked back across the street to daycare I spoke with her softly about how hard it is to end our time together. I continued to speak about how she was able to feel very, very angry with Mommy but at the same time love her and want hugs and kisses from her. Once in her classroom she refused to allow me to put her down. It was not until a beloved teacher's aide entered her room that I was able to transfer her to this woman's arms and leave her.

As it turned out Carina quit that job before she finished even one day and so the next morning she was home getting her girls ready for daycare when I arrived to get Cathy for her session. In speaking with Carina about the previous day's drama, I reminded her how just three days ago I witnessed how she woke Cathy up with a kiss and how her child opened her eyes to see her mommy and awoke with a smile. I explained that there is no replacement for her. That she is the most important person to her children and they need her to be there for them to do little things like kiss them awake in the morning.

In my office Cathy sat on my lap facing me with arms folded and her head down. She began to mutter without opening her mouth. It was very difficult to understand her but I figured out she was saying: "I want my mommy." I spoke with her about what it feels like to just want your mommy. We became engulfed by her sadness. I was able to sit with her for 15 minutes in this terrible sadness. It felt like hours. A single tear escaped from her eyelash and fell to my lap. I began to talk about what had occurred the previous day. How she woke up and Mommy was gone, how angry she was and scared and sad.

All she wanted was Mommy and how today she was feeling so very sad that she could not even move. She shook her head in agreement, but seemed to no longer be able to be with me. She slid off my lap to the floor, crawled over to the farthest corner of my office by the door, and curled into the fetal position with her back toward me. I said: "Let's go find Mommy." Carina was still in her apartment getting her other children ready for daycare. I told Carina that Cathy was feeling dreadfully sad and simply needed her mommy. I put Cathy into her mother's arms and the floodgates opened. Vast sobs exploded from her tiny body. I had never seen Cathy cry like this. Carina held her like an infant and caressed her face and cooed softly to her as her own body began to rock in rhythm to her child's tormented sadness. I was no longer needed and left them to be alone with each other.

Later that day I met with Carina and we spoke about how when Cathy awoke to find her mother already gone it stirred strong emotions in her. She could not bear the feeling of losing her mother. To Cathy the loss of her mother that morning may have been experienced as annihilation anxiety. In Winnicott's words "going to pieces; falling for ever; dying and dying and dying" (Winnicott, 1987, p. 86). I reiterated to Carina that there is no replacement for her and that all Cathy wants is to be loved and cared for by her mom. I commented on how well Carina had handled her daughter's sadness and she said: "When I was a little girl nobody cared when I was sad. If I was sad they would just yell at me and tell me to get away." I told Carina how special it was that she was able to give something to her children that she never had, that was always denied to her.

In the final weeks of the analysis Carina came to many of the sessions or the last few minutes of a session to take her child back. Winnicott speaks of "giving back to the baby the baby's own self" (Winnicott, 1971, p. 118). I was the attuned mother/therapist who allowed Cathy to begin to trust and begin to develop once again. I facilitated Carina's own natural abilities to be able to accept and nurture her child's true self. And that is what it felt like . . . I had simply given her back her child . . . maybe for the first time.

CONCLUSION

For a first-year child and adult psychoanalytic candidate, this case presented several dilemmas. It was certainly not the classical psychoanalytic control case. Much of the work was conducted in a homeless shelter apartment, sitting on a pullout couch, surrounded by naked children. In addition, another portion of our work occurred on the sidewalk of an inner-city street as we traveled back and forth to my office. At first I worried, as I sat in continuous case conference and listened to my fellow candidate present her case, that what I was doing was not an analysis. Cathy's analysis taught me that the internal experiences of middle-class children are not so different from those of homeless children. I had to close that gulf of difference within myself. Cathy and her mother became my teachers as my supervisor guided me and joined with me in this journey. My psychoanalytic training has helped me to understand the profound effects of trauma and deprivation on the inner worlds of mothers and their children and guided my efforts to provide a safe holding environment for the work of learning, feeling, and healing.

It is difficult to discern who benefited most from this relationship. I feel a deep gratitude toward Carina and Cathy. Cathy's analysis forced me to re-examine events in my own life that were preventing me from being a good enough analyst. I learned that all of the analytic theory that I internalize guides my thinking but being-with the patient in her deepest sadness and most hostile anger is what matters most, whether on a pullout bed in a homeless shelter, walking on an inner-city sidewalk, or sitting in a beautifully furnished office.

This case shows how the intensive psychoanalytic work with the young child led to interventions with the mother, and demonstrates how both are needed in order for the child to get back on track developmentally, and for the attachment between mother and child to solidify, improve, and continue to develop.

Chapter Four

Mothering without a Home

Homeless women and their children, prior to residing in a transitional housing facility or long-term shelter, usually have experienced multiple traumas. These numerous, chronic traumas often result in disorganized patterns of attachment, which in turn affect all future development. There are few studies that explore the difficulties that homeless mothers experience in forming positive attachments with their babies. There are also a dearth of programs and interventions that address disturbed attachment patterns within this marginalized population.

The work I describe here was with five very special mothers and their six children. They met at a transitional housing facility or shelter for homeless women and children where they were able to live and receive multiple services for up to two years. When we think of the homeless we rarely think of a young mother pushing a baby stroller down the street with all of her essential belongings in tow. We cannot allow ourselves to think that a mother and baby have nowhere to sleep that night: it is too terrible a thought to allow ourselves to have.

Women with young children are rarely seen living on the street because they know that they will have their children taken from them. When a young woman has two or three little children under the age of four, she will try to rely on different family members but quickly wears out her welcome. These mothers go from family member to family member, couch to couch, or even sleep on someone's floor with their children, never really knowing what to expect the next night. Other homeless mothers may even find themselves sleeping in abandoned buildings or cars, or seeking shelter in a public bathroom, their safety at stake.

How do you end up with a baby and no home? Each of the women in our group had their individual unique story, but there are many common background factors. Almost none of the women who come to live at homeless shelters come from stable families. Many have experienced abuse and neglect and never had a safe place to call home. Often their parents were not able to provide the basics of emotional security and a decent education. Abject poverty, oppressive racism, and dangerous living situations are traumas that get handed down from generation to generation.

As we are all aware, a good home is not just a physical structure but is where we build nurturing relationships that support us as we grow. Home is where we feel cared for, and where we learn to trust, to love, and to feel loved. What happens when our earliest relationships are laden with hurt, fear, and anger? Then home becomes a terrible place, a place to avoid.

Child psychoanalysts and infant researchers who study attachment patterns in infants and young children have much to tell us. Neglect and abuse early in life have long-term harmful effects. The infant brain is shaped by its early experience in the world of relationships. Children who are afraid of their caregivers, or cannot rely on them, cannot learn to trust. They often have grave difficulties in loving and accepting love. These children learn to protect themselves by avoiding or resisting others. As they grow they may continue to distance themselves from others by violence or by drugs.

For some women, this shelter is their first good home. It is a place where they can feel safe and cared for, and for many a place where they come to know themselves and their babies for the first time. In our psychoanalytically informed mom/baby group the women were given a unique opportunity to share their stories with each other in an atmosphere that encouraged trust and hope. In the group the women were able to reflect on their own childhoods and I encouraged them to reflect on themselves as mothers. As they did this they were able to connect the past with the present. With the help of each other and the therapist, they began to explore new ways of being with their children, ways that promote more secure attachments and healthy emotional and physical development.

PURPOSE OF STUDY

This study identified and described the attachment style of homeless mothers, and explored its effect on the resulting attachment style of their children. It incorporated psychoanalytically informed interventions with the goal of aiding the women to develop a deeper capacity to understand and be attuned to their babies' emotional needs. Within these interventions, the women began to learn to recognize attachment behaviors in their children.

Based on the current attachment literature, I hypothesized that my study would demonstrate that mothers with unresolved past trauma and loss tend to have children who have developed disorganized attachment styles. This did not hold true for the small group of mothers and children who participated in the study.

I also hypothesized at the onset of the study that by employing several psychoanalytically informed interventions with both the mother and her child, the child's disorganized/insecure attachment style would improve to an organized/insecure attachment style, and that the mother's attachment style would remain unchanged. These hypotheses were also untrue. These findings will be explored in depth in a later chapter.

This was a valuable study that clearly demonstrated the benefit and cost-effectiveness of using psychoanalytically informed methods to help young mothers and children who are at risk. For instance, such mom/baby groups could easily be implemented in transitional housing facilities, shelters, and daycare centers or nursery schools, as well as in outpatient mental health centers and community centers. In addition to the research findings and the benefit to the study participants, the study produced two films:

1. A parenting film written and acted by the homeless mothers and their children, intended for other homeless families. This film could be used in general parenting classes, but is also useful for all young women who are faced with poverty, homelessness, and marginalization by society at large.
2. A documentary that tells the stories of these women as they come to understand what it means to parent without a home.

This study had both an Intervention Group and a Control Group. Each group was made up of five women and six children. Position in the groups was completely voluntary.

HYPOTHESES

At the onset of the study I had the following hypotheses:

H_1 Adult attachment style will remain the same in both the Intervention and Control Groups.

H_2 The Intervention Group children's attachment style will change from disorganized to insecure/organized.

H_3 There will be an increase in cognitive function in the intervention group children, with less of an increase in cognitive function in the Control Group.

H_4 Experience Scores will improve in the AAI for the women in the Intervention Group but not for the women in the Control Group (see appendix D for detailed descriptions of AAI and Strange Situation measurements).

H_5 State of Mind Scales will improve on the AAI for the women in the Intervention Group but not for the women in the Control Group.

H_6 Scales for Overall States of Mind will improve on the AAI for women in the Intervention Group but not for the women in the Control Group.

Each of the hypotheses will be explored and explained with detailed data in later chapters.

RESEARCH METHODOLOGY AND RESEARCH TOOLS

This study included an Intervention Group and a Control Group. Each group included five women and six children. All of the women and children were residents of a transitional housing facility for homeless women and children located in a large metropolitan city.

At the onset and termination of this project I administered the Adult Attachment Interview (AAI) to all of the adult participants in both the Intervention and Control Groups. All of the children in both the Intervention and Control Groups underwent the Strange Situation at the onset of the project and again at termination of the project. In addition the children in both groups received the Bayley Cognitive Infant Assessment Measurement at both the onset and termination of the project.

I met in a mom/baby group with five homeless mothers and their six children, who ranged in age from one week to three years old. We met twice weekly for two hours, over six months. For the first hour the children played together in a playroom with a child therapist employed by the shelter and supervised for this project by myself. During this time away from their mothers, we focused on attachment concepts and concerns of the children. For example, if a child demonstrated anxiety during the separation from his mother, the therapist addressed these difficult feelings in the presence of the other children, and helped the anxious child put words to how the separation from mother felt. The child therapist promoted recognizing complex and painful affects and putting words to these feelings. In addition, her work with the children promoted empathy and facilitated the development of the ability to mentalize.

While the children were in the playroom with the child therapist, I met with the mothers. During this hour the women had the chance to view themselves on videotape from previous sessions. Normal child development was addressed as the women learned to recognize attachment behaviors in their children. In addition they were given the opportunity to talk about daily problems and issues they experienced with their children.

As we talked, the mothers made "baby" books using photographs that were taken during our group play-sessions. The women were given cameras to capture important moments outside the group, in addition to photos of their other children. In these books the women wrote about hopes, wishes, worries, concerns, and dreams.

In the second hour the mothers and children "played" together. Attachment behaviors were addressed as they appeared within the group interactions. There was some structured time with the mothers and babies together where dance movement and singing became an important ritual. This portion of group ended with snack and reading, which was eventually anticipated and enjoyed by both mothers and children.

The whole project was filmed in order to fulfill the goals of the study: a documentary, and a parenting video. More will be said about these films in a later chapter.

INTERVENTION AND CONTROL GROUPS

Every family who lived at the shelter with a child under age three was offered the opportunity to participate in either the Intervention or the Control Groups. The project was explained at a shelter meeting where I asked for volunteers, and I met individually with each woman to discuss the project in depth and explore any concerns. Of those that volunteered, the children were between birth (one mother was nine months pregnant at the onset of the project) and 42 months of age. Both the Control and Intervention Group participants were given the AAI, Strange Situation, and Bayley Scales of Development measures. The families in the Control Group did not participate in the psycho-analytically informed group intervention but did receive all available services offered by the agency. All residents of the transitional housing facility have access to the following services:

1. Life Skills classes to help with cleaning and taking care of a home and children as well as teaching money management.
2. GED preparation
3. Aid in finding additional educational programs
4. Parenting classes
5. Book club
6. State-of-the-art daycare
7. After-school care for school-age children
8. Drug counseling
9. Family trips, such as to the circus and amusement parks

10. Clinical mental health services for both mothers and children
11. Case management

RESEARCH METHODS AND INSTRUMENTS

This study made use of both quantitative and qualitative measurements such as the Adult Attachment Interview (AAI), the Strange Situation, and the Bayley Infant Assessment Measurement. I chose the AAI (Main, 1991, 1995, 1996, 2000) because it is used to measure attachment in adults and is best known for its external correlates. The AAI is able to predict parental sensitivity and infant Strange Situation attachment patterns (Main, 1991). It has been used as an assessment tool in several studies, which demonstrate its strong reliability and validity (Main, 1991). It has been documented that adult attachment is stable in repeat interviews across times ranging from two months to four years In addition, inter-judge agreement on classification is high and the responses to the questions do not change with different inter-viewers (Main, 2000).

I explored the relationship between the attachment styles of the mother/child dyads, using the Strange Situation because there is a strong relationship between the mother's attachment style and that of her child and because the Strange Situation is a valid measure of the child's attachment style. By looking at differences in pre- and post-tests of both the AAI and the Strange Situation, I was able to quantify changes in attachment between the mother and her child and determine the correlation between them.

THE ADULT ATTACHMENT INTERVIEW

The Adult Attachment Interview (AAI) relies completely on the study and coding of verbatim transcripts. The interview measurement is organized into three "states of mind with respect to attachment" (Main, 2000, p. 1078), and is designed to assess an individual's overall "state of mind" (Hesse, 1999). It is vital to note that security in adulthood is not established in relation to a specific relationship. Instead what is coded in this study measurement is "individual differences in *state of mind* with respect to overall attachment history" (Main, 2000, p. 1079). What matters is not the content of life histories but how the individual narrates their story. As Main says, "an individual's life history cannot change [however], it can be told or reconstructed in many different ways" (Main, 2000, p. 1083).

The AAI has proven to be highly reliable in predicting parental sensitivity. There is also a high correlation between AAI results in parents and Strange

Table 4.1. Adult Attachment Interview Categories

F	Securely Autonomous
D	Dismissive
E	Preoccupied
U/d	Unresolved for Trauma and Loss

Situation category in children. The adults whose children are deemed secure in the Strange Situation tend to answer questions in a clear, coherent, and collaborative way (Main, 2000).

The AAI is a semistructured interview that takes between 45 and 90 minutes to administer. It involves about 20 questions and has extensive research validation to support its findings (Shaver & Cassidy, 1999).

Adult attachment representations have been classified into four groups, with each category corresponding theoretically and empirically to attachment traits and behaviors of children as observed in the Strange Situation. Adults who fall into the *autonomous secure* category are able to give a coherent narrative of their childhood memories and experiences, to provide both positive and negative examples, and reflect on them. Adults who are *dismissive* give incoherent examples where attachment figures are either demeaned or overly idealized as a defensive strategy against painful childhood memories. The adult who is classified as *preoccupied* tells her story through anger. Her narrative is a never-ending tale of conflict with her attachment figure, and childhood memories appear as if currently happening. These adults often contradict themselves. Adults who are *unresolved* seem disorganized in speech and confuse time sequences. Their narrative contains long silences and unusual details and may be incoherent and irrational (Kachele et al., 2001).

The results of longitudinal studies demonstrate an unmistakable relationship between the attachment styles and representations of mother and child (Main, 1991; Fonagy et al., 1991). From these results a transgenerational transmission of attachment can be inferred (Kachele et al., 2001). Fonagy et al. conducted a study where the predictive quality for the child of mother's attachment is clearly shown: "The attachment quality of the child could be predicted from the attachment representations obtained during an interview conducted when the mothers (n = 100) were pregnant (I = .44 [69%])" (Fonagy et al., 1991 in Kachele, 2001, p. 375).

THE STRANGE SITUATION

As noted above, infants are inherently driven to form attachments. Mary Ainsworth (1978) developed the Strange Situation through which four infant attachment styles have been identified: secure, avoidant, resistant/ambivalent, and disorganized. These attachment styles are determined by the infant's response to brief separations and reunions with the caregiver. It has been determined that infants who demonstrate secure patterns of attachment are upset when separated from their caregiver, but actively regain closeness upon reunion. The infant who has an avoidant attachment style will often behave in ways that are rejecting, may ignore their caregiver's departure, and then may avoid closeness upon reunion. The resistant/ambivalent child is fixated on the caregiver, alternately seeking out soothing or rejecting offers of comfort from the caregiver.

Children who have been abused and maltreated by their major attachment figure often show a disorganized style of attachment. These children will show conflicting behaviors such as simultaneously seeking comfort from and turning away from their primary attachment figure (Hardy, 2007), because when the caregiver is both the major attachment figure and the cause of distress it causes an inherent conflict. The disorganized style of attachment is the one most correlated with psychopathology (Main, 1996).

It has been established that mothers who are sensitive to their infant's communications and signals tend to have children who are securely attached. Mothers who show rejecting behaviors tend to have avoidant infants, while mothers who behave in unpredictable ways have children who are resistant/ambivalent in their attachments (Main, 2000). These three categories of attachment are regarded as organized, in that "behavior and attention (whether flexible or inflexible) is consistent and in addition is comprehensible as an adaptive strategy with respect to the condition (i.e. the care giving situation) in which the infant finds itself" (Main, 2000, p. 1077). Main argues that the insecure attachment patterns of organized attachment are used by the child to maintain closeness to the parent who is otherwise emotionally unavailable, inconsistent, or unpredictable (Main, 2000).

The Strange Situation is a laboratory procedure used to assess infant attachment style. The procedure consists of eight episodes:

1. Parent and child are introduced to the experimental room.
2. Parent and infant are alone. Parent does not participate while infant explores.
3. Stranger enters, converses with parent, then approaches infant. Parent leaves inconspicuously.
4. First separation episode: Stranger's behavior is geared to that of infant.
5. First reunion episode: Parent greets and comforts infant, then leaves again.
6. Second separation episode: Infant is alone.
7. Continuation of second separation episode: Stranger enters and gears behavior to that of infant.

8. Second reunion episode: Parent enters, greets infant, and picks up infant; stranger leaves inconspicuously.

The child's behavior upon the parent's return is what is most important in assessing attachment and classifying into attachment categories (Connell & Goldsmith, 1982; Ainsworth, Blehar, Waters, & Wall, 1978). Ainsworth designed the "Strange Situation" to observe attachment relationships between caretakers and children (Ainsworth, 1978), and identified four patterns of attachment.

The first pattern is the *securely attached (B)* group. When these children are separated from their mother they show distress but are easily soothed upon reunion. They recover quickly and are able to return to play and exploration.

The second group is the *insecure-avoidant (A)*. These children have experienced rejecting interactions with their attachment figure, and avoid the rejection by concentrating on their play in a seemingly untouched manner. They show no distress when the parent leaves the room, nor do they show any emotion upon reunion.

Cortisol levels were measured in these children and showed them to be extremely stressed, indicating that the avoidant strategy is maladaptive.

The third group is the *insecure-ambivalent (resistant) (C)*. These children have had unpredictable experiences with their attachment figure. Sometimes the interactions are responsive and sensitive but at other times the mother is rejecting and/or neglectful of the child's needs. At separation this child is extremely upset and difficult to comfort, and they show anger or passive despair.

The fourth group, described in the 1980s (Main & Solomon, 1986), is *disorganized*. These children are unable to cope when separated from their attachment figure and on reunion they are unable to approach their mother. They exhibit "unintegrated behaviors, such as stereotypic movements after seeking proximity, phases of rigidity, so called 'freezing' and an expression of fear towards their parent" (Kachele et al., 2001, p. 372). Most commonly, disorganized-disoriented attachment style is seen in children who have experienced maltreatment or whose parent has unresolved losses or trauma. The distribution internationally is *secure* (66%), *avoidant* (20%), and *ambivalent* (12%). In nonclinical populations *disorganized* is 15–35 percent but in a

Table 4.2. Strange Situation Categories

B	Securely Attached
A	Insecure-Avoidant
C	Insecure-Ambivalent-Resistant
D	Disorganized

**Table 4.3. Relationship between AAI Categories and
Corresponding Strange Situation Categories**

AAI		Strange Situation	
F	Secure-Autonomous	B	Securely Attached
D	Dismissive	A	Insecure-Avoidant
E	Preoccupied	C	Insecure-Ambivalent/Resistant
u/d	Unresolved for Trauma and Loss	D	Disorganized

clinical population of abused children the frequency of disorganized-disoriented attachment is 80 percent (Main, 1995).

Table 4.3 shows the relationship between the AAI categories and the corresponding Strange Situation categories.

THE PHYSICAL SETUP OF THE STRANGE SITUATION

There are two rooms: a playroom and a camera/observation room, and videotaping is done through a one-way window. The furniture consists of two chairs, for the mother and the stranger, and toys in a triangular configuration. When the child is in the center of the triangle, he/she should be equidistant from the mother and the toys. A digital clock is placed where the stranger can view it. The following toys are necessary: pull toy, plastic milk bottle, toy phone, peg bench and hammer, silver measuring spoons and cups, stacking rings, bus plus driver and passengers.

BAYLEY SCALES OF INFANT DEVELOPMENT II (1993

The Bayley Scales of Infant Development are a standardized assessment of cognitive and motor development for children ages 1 month–42 months. This measurement tool has been renormed (1993) on a stratified random sample of 1,700 children (850 boys and 850 girls). It contains three scales: the mental scale, motor scale, and behavioral rating scale.

Mental Scale: The normalized standard score is called the Mental Development Index, and it evaluates sensory acuities; acquisition of object constancy; memory; learning; problem solving; verbal communication; basis of abstract thinking; and mathematical formation.

Motor Scale: This scale assesses degree of body control, large and small muscle control, manipulations of fingers and hands, and dynamic movement.

Behavioral Rating Scale: This scale measures attention/arousal, orienta-tion/engagement, emotional regulation, and motor quality in children be-tween 1 month and 42 months of age (Bayley, 1993).

I chose to use the Bayley Infant Assessment to demonstrate improve-ments in cognitive development in the children. Cognitive development is contingent on attachment relationships, and the attachment literature asserts that children who are deemed *Disorganized/insecure* often exhibit delays in cognitive development (Brisch, 2002).

PSYCHOANALYTICALLY INFORMED GROUP INTERVENTION

The women and children in the Intervention Group met twice per week for two-hour sessions with the therapist (myself) in a mom/baby group. Within this group the women, with the help of the therapist and of each other, came to know themselves and their babies, perhaps for the first time. As part of the Intervention Group the women had the opportunity to make photo journals of themselves with their children. They were also given cameras to take home. One purpose of the use of photographs was to help the mothers focus on and really *see* themselves and their babies. In addition, the mothers were encour-aged to write in their journals and record hopes and wishes for the future as well as worries and concerns.

The women in the Intervention Group participated in making a docu-mentary where they were given the opportunity to tell their story and speak about how they came to be homeless. They were encouraged to speak about their hopes for the future for their families. The women also collaborated and wrote the script for, and acted in, a parenting film where they tell young women in situations like their own what they wish someone had told them, and what they have learned from their experiences.

First Hour

In the first hour the women spoke about their children's current developmen-tal issues and other relevant concerns with each other and the therapist as they made photo journals of themselves and their children. The photographs were taken during group time, when mothers and children played together. In these books the women wrote about hopes and wishes for their children. Some of the women included pictures, poems, and photos of their other children. In the early weeks, the women had difficulty finding words to describe their in-ner lives and the inner lives of their children. Within the group they began to learn about themselves and discover their children for the first time, beginning to think of their children as separate selves with complex emotions. Most of the women in the group had been abandoned emotionally or even betrayed by their own mothers when they were little. They grew up in crisis amid a backdrop of trauma. "Knowing others and their minds had been fraught with terror, disappointment, and rage. And now they were faced with the enormous challenge of holding their own children in mind" (Slade et al., 2006, p. 76).

The women watched their interactions with their children on video. I was careful to choose one good interaction and one interaction where there are difficulties. Viewing themselves on video is a powerful experience and can affect change quickly. However, the video was viewed as a group so the other women's observations were a crucial component of the discussion.

Second Hour

In the second hour the children joined their mothers in play. Ritualized structure was introduced at this time. All of the group meetings were videotaped, with the video footage used in several different ways. First, it was used in interventions with the mothers: making the films was an empowering experience for the women as they told their stories and offered advice to other young women in similar circumstances. It was also used by the mothers in making a documentary and a parenting film for use outside the study itself.

RITUALS

Structured activities were introduced in the mom/baby group. When I undertook an earlier exploratory study with homeless mothers and children it was evident that although the transitional housing facility provided stability and safety, and is an excellent "holding environment," many of the women continued to live chaotic lives. Perhaps because they lived with a background of violence and trauma as children, they never experienced what it is to have a *bedtime* or a *goodnight story*. For many of the women, ritual was mostly absent from their childhood experiences.

As described earlier, in the first hour of group the women met with the therapist without their children. In the second hour they joined the children, and were instructed to play with their children as they might do in their living units. After this period of undirected play, the therapist introduced structured activities that were repeated in every session. The group always ended with singing and movement and then a snack and a story.

The goal was for the mothers and children to find safety and comfort in the rituals as they took on individual significance and meaning. The children might not understand the words of the story or the song, or they might not be capable of manipulating the symbols for communication, but I predicted that as the ritual took on meaning the baby would be able to respond to it. Because the mothers participated with their children in the ritual activity, each learning their own part of it, the meaning became shared. However, for this shared meaning to occur the mother first had to be able to "accurately identify her infant's feelings" (Brinich, 1982, p. 6). Importantly, it is not the specific content of the ritual that is valuable, but the "sense of understanding and being understood: infant by mother and mother by infant" (Brinich, 1982, p. 6).

VIDEO INTERVENTION

The use of video feedback as an intervention is powerful, because it allows the mother to watch herself interact with her baby. As we watched the mother's interactions with her child on videotape, I put words to the actions, addressing her "representations of her transferences to the infant" (Beebe, 2007, p. 9). This "translation" of the interaction helped the mother to learn to recognize the baby's nonverbal language, to better comprehend her baby's communications, and to respond to them.

SETTING: THE TRANSITIONAL HOUSING FACILITY

The shelter is a transitional residential facility for homeless women and their children. It is located on a quiet residential street in a Latino neighborhood in a neglected section of a major metropolitan city. Each family in the agency has its own living unit equipped with a partial kitchen, bathroom, and up to three bedrooms. Families may never have had a safe place of their own, experienced what it is to feel protected, or had a sense of privacy, so the setting of this shelter is important to them.

Thirty families are in residence. The majority of the residents are African American but there are also Caucasian and Latino families. Mothers must be at least 16 years old, and her children must be under 12. Families are referred by either the city's Office of Emergency Shelter System (OESS) or Housing and Urban Development (HUD). The OESS families remain at the agency for one year; families referred through HUD may remain for up to two years.

This agency provides intensive case management, along with subsidized daycare and after-school care, parenting classes, life skills workshops, and psychodynamic psychotherapy for both the mothers and their children. The daycare facility also serves the general community when space is available, and all of the children enrolled in daycare are eligible for clinical services. Most of them attend weekly therapeutic groups, with specific children identified for individual therapy. After families graduate from the program they are eligible for all services for up to seven years, so that a particular child may remain in treatment for several years if needed.

The agency provides a safe environment that helps the families maintain a feeling of control and relative calm. When families enter—many times after living on the street or in poorly staffed shelters—they often feel silenced, invisible, and powerless. These fragmented families present as disconnected not only from their communities and society at large, but also shattered within themselves. This fragmentation contributes to "a sense of powerlessness and to the individual, family, and societal problems so prevalent today" (Pinderhughes, 1995, p. 132), including child abuse, domestic violence, and substance abuse. One of the main goals of all staff members is to facilitate empowerment among clients: "Empowerment is defined as achieving reasonable control over one's destiny, learning to cope constructively with debilitating forces in society, and acquiring the competence to initiate change at the individual and systems level" (Pinderhughes, 1995, p. 132). But most important, this agency provides a "holding environment" (Winnicott, 1996) so that these families may begin the arduous work of healing.

LIMITATIONS OF STUDY

At the onset, as I undertook this ambitious study, I was aware of numerous limitations that were likely to arise. The following list of limitations were anticipated:

1. There might be a high dropout rate as mothers obtain housing and move out into the city.
2. Homeless women might not want to participate due to worries about confidentiality.
3. It would be impossible to randomly select study participants, so that the sample population would be self-selected, weakening the study.
4. The women must be available in the mornings for the study, but many of the women had full-time jobs that would not allow them to participate.
5. Several of the women might not wish to participate for personal reasons.
6. With only 30 women living in the shelter, not all with children three years old or less, it was extremely difficult to get a large enough group.

7. There is no way to control for age except to limit the study to families who have children three or younger. Because there are a limited number of families available to participate, there is no way to know how many of the children will be in each age group.

8. Because of insufficient funds, as Principal Investigator, I had to take on many of the tasks of this study, including:
   a. AAI interviewer for both the pre- and post-tests
   b. Transport mothers and children to the Strange Situation lab
   c. Administer the Bayley Infant Assessment
   d. Group facilitator/therapist
   e. Supervise both the adult therapist who helped in group and the child therapist who worked with the children

DATA ANALYSIS

The pre- and post-test AAI transcripts were coded by three certified coders in Canada, who completed an inter-coder reliability test. Three certified coders, also in Canada, coded the Strange Situation tapes; one of these coders is certified in coding children between the age of 27 months and 48 months of age.

I interpreted the data from the AAI by noting movement in the subscales of the measure (see appendix for explanation of subscales). Before the study began, I had hypothesized that the children who took part in the Intervention Group would be coded *Disorganized/insecure* in their pre-test Strange Situation but would show improvements toward a less disorganized and more secure style of attachment in their post-test. In this way I demonstrated quantitatively that change occurred in the mother's and children's attachment relationships.

The scores from the Bayley Infant Assessment were used to determine if there was a measurable difference in cognitive function between the children in the Intervention Group and those in the Control Group. I observed differences and change in the women and children who took part in the Intervention Group, examining the value and importance of the relationship that forms between each mother/child dyad and myself. In this way I showed qualitatively that change in attachment relationships occurred.

I used a Group Survey to determine which experiences were most beneficial to the women therapeutically. Through participant observation I determined the value and merit that the filmmaking had for the women and its contribution to change. In addition, I included a detailed history of each woman and child and their journey through the six months of this project.

Chapter Five

Literature Review

Mothers with young children are the fastest growing segment of the homeless population (Baumohl, 1996). When there is chronic stress as a result of extreme poverty and racism, how do families stay functional and cope? What happens when family structure breaks down, leaving young single mothers alone to care for these children? What happens to parenting skills when the mother is poor, homeless, and isolated from family and community support? How do mothers parent when addicted to alcohol or drugs? The combined stress of extreme poverty and homelessness can greatly impair the ability of single mothers to parent their children effectively. A history of poor attachments and abusive relationships, added to the chronic stress of poverty and homelessness, may cause the mother to feel powerless and inadequate.

It has been documented that infants whose mothers are unable to provide comfort and protection, and who do not foster an interest in the world, will not develop the ability for self-regulation. Greenspan tells us that these babies show increased tendencies toward muscle rigidity, gaze aversion, disorganized sleep, and poor eating patterns (Greenspan, 1990). Moreover, the homeless mother is preoccupied with daily, and sometimes hourly, survival; when the homeless infant is overwhelmed, sleep brings peace from an over-stimulating and abusive environment (Koplow, 1996).

The mother without a home is unable to provide an intimate environment in which the infant may experience her as provider and protector. The mother often feels helpless and inadequate in her ability to care for her child in terms of the most basic provision of shelter. Because she herself is totally dependent on others for survival she may defensively detach from her child's dependency needs (Koplow, 1996). Opening herself to her infant's emotional needs requires her to become reacquainted with painful experiences in the present and the past. If her experience was one of rejection and neglect it may be too painful and dangerous to *feel* in the absence of family and home. Karen states that "when one becomes a parent, unresolved pain is shaken loose, the defensive wall is breached and new defensive efforts are required" (Karen, 1998, p. 374). When a homeless mother gazes at her child, her own pain and sadness is mirrored back. Unable to bear her own painful feelings, the mother is also unable to feel empathy for her child's plight: her new defense is to distance herself from her child, and the mother's own depression and powerlessness become overwhelming. Stern calls this the "dead mother complex." He explains that the mother's depression allows her to be physically present but emotionally absent (Stern, 1995). It is easy to understand that both mother and child use most of their energy to survive, with little left for healthy intimacy.

INFANT RESEARCH

In the last 50 years there have been vast changes in our understanding of child development and parent-child relationships. It is useful to view current infant research and its contribution to the evolution of new theory within an historical context. Several infant researchers have made major contributions to theoretical changes based on an interactional point of view, focusing on the dyadic relationship rather than the drive-conflict model. This paradigm change promotes an integration of ethology and communication, and contributes to major changes in clinical technique as well as social policy (Buchheim & Schmucker, 2001).

SPITZ

The earliest empirically based mother-infant research is credited to René Spitz, who was one of the few researchers of his time working predominantly with direct observations of infants and young children. His most famous and prestigious studies were on severe early deprivation of mothering, which often resulted in "Hospitalism," "Anaclitic Depression," or "Autoerotisim" (Emde, 1985). Spitz's first interest was in studying the smiling response in infants. His observations led him to state that the social smile in the infant gave the "impression of striving for, and of pleasure in reciprocity" (Spitz, 1965, p. 99). He was the first researcher to speak of affective discrimination as the earliest mental activity that then set the trajectory for further development.

Spitz wished to understand "the psychological meaning inherent in the child's emotional relations with his human partners" (Spitz, 1983, p. 123), as

he described the consequences of maternal deprivation and maternal overpro-
tection. He contemplated the critical impact of the environment and the mother's psychology on development. Spitz was the first theorist and researcher to
look at the "mutual exchanges in a give and take action and reaction between
two partners which requires from each of them both active and passive responses" (Spitz, 1983, p. 178), and he was the first to acknowledge and stress
the importance of the interactions between the mother and infant as he described their circular process. Spitz said that "the child's initiatives provoke
reverberations in the mother . . . which in turn evoke an answering behavior in
the child and so on, producing ever new constellations of increasing complexity, with varied energy displacements" (Spitz, 1965, pp. 183–184). From this
data he discussed the implications for brain development, the development of
the self, and the development of language (Emde, 1985).

One of Spitz's most important contributions to psychoanalysis and to society was his work with institutionalized infants, from which he coined the
term "hospitalism." (Spitz, 1965). Spitz studied children from two institutions. In the first, the children were in a foundling home, and in the second
group the infants were institutionalized because their mothers were in prison.
In the foundling home, only the children's physical needs were attended to.
He observed a huge contrast in the development of the children based on maternal deprivation. Spitz discovered that children who were institutionalized
from infancy developed significant psychopathology, and stated that "there
is a point under which the mother-child relations cannot be restricted during
the first year without inflicting irreparable damage" (Spitz, 1945, p. 70). He
set out to determine the "pathological factors responsible for the favorable
or unfavorable outcome of infantile development" (Spitz, 1945, p. 56). He
determined, following children in the Foundling Home, that in spite of good
physical care such as hygiene and feeding, the children showed "from the
third month on, extreme susceptibility to infection and illness of any kind"
(Spitz 1945, p. 58). He made the claim that the presence of a mother or primary caretaker compensated for all other environmental deprivations, stating
that "they suffered because their perceptual world is emptied of human partners" (Spitz, 1945, p. 68).

Spitz hoped that his study of institutionalized infants and children would
offer answers for how to help orphaned infants. He also felt that his work
had social implications as women entered the workforce because of World
War II.

Two years after his first study comparing institutionalized infants from
two different institutions, Spitz did a follow-up study and found that out of
the original 91 children in his study 27 had died by the end of the first year.
At the end of the second year another seven children had died, with a total

mortality rate of 37 percent. The remaining 21 children were found to show extreme retardation in development in comparison to their peers raised by a primary caretaker. In this follow-up study Spitz was concerned that "damage inflicted on the infants by their being deprived of maternal care, maternal stimulation, and maternal love, as well as by their being completely isolated is irreparable" (Spitz, 1946, p. 114). He was unsure if these children would benefit from therapeutic interventions.

Spitz built his theory on the idea that in the beginning there are no objects. He considered the psyche to be unstructured. Like Freud, he felt that the infant reacted to the object purely through physical needs. He divided development into stages stating that in the first stage "emotional organization varies from excitation to quiescence, in the second stage the manifestations of unpleasure and pleasure become unmistakable" (Spitz, 1950, p. 67). However he was the first theorist and researcher to claim that during the first year of life a "twoness rules the development of every new behavior and activity" (Spitz, 1950, p. 68), demonstrating that by the eighth month the libidinal object has been established.

Spitz's groundbreaking research demonstrated that there is a vital relationship between the nature of the environment and the etiology of pathology. He claimed that poor environmental conditions made it almost impossible to shift from "narcissistic cathexis into neutralized libido" (Spitz 1950, p. 70), which in turn makes the formation of healthy object relations impossible. Spitz's work was a great contribution to preventive psychiatry and to providing new ideas in how to work therapeutically with children who experience gross early deprivation.

The term Anaclitic Depression was first formulated by Spitz (1946). Infants after six months of age who experienced prolonged separations from their primary caretaker developed symptoms of weeping, apathy, inactivity, withdrawal, sleep problems, weight loss, and developmental regressions, which he gave this label. In addition, feelings of loneliness, helplessness, and fear of abandonment are now understood to be a part of the syndrome. If adequate mothering is reestablished within a reasonable time period, the infant is expected to recover. Spitz also described this as an "emotional deficiency disease" (Spitz, 1965), The occurrence of an anaclitic depression was linked by Spitz to the "developmental milestone of the mother's becoming a consistent and recognized object for the infant" (Wagonfeld & Emde, 1982, p. 66). "Anaclitic" means "leaning upon," and in anaclitic depression the infant becomes depressed because the mother is not experienced as available to lean upon.

Spitz (1965) stated that the manifestations of aggression such as biting and hitting, normally demonstrated in the infant in the second half of the first year of life, are absent in anaclitic depression, and he postulated that the aggressive drive had been turned back onto the self. Many of these infants develop self-injurious behaviors such as head banging and tearing their own hair. Thus the expression of both libidinal attachment and aggression are inhibited.

Anaclitic depression is related to the establishment of an object tie. Spitz emphasized that the children who develop anaclitic depressions are those who had once developed satisfactory object ties. A good object attachment must first be established in order for its loss to be mourned. Erikson (1950) spoke of the loss of maternal love as a cause of anaclitic depression, which he described as a "chronic state of mourning." He further speculated that infants and young children who suffer from the loss of the libidinal object during the second half of the first year might experience a depressive undercurrent for life.

Bowlby (1960) wrote of the effect of maternal loss on the developing infant and observed the sequence of protest, despair, and detachment behaviors from prolonged separation. Mahler (1968) understood anaclitic depression in terms of separation-individuation. She stated that after six months, once a symbiotic relationship with the mother has been established, she is no longer transposable, and her loss produces an anaclitic depression in the infant.

In recent years, attachment research has hypothesized that secure attachment is negatively related to depression, while insecure attachment may predict anaclitic depression.

MAHLER

Margaret Mahler made use of Spitz's work, which highlighted the tremendous trauma that can occur with certain types of separation from the primary caretaker. We know that in Spitz's research the infants were physically separated from their mothers for long periods of time. These separations were obviously out of the control of the infant. Mahler saw this as the child being passive in relation to the separation, and her work on separation took a different turn. She looked at the normal process of separation-individuation, "the child's achievement of separate functioning in the presence of the mother while the child is continually confronted with *minimal* threats of object loss" (Pine & Furer, 1963, p. 325). Mahler pointed out that normal separation-individuation is a developmental task of all humans, and stated that the child attains pleasure in his newfound independent functioning because the mother remains libidinally available (Mahler, 1963).

In the classic book *The Psychological Birth of the Human Infant: Separation-Individuation* (Mahler et al., 1975), the concept of separation-individuation phases, and the process itself, are outlined and extensively defined and described. Mahler's work with very young, severely mentally ill children first led her to describe a "symbiotic psychosis" of early infancy (Mahler, 1952, 1968). She took Spitz's work further and reported that the children she saw had demonstrated normal development to the point when they became separated from their mother. A "rupture [occurred] before he or she was emotionally ready for it, and (in predisposed children) panic, regression, and fragmentation were the result. Stark, panic-driven and overwhelming clinging behaviors (linked to the symbiosis) were often seen, but *secondary* withdrawal into noncontact (autism) was also seen and understood as protective shield against the panic of loss of merger fantasy" (Pine, 1992, p. 104).

Mahler made use of systematic observational research. She studied normal, middle-class children. She observed how they "negotiated the task that the symbiotic psychotic child presumably failed at—that is, the move from symbiosis to self-other differentiation and object relationship" (Pine, 1992, p. 104). In their extensive observational research of mothers and their children, Mahler et al. demonstrated the process of the separation-individuation phase that takes place from five months to 36 months of age. They divided the separation-individuation phase into four sub-phases: "differentiation, practicing, rapprochement, and the move toward object constancy" (Pine, 1992, p. 104).

Mahler's incredible research produced a new theory (separation-individuation theory) and had vital importance to clinical technique as therapists came to understand and make use of it. In past years Mahler's work has been criticized based on newer infant research, which demonstrates that infants are born with "a degree of perceptual and cognitive sophistication too substantial for the infant ever to have been in a phase where he or she failed to differentiate between self and mother" (Pine, 1972, p. 103). Stern states that symbiosis is only a fantasy that emerges later in life and that the infant is born with an awareness of self and other (Stern, 1985).

FRAIBERG

Selma Fraiberg was a pioneer in her efforts to help the underserved population who were at high risk for abuse. In her paper "Ghosts in the Nursery" (1975), she and her colleagues used psychoanalytic concepts to understand and help young mothers who had been identified as rejecting toward their infants. They understood the mother's unhappiness and saw that the mother's troubled history needed to be addressed in order for her to not unconsciously pass on past abuse and rejection to her own infant. What was perhaps most striking is that this work was not done in offices or clinics but in the kitchens of the young families. This was the beginning of bringing psychoanalytically informed therapy off of the couch, out of the office, and to the young families who needed it most.

PARENS

Henri Parens conducted his mother-child observational research from 1970–1977, publishing a 19-year follow-up study and a 39-year follow-up study. He saw mothers and children from the Philadelphia Projects twice per week in a mother-child group. Parens began his research determined to correlate three separate ego functions with mother/child interactions. He initially followed Spitz and Mahler, using an observational frame. However, psychiatric fellows and residents attended some of the sessions and he would point out developmental issues to them. Because he intentionally did not lower his voice, thinking it rude, the mothers overheard and asked to be included in the discussions. Thus his strict observational frame, only answering questions when asked, evolved into teaching the mothers about their children's development. Like Mahler and Spitz before him, he taped all of the sessions with a handheld movie camera.

Parens began to notice what he believed was neutralized aggression in babies as young as 15 weeks. All theory to this point stated that the ego of such a young infant was not mature enough to neutralize aggression, and he commented: "The babies had not read Freud!" (Parens 2006, personal communication). He began to ponder Freud's theory on aggression, discarding the old model and focusing on the behavior of the infants he was observing. This struggle took many months, and culminated in a dream. When he woke he had discovered a new model of aggression (Parens 2006, personal communication).

Parens described four categories of aggression, all postulated on the position that hostile aggression is generated by extreme pain (Parens, 1979). These are: "(1) the unpleasure-related discharges of destructiveness, (2) the nonaffective discharge of destructiveness, (3) the nondestructive discharge of aggression, and, (4) the pleasure-related discharge of aggression" (Parens, 1979, p. 4). His research looking at correlations of ego functions and mother-child interactions had been derailed, and in its stead he formulated a totally new theory of aggression.

Parens was also the first researcher to incorporate parent education with mother-child observation, beginning there and evolving into a program for parent education. From his extensive research he developed a new theory of aggression and suggested a different path by which the little girl enters the oedipal complex (Parens et al., 1976). His findings add to and change technique as the analyst thinks differently about aggressive behaviors and understands the little girl's oedipal phase of development in a new way.

GREENSPAN

Perhaps the most important contribution from Stanley Greenspan has been his longitudinal research study with NIMH, where he explored the parent-infant relationships defining multiple variables. His work involved helping mother/ infant dyads at high risk for attachment difficulties. Greenspan developed an approach where many services were put in place for these high-risk families. In addition to studying the parent-infant dyad, Greenspan was dedicated to developing intervention techniques. He developed a theoretical structure which he termed "the developmental structuralist" approach, basing his theory on two assumptions: "that the child's organizational capacity changes over time to higher levels, so that stimuli (internal and external) of increasing complexity are processed in such a way as to lead to the development of structures of parallel complexity; and that each succeeding stage of development epigenetically builds on the resolution of the characteristic tasks of the preceding stage" (Shopper 1984, p. 122). Greenspan formulated the following five stages:

1. Somatic Level of Organization, Phase I, Homeostasis (birth–3 months)
2. Phase II Attachment (2–7 months)
3. Phase III Somatic-Psychological Differentiation (3–10 months)
4. Phase II Behavioral Organization, Initiative and Internalization (9–24 months)
5. Representational Capacity, Phase I, Representational Differentiation and Consolidation (30–48 months) (Greenspan, 1981)

Greenspan states that at each stage an adaptive structure must form in order to move ahead to the next stage. Most interesting in this work is that once disordered development has been identified a preventive intervention can be designed for the individual parent-child dyad (Greenspan, 1981).

Like Parens, Greenspan worked with an underserved population who presented with multiple problems. These families required a special support staff and outside services. Greenspan differed from other psychoanalytic clinicians in that he did not focus on the parent's past experiences, but instead concentrated on the parent/infant maladaptive fit (Greenspan, 1981).

TRONICK

Central to Edward Tronick's research is the integration of mutual and self-regulation. Tronick (1989) argued that initially the infant needs to regulate physiologic states such as hunger, sleep, and activity cycles. However, following close behind this accomplishment the infant then must learn to regulate affective states. All regulation is accomplished between two people and is "based on the micro-exchange of information through perceptual systems and affective displays as they are appreciated and responded to by mother and infant over time" (Stern et al., 1998, p. 907). Tronick states that self-regulation and mutual regulation occur simultaneously, and explains that the same interactive repertoire, which the infant uses to maintain and repair interactions is also used to perform self-regulating functions (Gianino & Tronick, 1988).

Tronick collected his experimental data on self and mutual regulation by way of the "still face" experiment (Tronick et al., 1978). In this experiment, after two minutes of interactive play the mother is instructed to remain in the infant's sight without moving her facial expressions—in other words, she remains dead-faced and unresponsive. When the mother presents her "still face," the well-adapted infant continues to signal the mother by smiling and making sounds, while the less-adapted infant will turn to self-comforting behaviors and may withdraw and become disorganized (Tronick, 1989). Tronick's still-face experiment led him to the view that while there are always disruptions in the mother-child relationship, the repair is crucial. His data showed that even after the mother returns to her normal self the baby's disturbed mood continues. Tronick concludes that "this finding suggests that even three month old infants are not simply under the control of the immediate stimulus situation, but that events have lasting effects, e.g., are internally represented" (Tronick 1989, p. 114).

Studies of depressed mothers show that disruptions without repair are common in depressed mother-infant dyads. It is then that the balance between self- and mutual regulation becomes unstable (Tronick, 1989). Tronick further states that when self-regulation becomes the overwhelming job of the infant, psychopathology is a likely outcome. Tronick added that dysregulation patterns set the stage for all further interactions and relationships. The infant begins to expect disruption without repair, which in turn organizes further interactions (Tronick, 1989).

Tronick's research on disruption and repair in the mother-infant dyad has led to predictions as to the "future course of the quality of the infant's attachment to his mother" (Beebe & Lachmann, 1994, p. 144). Tronick's findings help to understand how valuable the availability of the caretaker is, that consistency and predictability of the object stimulates an organizing process in the child. Along with understanding and predicting attachment styles, the disruption and repair model has had "wide-ranging influence on psychoanalytic theories of internalization and structure formation" (Beebe & Lachman, 1994, p. 145).

Tronick has suggested that in mutual regulation, each partner affects the other's "state of consciousness." He states that "each individual is a self-organizing system, which creates its own states of consciousness—states of brain organization—which can be expanded into more coherent and complex states in collaboration with another self-organizing system" (Tronick, 1996, p. 9 in Beebe & Lachman, 1998). Tronick's development of the disruption-and-repair model has had a tremendous impact on the evolution of psychoanalytic theory. For example, several influential theorists such as Freud (1917), Kline (1967), and Kohut (1971) all discuss the effect of disruption and disequilibrium as major contributors to structural organization (Beebe, Lachman, & Jaffe, 1997).

Tronick's findings have technique implications, as we come to understand that "both analyst and patient create and transform unique dyadic states of consciousness through mutual and self-regulation" (Beebe & Lachman, 1998, p. 491). As the analyst attends to the patient's self-regulating behaviors, they may be misunderstood as evasive or dissociative without an understanding of this concept.

Tronick's research on self and mutual regulation, and disruption and repair, has contributed critically to understanding the pathology that results when the infant is faced with a chronically depressed mother. His research has furthered psychoanalytic understanding of the patient-analyst dyad and aids our understanding of what cures. In addition, Tronick's work has set the stage for other researchers to expand on his work.

BEEBE

Beatrice Beebe addressed Tronick's work on self and mutual regulation and took it one step further, examining patterns of mutual regulation between mothers and their infants. She films these interactions, and slows down the film so as to make microanalyses possible. Beebe sees patterns in the mother-child interactions, and conceptualizes the various ways of interrelating, suggesting that "the dynamic process of reciprocal adjustments is the substance of these earliest interactive representations" (Beebe & Lachman, 1988, p. 305). Tronick focused his work on self and mutual interactions, while Beebe's research explores mother-infant interaction. Her data helps us to understand the developing self and other representations in the infant (Beebe & Lachman, 1988).

Beebe studied normal mothers and infants (3–4 months old) at play. The baby is placed in an infant seat with the mother facing her infant, and mother and infant are left to play alone as they are filmed using the split-screen technique. This specific research examines social interactions during periods of alert attention (Beebe & Lachman 1988, p. 312). By slowing down the film the researcher is able to observe interactions between the mother and infant that are not visible to the naked eye. Beebe developed a scale that describes the subtle variations of facial expressions that the infant and mother used to interact. She revealed through these films that the mother and infant live in a "split-second" world. In her words: "These split-second mutual adjustments are so rapid that the temporal relations, and many of the fleeting behaviors themselves cannot be fully grasped with the naked eye" (Beebe & Lachman, 1988, p. 316).

By following the direction of affective changes in the mother and infant, Beebe matched patterns that she felt provided the capability to share subjective states (Beebe & Lachman, 1988). Beebe then proposed that these "interaction structures are represented over the early months of life and play a major role in the emerging symbolic forms of self-and object representations" (Beebe & Lachman, 1988, p. 326). She further argues that "characteristic patterns of self and interactive regulation form early interaction structures, which provide an important basis for emerging self and object representations" (Beebe, Lachman & Jaffe, 1997, p. 133). She defines *interactive structures* as distinguishing patterns of the different ways that mother and infant impact one another, "patterns of the ways the interaction unfolds" (Beebe, Lachman & Jaffe, 1997, p. 134). Unlike other researchers, Beebe and her colleagues examine the dyad, not only the individual infant. By looking at the interaction within the dyad, the researcher views the information that is sent and received by both the mother and the infant simultaneously (Beebe, Lachman & Jaffe, 1997). This valuable research demonstrates that there is a very early organizing process occurring as ways of relating are laid down and stabilized, and that this process in turn has important consequences for further development.

In another research project Beebe explores distressed infant-mother interactions. She defines her theory of interaction as examining how "each partner is affected by his own behavior, self-regulation, as well as how each partner is affected by the behavior of the other" (Beebe, 2000, p. 421). She explores how maternal impingement, which causes infant withdrawal, occurs within a co-constructed process. Beebe analyzes split-second videos that showed that "regardless of whether the interaction was positive or disturbed, each person's behavior could be used to predict that of the other, second by second" (Beebe, 2000, 423). Beebe proposes that all individuals are always trying to self-regulate in relation to what is going on in the environment, within an interactive process in the dyad. One of her most important points is that it is "not the presence of disruptions, but the balance between disruption and repair" (Beebe, 2000, p. 426). She postulates that when repairs are made after disruptions occur, the infant is more likely to be securely attached.

Beebe's findings have added to the understanding of the emerging self of the neonate, making it almost impossible to continue to view the infant as undifferentiated. She has demonstrated that the earliest interactive patterns are represented presymbolically: "The infant forms expectations of how these interactions go, whether they are positive or negative. They organize the infant's brain, and they set up a trajectory for development" (Beebe, 2000, 437). Like Parens, Beebe makes use of her theoretical findings clinically. She teaches the parent to be a "baby-watcher," demonstrating how each person's behavior affects the other. Beebe encourages the parent to speak of their own childhood, and attempts to "link the stories of the presenting complaints, the video interaction, and the childhood history" (Beebe, 2000, p. 433). She has also developed her own clinical interventions. For example, when the infant presents as gaze avoidant she teaches the mother to do vocal rhythm coordination, helping the infant to engage (Beebe, 2000).

Even though Beebe's research is based on mothers and their infants, she argues that her findings are relevant to work with adults. She claims that her research documents the slightest variation in self-object interactive regulation patterns. Beebe states: "Observing and owning this process enriches our range and flexibility as analyst. Attention to this self and interactive interface is critical to restoring, expanding, and in some cases, creating access to inner experience as well as interpersonal engagement" (Beebe, 2000, p. 510).

HARRISON

Alexandra Harrison, like those before her, has made brilliant use of film. The difference is, she has taken it out of the research laboratory and brought her camera directly into the treatment room, where she is able to watch in microseconds the dance between the analyst, the mother and child, and/or the interactions of a family. In our field we are used to hearing about a case as the analyst describes it, but Harrison gives us the unique opportunity (when she presents her work) of being, not only invited into the room but also invited to watch the back-and-forth as each individual responds, rejects, repairs, or reflects on the other's words, facial expressions, sounds, and movements—as

Harrison and Tronick (2011) call them, "polysemic bundles" that many psychoanalysts do not often think about because these things occur simultaneously and in real time. Harrison emphasizes that the benefit of film is being able to repeatedly watch it slowed down into microseconds and pick up what is missed in the moment. Viewing the film segments "allows one to uncover key verbal and non-verbal interactions" (Harrison, 2005, p. 128).

Through her use of microanalysis of video, Harrison describes the "something more" than interpretation that brings about therapeutic change (Stern et al., 1998). Using infant observational research data, she adds to psychoanalytic theory and technique by suggesting, "infants interact with caregivers on the basis of a great deal of relational knowledge" (Stern et al., 1998). Infant research has demonstrated that infants anticipate and have expectations, showing surprise and a great deal of upset when expectations are not met (Stern et al., 1998). Through interactive experiences, the infant builds "adaptive strategies . . . [that] constitute the initial organization of his/her domain of *implicit relational knowing*" (Stern et al., 1998). Stern and Harrison point out that *implicit relational knowing* is not reserved for the pre-verbal/pre-symbolic infant, but that all of us interact on this level, including the therapist/patient dyad within the transference. They call this "the 'shared implicit moment' . . . with its roots in the earliest relationships" (Stern et al., 1998).

Harrison has developed the Parent Consultation Model (PCM) using microanalysis of video of family meetings "as the basis for formulations concerning the child's psychological problems" (Harrison, 2005, p. 129). PCM is based on developmental theory, making use of microanalysis of filmed interactions to offer a clinical "assessment of relationship, the mother-child relationship, the sibling relationship, and the marital relationship" (Harrison, 2005, p. 137). Harrison states that "time spent in the family session is short, but videotaped transcription makes possible the recognition of repeated patterns on a micro level, contributing to the larger level behaviors that constitute an adaptation" (Harrison, 2005, p. 138).

ATTACHMENT THEORY

Bowlby (1969, 1973, 1979, 1988) is recognized as the *father* of Attachment Theory. He moved away from the traditional psychoanalytic idea of fantasy life in childhood, as his focus became the impact of real-life experiences of loss and separation on the emotional life and subsequent development of the child. Bowlby believed that the relationship with the primary caretaker was the most significant predictor of the child's future personality development (Kachele, Buchheim & Schmucker, 2001; Hardy, 2007).

Attachment theory postulates that "infants are evolutionarily primed to form a close, enduring, dependent bond on a primary caregiver beginning in the first moments of life" (Hardy, 2007, p. 27). Neonates know their mother's voice, are capable of recognizing faces, and gaze into their parent's eyes while being fed. It is felt that infants are driven to form attachments at birth, to seek protection "by maintaining proximity to the attachment figure or parent in response to real or perceived danger" (George & Solomon 1999, p. 650).

One of Attachment Theory's most valuable contributions has been determining attachment styles. It has been determined through empirical research that "patterns of attachment between infants and parents have proven to be one of the most robust predictors of subsequent development" (Zeanah, Larrieu, Heller & Valliere 2000, p. 223). Two measures of attachment, The Adult Attachment Interview and The Strange Situation, were discussed in chapter 2.

NEUROBIOLOGY AND ATTACHMENT

The neuropsychoanalytic perspective of attachment theory adds a neurobiological component. The affective interactions between infant and caregiver "provide a foundation for neurological development and lead to the creation of neural networks (particularly in the right hemisphere) that will influence the infants' personality and relationships with others throughout life" (Hardy 2007, p. 28). It is interesting to note that the right hemisphere is vital to the communication and reception of emotion. Empathic interpersonal experiences depend on optimal performance in this area of the brain.

Schore states that attachment constitutes "*synchronized dyadic bioenergetic transmissions*" (Schore, 2002, p. 444) between caregiver and infant. This is the capacity of the caregiver to "modulate and process affective states and provide this structure to the infant" (Hardy, 2007, p. 28), and is vital to the infant's early brain development. The attunement of the mother to her infant provides maintenance of "homeostasis and equilibrium in the infants' central and autonomic nervous systems" (Schore, 2002, p. 445). When this homeostasis is disturbed the baby's nervous system must work very hard to maintain equilibrium on its own. If the homeostasis fails, the right brain is "unable to maintain coherent neural connections and goes into a state of shock that leads to dissociation and stalls normal development. When both internal and external regulatory systems fail, a sense of helplessness and hopelessness could result" (Schore, 2002, p. 445). Perhaps this is what occurs in the infants who exhibit disorganized attachment patterns.

In order for the infant to be able to develop a symbolic representational system of mental states that includes the ability to mentalize, the infant needs to bond to another person. When these affectional bonds are disrupted, mal-adaptive attachment patterns develop, challenging further social development (Fonagy et al., 2003). Infant researchers (Stern, 1985; Morton & Johnson, 1991; Meltzoff & Moore, 1977, 1989; Trevarthen, 1979; Brazelton & Tron-ick, 1980; Beebe et al., 1985; Tronick, 1989; Jaffe et al., 2001) have demon-strated that infants can tell people apart from birth. They are able to recognize their mother's voice and imitate facial expressions from birth. There is a "turn-taking" structure to infants' interactions with their caregivers and the "mother and infant are engaged in affective communication from the begin-ning of life in which the mother plays a vital role in modulating the infant's emotional states to make them more manageable" (Fonagy et al., 2003).

The contributions of Meltzoft (1998) demonstrate that the newborn in-fant's imitation, such as opening his mouth or sticking out his tongue, is the infant "comparing his own action . . . against an internal memory, schema, or representation of the action" (Beebe et al., 2003, p. 810) that he saw the adult make. "By six weeks, the infant can observe the model one day and then return 24 hours later and imitate action" (Beebe et al., 2003, p. 810). We speculate that this capacity may be based on mirror neurons.

There seems to be a connection between mindfulness and attachment: "The caregiver's mindfulness about the child's mental states appears to be a signif-icant predictor of the likelihood of secure attachment" (Fonagy et al., 2003), and there is evidence that secure attachment is necessary for the optimal development of cerebral structures supporting mentalization (Schore, 2001). "The right hemisphere is specialized for emotion and social cognition, and the right hemisphere is dominant in the first three years of life, providing an opportunity for attachment relationships to participate in the sculpting of the cerebral substrates of socioemotional behavior and emotional self-regulation" (Fonagy et al., 2003, p. 432). When the attachment relationship is poor the development of cortical structures may become compromised. "These are the same structures that are essential to the activity of mentalizing. Thus, we have potentially interlocking, vicious developmental circles in which attach-ment disturbance, affective hyperarousal, and failure of mentalization are all intertwined" (Fonagy et al., 2003, p. 434).

Early stress and maltreatment inflicted on the infant cause multiple neuro-biological events that could produce lasting changes to the developing brain. Structural consequences of early stress and maltreatment include "reduced size of the mid-portions of the corpus callosum and attenuated develop-ment of the left neocortex, hippocampus, and amygdala. Major functional consequences include increased electrical irritability in limbic structures and reduced functional activity of the cerebellar vermis" (Teicher et al., 2003, p. 33). In addition, early maltreatment and chronic stress affects "neurogenesis, synaptic overproduction and pruning, and myelination during specific sensitive periods" (Teicher et al., 2003, p. 33). The above neurobiological events play a significant role in the later development of psychopathology.

TRAUMA

It is known that cumulative/strain trauma (Kris, 1956), which is frequently silent, often goes unnoticed by all. It is only in retrospect that we are able to view it. Children who experience abject poverty and homelessness are often parented by depressed mothers. Normal life experiences can be limited as there is often no safe place to explore the world: experience is necessary for proper brain development, and a lack of experience can have profound consequences. We know that stressful life events are the strongest predictor of depression in women. Poverty, domestic violence, lack of support, alcoholism and substance abuse are examples of life stressors that can affect the brain's biochemical balance. Strain trauma promotes the development of rigid ego defenses, but in addition it renders the person more vulnerable to shock trauma (Krystal, 1978). When an infant lives with strain trauma (such as poverty, neglect and homelessness), an acute trauma becomes magnified because the infant does not have the ego defenses, self-structures, and actual relational and social support necessary for flexible adaptation to challenges from the environment. It is known that an acute trauma can change the brain's pathways for mood regulation (Van der Kolk et al., 1996); it is also believed that inadequate mothering can have comparable effects.

Parents who have unresolved traumatic histories often find their children's emotional needs overwhelming. As a result, the child's needs and fears may be misinterpreted and distorted (Fraiberg, 1981; Lieberman, 1997). Fonagy points out that trauma interferes with the parent's capacity for reflective functioning, which then adds to distortions and misattribution of the child's affects (Fonagy et al., 1995, 2002). "At a most basic level, the defensive processes enlisted in the face of trauma fragment the development of stable, coherent representations of the self and other" (Slade et al., 2006, p. 77). Infants who experience maltreatment are more likely to develop insecure attachments (Bacon & Richardson, 2001). Attachment researchers connect maltreatment with the formation of the disorganized pattern of attachment arguing that this occurs when there is a "collapse of behavioral strategy" by the infant, when the infant is unable to integrate conflicting behaviors on the part of the attachment figure who is simultaneously the supplier of closeness and the cause of extreme distress. These babies often display contradictory behaviors, such as approaching their caregiver asking for comfort while simultaneously turning away. These infants may also exhibit a frozen, trance-like expression (Main, 1996). Approximately 80 percent of maltreated infants within a sample of children who have experienced abuse are disorganized, and often become adults who are unresolved/disorganized. Both children and adults who are disorganized in their attachment patterns have a greater risk of psychopathology (Hesse & Main, 2000).

A child who is securely attached to his or her primary caretaker usually develops flexible emotional relationships and, if all goes well, the preoedipal and oedipal stages of development proceed smoothly as the child individuates and acquires a strong sense of self. When the mother is emotionally unavailable or rejects and ignores her child's requirements, the child is unable to develop an efficient and adaptive method of communicating his or her needs. Very quickly a system of gross misattunement is established, setting the stage for dysregulation and distress (Stern, 1985; Slade, 1998).

As the mother recognizes and finds meaning in her child's affects, the child is then able to see herself as a thinking, feeling, separate self. When the mother is unable to contain and reflect her infant's affects the infant then becomes unable to self-regulate and normal development is at risk (Slade, 1998). Crucial to an infant's development is the mother's ability for attunement. In order to be properly attuned to her child the mother must be able to differentiate her infant's needs from her own. She must provide a "holding environment" (Winnicott, 1974) "wherein the mother is sensitive and responsive to her infant's needs which will gradually promote the child's slow internalization of the maternal soothing function to help organize beginning ego functioning and modulate the intensity of the drives" (Beebe & Sloate 1982, p. 601). This, in turn, affects all future development.

Stern defines attunement as the "intersubjective sharing of affect" (Stern 1985, p. 141). Several developmental and attachment theorists (such as Bowlby, Ainsworth, Winnicott, Stern, Karen, Fonagy, Beebe, and Steele) all consider attunement to be critical to the psychological and physical development of the infant. As the infant cries and demands to have his needs met, the mother responds and thus gives meaning to the infant's signals. Eventually the infant begins to know what he wants and how to signal with intent. This harmonized mother/infant pas de deux is a form of mutual regulation, and as a result the infant learns to regulate himself. In addition, between birth and five months of age, the face-to-face interactions between mother and infant, with exchanges of affective signals, are key in the baby's development of self-representation of affect (Fonagy & Target, 1997).

First, the infant is able to self-regulate biological functions such as sleep patterns, elimination, and eating. Gradually, as the mother/infant dance continues to develop, the baby learns to self-regulate on a psychological level as well. Shared social experiences (such as playful interchange and mirroring) give the child a sense of being appreciated and cared for. His emotions and affects are accepted and validated. He feels approval. These early social experiences usher the child into the richness of object relations and what it means to relate to another person.

A parent who does not have the capacity for self-reflection is unable to reflect on the inner states of her infant. This child will, in turn, be unable to relate to his or her own inner world. Attachment research has shown that insecurely attached adults tend to persist in strategies and schemas that they first learned from their own rejecting parent. In an effort to avoid an empty inner world devoid of objects, people incorporate malevolent inner objects. This loyalty to the early depriving caregiver causes a parent to continue rejecting patterns in her own interaction with her own children (Eagle, 1995; Karen, 1998). The infant who does not experience attunement and mirroring may experience his emerging preverbal self as defective. He is left to feel empty, helpless, and perhaps even without hope.

Scholars, researchers, and theorists have addressed the essential importance of the early primary object as the basis for physical and psychological development. Winnicott (1960) "conceptualizes the earliest parent-child relationship as a 'holding environment' and emphasizes the importance of empathy, continuity, stability, and safety to the well-being of the child. Being held in an embrace of safety is essential in nourishing the development of healthy intrapsychic structure and a sense of trust" (Paret & Shapiro, 1998, p. 302).

Infant researchers and clinicians who observe the earliest interactions between mother and baby describe the delicate dance between the two, the finely tuned rhythms that develop between the couple as the tiniest nuances of nonverbal communications take place. When misattunement occurs, when the beautiful pas de deux falters and the mother is unable to accurately respond to the baby's affective signals, the child has no choice but to resort to defensive behavioral strategies. It is important to note that mother-infant relationships constantly oscillate between attunement and the cycle of disruption-dysregulation-repair. These disruptions are part of all normal relationships; it is the repair that leads to hope and the expectation that differences can be negotiated and disagreements and misunderstandings repaired. Beebe has demonstrated in her infant-mother research that maternal impingement without repair is highly anxiety provoking for the infant and contributes to "defenses of dissociation, fragmentation, and, in extreme instances a disruption of the very capacity to think itself" (Beebe, 2000).

HOMELESS FAMILIES

In 1997, a study was done to explore the association of stress to behavioral difficulties. Seventy-seven homeless women and children and 90 low-income mothers were assessed using a comprehensive interview protocol, with standardized instruments used to determine the mental health of the mothers and their children's behavior. Multiple linear regression was used to explore the association of stressors to behavior. This study found minimal difference between the homeless children and the low-income children. The researchers concluded that "both homeless and low-income children experienced significant adversity in their lives, with homeless children facing more stress. . . . Mothers' emotional status . . . strongly predict children's negative outcomes" (Bassuk, Weinreb, Dawson, Perloff & Buckner, 1997, pp. 92–100).

A second study conducted a comparative analysis of transcribed interviews that led to the identification of homeless mothers' caring behaviors for their children. These behaviors were: "sacrificing for children, struggling with limitations, guarding from harm, and seeking answers" (Hodnicki & Horner, 1993, pp. 349–356).

In a third study, tape-recorded interviews were analyzed of 16 homeless mothers. The themes that developed in the interviews were "loss of freedom, a sense of being different, feeling down, maternal survival, and living under pressure" (Menke & Wagner, 1997, pp. 315–330).

Two studies, both conducted in Massachusetts, studied 82 and 151 homeless mothers and their children respectively. Both studies, using interviews, determined that 50 percent of the homeless children exhibited developmental lags, anxiety, depression, and learning difficulties. All of these children were in need of psychiatric referral (Bassuk & Rubin, 1987, pp. 279–286; Bassuk, Rubin & Lauriat, 1986, pp. 1097–1101).

The *Keeping the Baby in Mind Project* is a home intervention study with disadvantaged mothers and their babies, which trains home visitors to model reflective functioning in the care and nurturing of infants. The social worker and nurse enter the home during the second trimester of the pregnancy and continue weekly visits until the baby's second birthday. A major goal is to help the mother put meaning to her baby's behaviors. There is also a focus on helping the mother to identify "her own affective experience and to recognize and respond to her child's experience" (Slade, 2002, p. 11). Their research results state that the mother's capacity for reflective functioning greatly affects outcome success toward the goal of helping the mother give her child a sense of safety and security. At the core of this model is the goal of helping the mother learn to "read" her child (Slade, 2002, pp. 14–16).

Another study examined the effectiveness of group-based parent training as a preventive strategy during the preschool years. These training programs are divided into two theoretical categories: cognitive-behavioral and relationship-based. The relationship-based training programs build on parents' communication skills, helping parents to communicate in a more open and accepting way. Research findings show that both cognitive and relationship-based parent groups show improvements in parent and child behavior. Parents who participated (n = 97) in the programs used less coercive discipline strategies, and were less critical and less directive with their children during free play than parents in the control group (n = 91) (Gross & Grady, 2002).

A study titled *Prevention of Insecure Disorganized Attachment (PIDA)*, was conducted at UCLA, starting with the concept that without intervention, trauma gets transmitted intergenerationally. Parents who have unresolved losses may suffer from PTSD and dissociation, tending to reenact their own experiences of trauma with their children and continuing to experience themselves as victims. The group-based intervention is divided into two parts. The first phase is psycho-educational, with information about infant development presented to new mothers, who then share their experiences. In the second phase the women apply what they learned in the first phase. This study determined that the optimal time for successful intervention is before the infant is four months old (Harwood, 2006).

Another important study looked at the usefulness of mother-infant psychotherapy with high-risk dyads. The goal was to increase family use of public resources, decrease the mother's isolation, enhance positive mother-infant interactions, and emphasize the mother's role as a source of emotional security for her infant. The families in this study were referred by social service agencies. The infants had been maltreated and the mothers suffered from depression and other mental health problems. Home visits were conducted. Outcome variables included measures of maternal depression and social isolation, the Strange Situation, and the Bayley Scales of Infant Development (Bayley, 1993). The babies in this study scored as disorganized/insecure in the Strange Situation. Study outcomes demonstrated that babies in psychotherapy with their mothers did better on the Bayley than those who did not receive the intervention (Lyons-Ruth, Connell, & Grunebaum, 1990).

Similar research focused on mother-infant psychotherapy with high-risk dyads has shown similar results. Nylen et al., looked at several studies that all showed that despite different approaches, psychotherapy with depressed mothers and their infants demonstrated improvements in the mother-infant attachment bond (Cicchetti et al., 1999; Cohen et al., 2002; Lyons-Ruth et al., 1990). Nylen et al. concluded that interventions that were designed to target the mother-infant relationship had potential for improvement in the attachment relationship of these high-risk dyads (Nylen, Moran, Franklin & O'Hara, 2006).

Lastly, Moran et al. studied 50 adolescent mothers and infants between the ages of 6–12 months in the intervention group and 50 dyads in the control group. Fifty-seven percent of the mother-infant dyads who received the intervention had secure attachments at 12 months of age compared with only 38 percent of the comparison dyads. The focus of the intervention was helping the mother to alter her behavior toward her infant. It was felt that by using an intervention that focused on increasing awareness, empathic responses, and sensitivity on the part of the mother, a more coherent internal working model of relationships would be facilitated. Within this study, both infant-parent psychotherapy and psychoeducational parenting interventions were effective in increasing attachment security and decreasing disorganization in the dyad (Moran et al., 2007).

Chapter Six

Project Findings

Because of the nature of this project, the quantitative measurements, the AAI and the Strange Situation, could not be made use of in the way they were developed and originally intended. Because of some unforeseen circumstances, and several variables that I was unable to control for, the study population (N) was much too small. In addition, the homeless populace is one of the hardest populations to reach. Even though this study cannot make use of the quantitative instruments to demonstrate change, change did occur within the women and children who participated in the Intervention Group. I believe that the changes were most likely a result of the many psychoanalytically informed qualitative interventions that the families received in the course of the project.

Tables 6.1 and 6.2 show the names (changed for confidentiality) and ages of each mother/child dyad in both the Intervention and Control Groups.

Table 6.1. Intervention Group

Case	Mother	Child	Mother's Age	Child's Age
1	Christa	Iris	20 years	28 months
2	Nina	Karl	21 years	42 months
3	Lena	Noel	25 years	26 months
4	Zoe	Melody	26 years	newborn
5	Fannie	Tom & Rob	23 years	32 months &17 months

Note: Names are changed for confidentiality.

Table 6.2.   Control Group

Case	Mother	Child	Mother's Age	Child's Age
1	Susan	Karen & Karina	28 years	28 months
2	Robin	Linda	32 years	36 months
3	Rose	Abby	20 years	39 months
4	Diana	Mindy	20 years	19 months
5	Helen	Erin	25 years	19 months

Note: Names are changed for confidentiality.

BRIEF SUMMARY

Five homeless mothers and their six children (ages birth–three years) participated in a mom/baby group, twice per week. Each session was two hours in duration. Each woman was given the AAI before the group began and a second time at the termination of the group intervention. The children underwent the "Strange Situation" in a strange situation laboratory located at Temple University. Each child participated in the Strange Situation both at the beginning and end of the project. Attachment style was analyzed and coded for both the mothers and their children at the beginning of the project and at the end.

The children were assessed by the Bayley Infant Assessment Scales at the onset and termination of the project. This measurement evaluates cognitive development. All interviews were tape recorded and filmed. The tape-recorded interviews were transcribed verbatim. In addition, the women actively participated in the making of two of the films: a documentary where they told their stories and a parenting film where they decided on the content and how it would be told.

A control group of five mothers and six children were evaluated with the AAI, Strange Situation, and Bayley Infant Assessment Scales at the beginning and termination of the project. The Control Group did not take part in the psychoanalytically informed group intervention, nor did they take part in the films. Both the Intervention and Control Groups were eligible for all services* offered through the transitional housing facility.

LIMITATIONS AND CONCERNS

My original research design called for a minimum of 8–12 mothers and children in the Intervention and Control Groups respectively. The study popula-

---

* See chapter 2 for description of services.

tion ended up being five women and six children in each group. This occurred for several reasons:

1. The participating child must be between the ages of birth and three years old. There are only 30 families residing at the shelter and only 15 of these families had children between the age of birth and three years old.
2. The Intervention Group took place from 9:30 a.m.–11:30 a.m. This time was chosen because the children were only available before lunch and I was unavailable in the late afternoons or evenings. In addition the women would not have childcare for their other children if we met after school. Therefore the women must be available in the mornings in order to participate. Many of the women had full-time jobs and several of the women were in school full-time.
3. Several women chose not to participate for personal reasons, such as having no interest in attending a mom/baby group. One woman did not want to be interviewed or filmed.

In the original research design I had planned to use random selection. It became evident quickly that this would be impossible, and the final study population for both the Intervention and Control Groups was self-selected. All of the women who chose to participate in the Intervention Group did so because they were excited at the prospect of making films and were interested in learning more about their children. One mother in the Intervention Group felt she was wiser than many of the residents and thought of the group as an opportunity to impart her wisdom to the younger mothers.

The women who chose to participate in the Control Group did so because they saw it as an easy way to make $50 and did not want to commit time and effort to a twice-weekly mom/baby group.

The self-selection component of this study alerts us to the possibility that change occurred in the Intervention Group as opposed to the Control Group because these women were predisposed to accepting what I had to offer. It seems obvious that women who wanted to participate in a mom/baby group did so because they were open to accepting advice and education. The women who chose to participate in the Control Group, for the most part, did so because they had no interest in learning more about their child's development, attachment behaviors, and parenting skills. However, two of the women in the Control Group wanted to be in the Intervention Group but their work schedules did not permit it.

With an N of five women and six children in each group I knew from the beginning that the quantitative measures would be statistically insignificant and meaningless from a research point of view. However, I was interested in what the AAI and Strange Situation would show, so I proceeded with the study. The measures may be interpreted psychodynamically.

From the very beginning of the project attendance was a problem. It began with the difficult task of getting both the Intervention and Control Group participants to schedule time for their initial AAI and Strange Situation test. Scheduling for the Strange Situation at Temple University was difficult, as I had limited use of the Strange Situation lab and was dependent on the intern's school schedule. There were a few times when a mother would forget that we had scheduled an appointment or something would come up and she would not be at the transitional housing facility when I arrived to take her to the lab at Temple University. A couple of times, when this happened, another mother and child just happened to be available and were taken instead.

Homeless families live chaotic lives. It was difficult for all of the women in the Intervention Group to arrive on time and to make a firm commitment to attend all of the sessions. I feel that the difficulties in getting the mothers and children to participate on a regular basis and make a commitment for the full six months parallels their chaotic lives, where they have difficulties keeping a job or finishing a school program or even getting their children to daycare on time.

Of the five women in the Intervention Group, not one had perfect attendance. Zoe and her infant daughter, Melody, were usually the first to arrive and for the most part were on time or even early. Zoe attended on a regular basis, missing one session when Melody was ill, until she was forced back to work by welfare. This occurred ten weeks into the project. After that she attended sporadically, sometimes alone, without her infant who was being cared for by the paternal grandmother. Zoe was excused from her welfare program to attend our group but once she found employment she attended when her work schedule allowed. Two weeks could go by and we would not see her, and then she would come for the next several weeks.

Fannie and her two little boys, Tom and Rob, entered the group two weeks after the project began. This occurred because she had just moved into the shelter. Fannie and her sons attended all but two sessions when she overslept. Fannie had some difficulty getting up in the morning and was usually at least 15 minutes late.

Christa and her daughter Iris attended on a regular basis but like Zoe she was forced to attend a welfare-to-work program and missed several sessions when her welfare supervisor gave her a difficult time about changing her schedule. While the welfare system allowed the women to attend the project, they were required to make up all of the hours they missed. This became a burden to the women in welfare programs. Christa attended 80 percent of our sessions. For the most part she was on time but on occasion could be up to an hour late.

Lena and her daughter Noel attended regularly for the first four months and were about 20 minutes late each session. However, Lena also was made to attend a welfare program, and disappeared from the group for a three-week period. During this time I spoke with her case manager, received the phone number of her welfare supervisor, and made daily calls to this person to explain the project. The supervisor never returned my messages and it was pure luck that one day he happened to answer his phone. Once I spoke with him, he was accommodating and Lena returned to group.

Nina and her son Karl were always available but Nina suffered from vast mood swings. If she was depressed it was a tremendous effort for her to get herself across the street from her living unit to our mom/baby room. She was never on time, and would sometimes arrive 45 minutes late and then not be able to participate and leave. Sometimes she came without her son if he was visiting relatives. There were times when she was feeling better and she would attend and be a very active member of the group. There were several times when I would bump into her before group as I was arriving to set up and Nina was taking her son to daycare. Nina would promise to come to group, stating she just needed to go back to her room and fix herself up, but then she would not make it back across the street. Later she would see me and feel terrible that she was unable to keep her word. Even though Nina's attendance was spotty she attended just under 80 percent of our sessions.

OTHER PARTICIPATION PROBLEMS

One young woman who had a one-month-old infant had agreed to participate and had taken her initial AAI when she was asked to leave the transitional housing facility for inappropriate aggressive behavior. Her dismissal did not affect group dynamics, as the mom/baby group had not yet begun.

Another mother and child contracted to participate in the Intervention Group, participated in the AAI and Strange Situation, and attended the mom/baby group for two weeks. At this point she received her housing and moved. The transitional housing facility offered to pay for transportation so she could continue to participate, but she declined. Her absence from the group was a disappointment as she was very verbal and actively involved in our discussions. In addition her little boy was aggressive and this mother needed help in understanding his behaviors. The other women spoke about her disappearance. At first they were angry that she did not make an effort to stay connected, but seemed to accept it as expected behavior.

POST-TEST SCHEDULING

It is interesting to note that when it came time to end the mom/baby group and once again schedule time for the AAI and the Strange Situation, the mothers in the Intervention Group were extremely cooperative. All five women scheduled their tests within two weeks. However it was quite different for the women in the Control Group. These women had no relationship with me and did not readily make their appointments.

Four of the five Control Group participants had moved out of the transitional housing facility before the study ended. It was extremely difficult tracking them down, as several of the women did not have working phones. Once again it took repeated calling and asking the shelter to help find the women in order to complete the project.

As stated at the beginning of this chapter, the lives of homeless families are often chaotic, making it difficult for them to behave responsibly and make a commitment to the project. However it was obvious that the women in the Intervention Group developed a caring, trusting relationship with me, and because of this relationship they did their best to fulfill their contract of participation. In sharp contrast, the women in the Control Group had no relationship with me and it was extremely difficult to get them to fulfill their limited commitment.

MULTIPLE ROLES: PROS AND CONS

Due to limited staff and financial assistance, I was forced to take on multiple roles in this project.

1. *Met with all perspective participants to describe the project and answer questions:* This was valuable, as the perspective participants were able to get an idea as to whether they wanted to work with me. They were also able to view my enthusiasm and dedication to the work, which gave them an understanding of the importance of their contribution.
2. *AAI interviewer for both the Pre- and Post-tests:* For the pre-test AAI interview I was a stranger: the women had met me only once when they signed up for the project. In the post-test interview the women in the Intervention Group had developed close, trusting relationships with me through the six-month, twice per week, mom/baby group sessions. In their post-tests they were more open and added details to their stories that they neglected to share in the first interview. This does not affect the outcome of the AAI, as it is how the story is told, not the content of the story, which

is measured. All of the women showed some improvement in their ability to tell their story in a coherent fashion. Two of the women improved to the point where they moved from insecure toward a more secure category.

3. *Strange Situation:* I scheduled and carpooled and filmed the Strange Situation. This did not affect the test, as I did not take part in the actual test.

4. *Administered the Bayley Infant Assessment:* For the pre-test I was a stranger to all of the children. However, for the post-test the children who had participated in the Intervention Group were clearly very comfortable with me, and this could have affected their scores. The children in the Control Group did not have a relationship with me.

5. *Therapist:* This was my most valuable role. The close relationships that developed between the group members and myself were the basis of all change that occurred for the women and their children.

6. *Supervised both the adult therapist who helped in group and the child therapist who worked with the children:* This was valuable as the shelter therapists were able to follow my lead and were trained to run future groups.

It is impossible to know how my various roles and relationships affected scores on the quantitative measurements, but it is a variable that I was unable to control for. This could be considered a flaw in the study, causing meaningless results on the standardized measures.

SHARING THEIR STORIES: INTERVENTION GROUP PARTICIPANTS

Christa and Iris

Christa, a pretty 21-year-old African American woman with long reddish braids, was a single mother living in a homeless shelter with her two young children: a four-year-old son, and Iris, who was two years old. Christa's large brown eyes, outlined by long thick eyelashes, were only outdone by her two young children, who had inherited the longest eyelashes I have ever seen. Christa's voluptuous body often became a soft climbing toy for her young daughter, as well as a perfect place for Iris to lay her head when in need of a hug.

Christa described how she had felt betrayed by her mother before she became homeless, and they had stopped speaking. Christa had been living with her mother when they were evicted and her mother moved into a tiny one-room apartment, leaving Christa with nowhere to go with her two babies. "I was just stuck. Um I just didn't have nowhere else to go. I was just stuck so it was going into a shelter or living on the street. I had no choice. It really hurt. I had to go to two shelters that were not safe. It was very very scary. I was very confused and it was depressing. Emotionally, physically, mentally. I was just depressed. And I thought the world was going to end. My world felt like it was going to fall apart."

When I first met Christa to speak with her about the project, she had been living at the transitional housing facility for 13 months and was working hard to finish her GED, pay off her outstanding debts, and move forward toward her dream of becoming a chef and owning her own restaurant. She was eager to join our mom/baby group and she was on time for her AAI and Strange Situation measurements.

History

Christa never knew her father, who died before she was born. She lived alone with her mother until she was three years old, at which time she and her mother moved in with her grandparents and aunt. Christa and her children lived with her mother until she became homeless. She described her relationship with her mother when she was a young child as good, saying that "she was my best friend." Her memories with her mother consisted of going shopping at the mall. As she spoke of these "fun" times with her mother she became hesitant and added "well, the time we did have together. She had to work. She worked nights." Christa felt supported by her mother, such as when she was eight and cut her finger and her mother stayed with her all day; or when she was 16 when her first child was born. "She always said it would be alright. I was only 16 and I was pregnant and going through all that pain and I had to leave school. And it hurt for a while cause I was only 16 and his dad wasn't there for me. So being that and everything, being 16 I thought she was going to disown me. But she had so much support she always told me I was strong enough to get through it."

Christa had only good things to say about her early relationship with her mother. Her memories were of fun shopping trips, getting their nails and hair done together, playing and singing and dancing. It all seemed lovely and happy until I asked her what she did as a little girl when she was upset. "I would punch the wall, write letters, write on the wall, rip stuff apart . . . I guess I wasn't good enough or something like that and I would put holes in the wall and make large circles. I would write my name to know that I did it. I didn't like my mom at the time. I didn't care." In response to the question of what would happen if she were physically hurt—for example, who would care for her—Christa explained that she would make it worse: "I would hurt myself. I remember one time I slammed myself into a door. One time I threw myself down the steps. Stuff like that just to get attention. Now it seems childish, I would get yelled at, but at the time it didn't seem childish." Christa often felt that her mother chose male friends over her, and she sadly stated, "I wasn't important enough to fit into her life." She also felt that she was always being blamed for things she did not do and always seemed to be in trouble. She was beaten by belts and brushes ("anything that would hurt") and was told that she was "bad."

Christa spoke about what it felt like when her mother chose to move into her own tiny apartment leaving Christa and her two babies to fend for themselves. "She just went out by herself and got an efficiency apartment and that really destroyed me because she knew I had the kids. And it was wintertime and I was so depressed emotionally. I had no one to help me, I had no money. It just about killed me. I just stop speaking to her."

Christa's older child had never met his father because he had been incarcerated since before his birth. At the time of our project he was due to be free within the year. Christa was excited that her son would finally get to meet his father. Both of her children were enrolled in the transitional housing facility's daycare where Iris received special services such as speech therapy. Christa was feeling less depressed as she finished up her GED and prepared for her future. She had learned to be "more open, to be open because I mostly shut down as a young child. To let people more inside instead of blocking everybody out cause that is what I mostly do. I block a lot of people out."

Christa and Iris in Group

In the "mother only" portion of our group, Christa was an active participant. She loved making pages for her photograph book and spoke about the journals she kept in her childhood and how important they were to her. Christa was engaged with the other group members, listening closely to what they had to say. She offered support and empathy when appropriate and was eager to give advice and share her own frustrations and concerns. She had creative advice for others and sought out their ideas when she was unsure of how to handle a certain situation. Christa seemed to integrate what I offered in the way of child development and parent education and was noticeably relieved when she became aware that it is normal to be frustrated and/or angry with your child at times. She also seemed open to figuring out better ways of expressing her frustrations and dealing with her own feelings of inadequacies as a mother. She spoke about wanting to be a better mother to her children and to be more available emotionally. It was most important to her that her children know that she loved them and that she would never abandon them.

Christa spoke candidly about how terrible it was for her when she was 15 years old and pregnant. She hid her pregnancy for fear of her mother's reaction; she was afraid she would be thrown out. She also spoke of the shame she felt when she had to go to the "pregnant" room in her high school. As she spoke her facial expression highlighted her words: "I used to see those girls with their big bellies and think bad of them. Boy, now it was me. I couldn't believe it. I was one of them and everyone was thinking bad of me."

Iris was 29 months old when the project began. She was tiny and appeared younger both physically and behaviorally. Her speech was delayed, as she possessed just a few single words and these were difficult to understand. Iris was easily upset. If things did not go her way she quickly fell into tantrums. These moments were accompanied by piercing anguished crying. Christa had a difficult time comforting her daughter during tantrums and stated that her child was just being unreasonable and spiteful. What was most striking was that Christa felt that her little girl wanted to hurt her. She would often say: "She beats me up. She goes after me. She hates me." It was interesting to watch Christa and Iris interact. Iris would approach her mother with excitement and vigor, jumping into her arms, kissing her face and playing with her hair. This lovely interaction would quickly turn "bad." Iris would begin to get overstimulated as she climbed all over her mother, using her as a jungle gym, and Christa would encourage this by holding her upside down or other exciting physical play. Iris would be so overstimulated that she hit her mother or hurt her in some other way, and instead of explaining to her child that her play had crossed a boundary, and helping her to regulate, Christa would fake cry in an exaggerated way, saying that her daughter was "killing" her. These interactions would always end up with Iris crying and being rejected by her mother.

Iris and Christa both enjoyed the singing and movement portion of our group. Iris learned the words to many of the songs and sang and danced, imitating my movements and making her own creative additions. She loved being read to, and would bring me books asking me to start story-time. Iris also loved posing for the camera and was called "the little model'" by the other mothers.

Over the course of the group I felt that Christa was the participant who most benefited from the project as a whole. She seemed to gain a better understanding of her daughter's developmental and emotional needs and she became more capable of being a "secure base" for her child. In our final interview her words spoke for her accomplishments when she told the following story: "Iris was at her father's house for three days last week and I really missed her, I mean I needed the break, don't get me wrong and she does drive me crazy but I did miss her. So I go to get her and she runs and grabs my leg and she's so happy to see me . . . "Mommy! Mommy! Mommy!" It was beautiful it really was. It was just beautiful." This was an incredibly meaningful statement. It seemed as if Christa was now better able to accept her daughter's affection without turning it into a bad situation.

As our project came to an end, Christa and Iris were experiencing many more enjoyable interactions. Christa was better able to set limits and keep appropriate boundaries and Iris was less overstimulated. In addition, Iris's vocabulary increased by leaps and bounds as she was now speaking in sentences and making herself understood.

Nina and Karl

Nina, an attractive, intelligent 21-year-old African American woman, was openly emotional. It was easy to determine how she was feeling on any given day. When she was feeling well her eyes were bright and her features were soft. Her smile and laugh were infectious as she made excellent use of humor in her communications and interactions. However, when she was feeling depressed, her affect became flat and her sadness was palpable. Karl, her three-year-old son, identified with his mother's moods and took them on as his own. When she was feeling bad, he also became depressed. When she was feeling well, Karl too seemed to come alive. Nina also had a one-year-old son who lived with his father's family, and Nina hoped to one day regain custody of her youngest child.

In our first interview, Nina spoke openly about the massive abuse she had endured throughout her childhood.

History

Nina's mother gave birth to her when she was only 14 years old. At 15 she married Nina's father, a man in his twenties. Nina described her early years: "I lived with my mom and dad and I guess they had a fight and stuff like that and then I guess they broke up and then I had a brother and a sister. I have doubts about my own dad. I don't think he's my father." She explained that there was a different name on her birth certificate and her mother was vague when Nina confronted her with her father's identity. Nina's mother was drug addicted and would often leave six-year-old Nina to care for her younger siblings for days at a time. She remembered having no food and making Kool-Aid in the sink for them to drink. When she was six years old Nina's infant sister died while sleeping in bed with her. She was haunted by her sister's death and felt it was her fault. At age seven, when it was discovered that Nina's mother was not taking her to school, the Department of Human Services (DHS) became involved and Nina was removed from her mother's home.

Nina was supposed to go into a foster home but instead her maternal grandmother was granted custody. This was not a safe home, and the abuse and neglect that Nina had experienced in her first seven years continued in her grandmother's home. Nina was sexually, physically, and emotionally abused from the time she was a very young child until she was 14 years old. At 12 she told a therapist about the sexual abuse that was occurring but he did not report it. She never received help as her family refused to believe her and allowed her abusers to remain in the home. In our first interview, Nina spoke openly about the horrific abuse she endured throughout her childhood.

Her relationship with Karl's father was also abusive. She described those years: "He dragged me down the stairs and pulled my hair. I was in the hospital three times. After my son was born, the last time he hit me he ran out and after he ran out I packed my stuff. I walked away and he didn't know I left and he walked into the room and I could hear him screaming but I was already in the elevator. And um he realized I wasn't in there and he chased me. He saw the elevator closing so he was running down the steps to catch me. I made it outside." Nina was able to walk away from her abusive relationship and managed to stay with various family members until her second son was born. At this point she was no longer welcome in her relatives' homes and she sought refuge in the shelter system.

Nina managed to finish high school and would like to continue on to college. She is a talented artist and often draws when feeling down. She also loves science and would like to pursue a career in the sciences.

Nina and Karl in Group

Nina had a difficult time getting to group on time and would often arrive over a half hour late. Some mornings the effort to walk across the street from the residence to our group room was so taxing that when she arrived she appeared exhausted and depleted. There were many sessions in the early months when she would sit silently and contribute in monosyllables only when prodded by me. When she did speak, her words were barely audible. Nina seemed to like the idea of making the mom/baby books and requested that jewels be purchased so that she could decorate the cover of her book. When the jewels were purchased she painstakingly covered every inch of her cover in multi-colored glass beads. While the other mothers were making pages for their books with photos of their children, Nina was unable to do this. She was very critical of herself in the photographs and would refuse to enter them into her book.

As the weeks wore on, Nina's depression waned and she seemed to come alive. As this happened, her wonderful use of humor surfaced. At times she was just plain silly and reminded me of a little girl. She would sit close to me and want to "play." She began to participate in group conversations, sharing her own experiences. One morning the group was talking about what it is like when you are a single mother with nobody to help you and you have a new baby who is fussy and is unable to settle down and sleep. Nina shared how difficult these weeks were for her when Karl was a newborn. She told her story: "I didn't have nobody and I was so depressed, I had postpartum depression, and his father was abusive. I didn't have nobody. At night he cried and cried and nothing I did helped. I wanted to throw him out the window. I really did. So I went in the other room and turned my music on real loud and calmed myself. Then I went back and picked him up and sat myself down in the rocking chair and I tried all over again. I started out new. That's how I did it. I really wanted to throw him out the window, but I didn't."

However, Nina easily slipped back into depression. One particular morning she came in more depressed than I had seen her in the past. She shared with the group that over the weekend she had visited her grandmother's house for a party for her brother. The man who had sexually abused her as a child was invited to this party. She was enraged: "I couldn't believe it! There he was. That's the thing they never believed me. He was always there. I stared at him and wanted to kill him. He just laughed at me. My cousin held me back. She said don't go to jail for him, he isn't worth it. I couldn't believe they let him come there. It was terrible terrible just terrible!" The other women silently listened and commiserated by shaking their heads in agreement with her pain. There was nothing to say. We sat with her and listened to her despair.

The first time I met three-year-old Karl was when I went to his daycare room to take him for his Bayley testing a week before group began. I knew him immediately; he looked just like his mother. His sadness was palpable as he was unable to engage with me and he performed poorly on the test. In group he would lean against his mother as she remained on the couch. The other mothers would get down on the quilt to play with their children. Nina was unable to do this. Karl was unable to leave his mother's side to explore with the other children. One page in their photo book described their participation in the early weeks of group. It is a picture of Karl standing close to his mother as she sits on the couch. Her caption reads: "Me and Karl look on." Karl's facial expression mirrors his mother's depression.

As Nina came out of her depression, so did Karl. A lively, sweet, intelligent verbal little boy emerged. Karl began to play with the other children, joined in the singing and movement, and especially loved snack and reading time. His anger also emerged as he had an occasional temper tantrum when something did not go his way. Nina handled her son's anger by remaining calm. When he was extremely upset (which happened only once) she took him out of the room to help him to calm down and then rejoined the group. Karl made up creative games and Nina was able to participate with him and encourage his creativity and accomplishments.

There was one session when Nina and Karl were the only group members who attended that day (this happened only twice, once with Nina and Karl and once with Fannie and her sons). A fort with chairs and the quilt was constructed. At first I helped Karl to build his fort but Nina quickly joined in as they both moved into their fort/home together. All had great fun as they made up a puppet show and played together. It was hard to tell who enjoyed this morning more!

It was extremely gratifying to once again retrieve Karl from his daycare room for his Bayley post-test a few weeks after the group had ended. He was engaged and animated as he sailed through the various activities. As I took him out to the playground to rejoin his class he asked when the group time would resume.

Lena and Noel

I met Lena for the first time in her living unit in the shelter. I was holding an open meeting for the eligible women to explain my research project and encourage them to participate. Lena's little girl Noel was sick in bed that evening, but Lena was interested in hearing more about the mother/child project and asked if I would speak with her privately in her rooms. Lena seemed exhausted from taking care of her sick two-year-old as she cleared a spot at her table to sit and talk.

Lena appeared older than her 25 years both in appearance and behavior. She felt she had lived a lot and wanted to impart her wisdom to the other, younger mothers. She expressed her shyness around cameras and was reluctant to be filmed but she quickly became comfortable and was one of the more articulate members of the group.

History

Lena responded to the question "who would you say raised you?" by stating that she raised herself. As she told her story it became painfully clear that she was not exaggerating and it seemed that indeed she had raised herself.

Lena's mother was drug addicted since before Lena was born. While her mother was in her life, Lena never lived with her. She grew up in a home that housed more than 25 people. A woman Lena referred to as "Grandmom" (she was actually a great aunt) was the head of the household. Lena's aunt and several cousins also resided in the house. Grandmom took in all of the children whose mothers were unable to care for them. Lena has a brother and a sister who were both placed in the foster care system. Lena was "tortured" by family members who did not like her mother and took it out on her. She was pushed down the stairs, had her hair cut off, was sexually molested, and was generally beat up. Lena spoke about how when she was only seven or eight years old she would head out into the depths of the inner city looking for her mother. She knew where to look; she knew all of the crack houses. She undertook these dangerous journeys late at night into the early hours of the morning. The people of the street knew her and made sure she found her mother and escorted her back safely to her home. Lena felt compelled to continue her nocturnal searches for her mother. She needed to reassure herself that her mother was alive.

When Lena was 13 years old her mother went into a drug rehabilitation facility and Lena lived with her for the several months while she was in that program. At 15 Lena was placed in a group home where she found out she was pregnant with her son, who at the time of our project was nine years old. Her son has a good relationship with his father and visited with him on a regular basis. Lena lived with the father of her two-year-old daughter for a year. When the domestic violence got intolerable she moved herself and her children into a "women against abuse" shelter. From there she received placement at a transitional housing facility. Lena worked hard to help both of her children maintain relationships with their fathers. She no longer had a romantic relationship with either of the men but kept them involved with the children. For example, she insisted on a nighttime ritual for her little daughter. Every night before bedtime, Noel called her Daddy on the phone and told him all about her day. After this bedtime call she was able to settle down and sleep. If her father was unavailable she had a difficult time going to bed.

Lena was working on completing her GED and hoped to one day obtain a degree in nursing.

Lena and Noel in Group

Lena gave the impression of a much older woman than her 25 years. There was a strength and toughness that emanated from within her. Lena had strong feelings about many issues and often could not be deterred. Above all she was determined to give her children a better childhood than she had. She often spoke about how she was never allowed to have a childhood. She had few memories of happy times as a little girl. She lived in an unsafe environment and was unprotected by the adults in her life; in fact, she was abused by just about everyone. What was remarkable about Lena was her ability to play with her child and understand her child's need to be a little girl even though she herself never had those experiences.

From the beginning Lena loved to talk. She was the most vocal member of the group. Lena gave the impression of possessing a tough, rough exterior but she was capable of a softness that came out when she interacted with her two-year-old daughter. Lena was extremely helpful to the other women on various topics, such as what to do when your baby is learning to crawl and you live in an unsafe environment, toilet training, and fathers.

On one particular day I asked the mothers about what to do if your baby is learning to crawl and you live in an undesirable place for your baby to explore his surroundings. Lena described an unsafe home where the floorboards were coming up and mice droppings as well as other garbage were on the floor. Lena told what she did: "Well, what I did for my daughter was I made my own safe place. I cleaned up a space on the floor and I put blankets down and I surrounded it in pillows and put toys down for her and she could crawl there." This was a helpful story for Christa to hear, who also experienced unsuitable living arrangements when her child was crawling but kept her from crawling. She thought that if she were ever in that situation in the future she would now know what to do.

Lena also was able to tell the group about her toilet training experience with Noel. Early on in group Lena was frustrated but patient stating that Noel must not be ready and she will just have to wait. When another mother said she beat her son so he would use the toilet, Lena became silent and pensive. Finally after a long pause she said to the woman who had just confessed to beating her son: "Well my brother was beat to go to the toilet and he is in jail now so . . ." This led to an intense discussion of beating and its ill effects on children as they all remembered their own beatings as children.

Lena was eloquent and made use of humor as she spoke about her children's fathers. She often had the group laughing about a difficult and sensitive subject. Lena was not going to take any nonsense from these men. She demanded that they pay attention to their respective children and she insisted that they deal with each other. Lena told the story of how the two men hated each other and were fighting in front of the children: "I told them they better get along for the sake of my children and where my children are concerned they better not mess with me. I don't care if they hate each other but they better not take it out on my children. I told them they can just go ahead and kill each other and I will take their bodies and cremate them and put their ashes together in a bottle and sit it up on my mantel and they can fight for all eternity and I'll just sit there and look at that bottle and laugh!"

When the project began, Noel, an adorable two-year-old little girl, stayed close to her mother, bringing her toys one by one from the toy container. She was an observer, and seemed shy around me and the other women. It was obvious that Lena took great pride in her daughter's appearance, as Noel's hair was always neatly done with barrettes to match her outfit. By the end of our project, Noel was actively engaged with others and was speaking in full sentences and was toilet trained.

Lena and Noel both enjoyed the singing and movement part of the group. One of our songs was "If you're happy and you know it . . ." One verse is "If you're scared and you know it give a scream!" Noel loved this song, especially the screaming. Lena would encourage her daughter: "You go girl! You scream it out!" It was all great fun.

Zoe and Melody

Zoe was in her ninth month of pregnancy with her fourth child when we first met. She had two sons, ages nine and seven, and a four-year-old daughter. Her appointment for her AAI was on her due date; that night she gave birth to a beautiful daughter. Zoe's radiant beauty was striking. She was Muslim and wore the traditional headdress. She had large brown eyes that sparkled when she laughed and shot sparks of fire when angry. Zoe told her story with frank honesty and seemed to possess the wisdom of an older woman. She accepted the hardships of her childhood and her parents' shortcomings with compassion. She had a clear understanding that she had to take responsibility for her own future.

History

Zoe grew up in a home with her mother, brother, sister, and maternal grand-mother. She described her mother as a "functional addict" who always seemed to be able to maintain a job. Zoe realized that her mother was a crack/ cocaine addict when she was eight years old, and she did her best to stop her mother. She would find her drug paraphernalia and throw it away. She often wrote her mother notes pleading with her to stop. She realized now, as an adult, that a little eight-year-old girl is no opponent against addiction. How-ever, at the time she could not understand why her mother did not listen to her pleadings, and she became enraged.

Zoe described how the adults in her life played favorites. Her brother re-ceived all of the good attention from her mother; her sister, "the bookworm," was her grandmother's favorite; and she was her father's favorite. Zoe's fa-ther was rarely around and she would sometimes go a year or two in between visits. His visits were never planned or announced. They occurred when she was out on the street playing and her father would drive by. She would hop into the car and that would constitute a visit. Zoe had numerous half siblings, 17 at last count. She had relationships with some of them but not all. She proudly stated that several of her father's women all knew that she was the favorite child that he bragged about.

When Zoe was 12 years old she was in the wrong place at the wrong time and was shot in the leg in a drive-by shooting. She described this traumatic event in detail as if it had occurred yesterday. She was in the hospital for well over a month and underwent multiple surgeries. A metal rod remained in her leg and she still experienced stiffness and pain periodically.

Zoe was sexually molested when she was eight years old by a "nasty cousin." This went on for some time. Zoe never spoke about it as a child, but in recent years she discovered that her sister was also molested by this same cousin and had received treatment. Zoe brushed off the idea of needing any help with this part of her past, stating that it was bad and wrong but it did not damage her. When the offending cousin died young, she felt no remorse and felt some sort of justice in his untimely death.

Zoe's mother was incarcerated when Zoe was a preteen for over a year. When she was 16 years old, Zoe herself was sent away to a group home, where she gave birth to her first son. These were all difficult times; however Zoe chose not to elaborate on them.

Zoe's mother was diagnosed with end-stage colon cancer two years prior to our project. This was an extremely painful time for Zoe. She was shocked by the diagnosis and stayed with her mother to care for her. Zoe stated that her mother remained "mean" up to her death, and it was very difficult to care for her as she pushed her away and would not accept comfort. Zoe was devastated by her mother's death. She attempted to continue living in her mother's home and took over the responsibility of paying her mother's debts. However this proved to be overwhelming when no help came from other family members. Zoe had no choice but to lose the house and enter the city's shelter system. Zoe's housing came through during the research project and she moved with her four children into a three-bedroom apartment one week after termination of our mom/baby group.

Zoe's children each had a different father. Her oldest son had a relationship with his father and spent weekends with him. Her second son had no relationship with his father, and it was difficult for this child. Zoe would often give him extra attention and time alone with her but she felt that this did not make up for his father's neglect. When he says that his father must not love him, Zoe feels at a loss for words and does not know how to help her son deal with his abandonment by his father. Zoe is grateful to her older son's father, who has included both of the boys on outings. Zoe's daughter spent time occasionally with her father and his family but Zoe did not have a friendly relationship with him. The baby's father's family is extremely involved with Zoe and her children. They have taken over childcare so that the baby does not have to go into daycare when Zoe works. In addition, because Zoe often works night shifts, the family cares for all four of her children. Zoe continued in a romantic relationship with her baby's father but had no plans for marriage.

Zoe and Melody in Group

Zoe was a dedicated member of the group. She was always the first to arrive, usually on time, and loyally attended until she was forced to enter the welfare-to-work program toward the latter half of the project. After her baby was placed in childcare, her attendance became sporadic.

Zoe had much to offer the group because Melody was her fourth child. She often spoke about her older children, especially around toilet training experiences and relationships with the children's fathers. Zoe demonstrated her understanding and empathy for her second son when the women were sharing how they arranged for their children to visit with their fathers. Zoe explained: "Well, my oldest son, he sees his father. His father is in his life, he buys him some things and takes him places. He don't stay there much, if at all. I mean

I never get a break, but he in his life. Now my second son, his father is just not there at all for him. I feel some kind of way about it but what can I do. He says: "My father must not love me" and this, that and a third. I'm not going to lie to him. It's just how it is. But I give him extra time alone with me. I might do something special just for him. The others understand that. They have fathers, he doesn't. It's good because my older son's father will include him. That's nice and I appreciate it. But I do feel some kind of way about it all!"

Zoe was wonderful with infant Melody. She was unrelenting about insisting that "meat spoils, not babies." Zoe felt that babies should be held, which she demonstrated by keeping Melody in her arms for most of group time. She was attuned to her baby and would pick her up out of her infant seat before Melody became uncomfortably upset. I was impressed with how quickly Zoe began to take some of my words as her own and incorporated the idea of thinking about what your baby was thinking into her interactions with her infant. This is beautifully illustrated in her photo book on several pages. For example, at times Zoe had a tendency to be overintrusive, kissing Melody all over her face many times. On a page where the photo shows Zoe very much in Melody's face, Zoe writes: "Too many kisses, Melody is thinking: Too many kisses." And on another page there is a beautiful photograph depicting Zoe and Melody gazing into each other's eyes and Zoe writes: "I wonder what Melody is thinking about? I wonder what is on her mind?"

It was difficult for Zoe to put Melody in daycare; however she was threatened with losing her welfare if she did not comply. Zoe spoke about finding appropriate daycare and how she needed to be nearby so she could just drop in at lunchtime and visit her baby. She also wanted to be able to make sure that her infant was being properly cared for. In the end, Zoe did not have to use a daycare but instead Melody's paternal grandmother took over her care. There were pros and cons to this situation. The good thing was that Melody was with a family member who loved and adored her and she got one-on-one attention. The unfortunate problem was that Zoe began to go several days at a time without seeing her baby. Zoe would come to group, stay until the children joined us and then she would go to her work program. Several weeks later Zoe brought Melody to group and there was a striking difference in her appearance. Melody seemed depressed, as it was difficult to get her to engage and to respond. Melody did not smile at all that week. I was concerned and wondered with Zoe how she thought her baby was feeling about this separation. This was very difficult for Zoe to allow herself to even think about, and she cut off the conversation with insisting that her baby did not miss her, and that she was absolutely fine. I certainly understood her anxiety, which caused her to become defensive. However, as the weeks progressed Zoe had her baby with her more often. In the last weeks of group, I observed six-month-old

Melody, who was developmentally advanced, bright eyed, happily verbal-
izing and engaged.

Fannie and Tom and Rob

Fannie moved into the shelter the week the mom/baby group began, missing
the first two sessions. She appeared years older than 23 as she attempted to
navigate her way through the system. Overwhelmed by her two little boys,
ages one and two years old, it seemed as if she was unable to take care of
herself as she was disheveled, while her living unit was immaculate and her
boys were dressed in matching outfits down to the socks and shoes. It was
not clear if Fannie completely understood the purpose of the group as she had
significant cognitive limitations, but she was lonely and there was no room in
daycare for her boys so she consented to join the group.

History

Her mother and father raised Fannie. Her older brother and sister lived
with them until Fannie was eight years old, when they were sent to live
with grandparents. She did not know why her siblings were removed from
the home. She remembered being very lonely as a child with nobody to

play with or talk to. Her first memory of separation was when she went to kindergarten. She remembered crying and being worried that her mother was leaving her forever and would never come back. Fannie had no other separations from her mother until her mother died when Fannie was 17 years old. Fannie did not experience her childhood as abusive in any way and saw it as ideal. She described two incidents that contradict her own views. When she was around seven years old she fell off her bike and then was pushed to the ground again by a man running from the police. She got a large cut on her leg that required stitches. Fannie told how her siblings held her down as her mother sewed up her leg with an ordinary needle and thread. Fannie remembered the excruciating pain and how angry she felt afterward. When she asked her mother why she did that to her, her mother replied: "I didn't want to go sit in the hospital." A second disturbing event was when Fannie killed the family cat by tying a rope around its neck too tight. She described how she tried to get the rope off but was unable to do so. Being sent to her room for two weeks punished her. She was only allowed to come out to use the bathroom.

Fannie was placed in a special education classroom for children with cognitive and developmental delays. She was able to graduate from high school but was unable to work outside the home or support herself and her children.

Fannie remembered fights between her parents and feeling extremely frightened. Her father divorced her mother and moved to another state where he remarried. Fannie was unable to get along with her stepmother. After Fannie's mother died she struggled with no one to guide her or help her make decisions. She moved from house to house and got involved with "the wrong people." When she got pregnant with her first son she moved in with the father's family, and quickly had a second child. Fannie's relationship with her children's father was physically and verbally abusive. She described how he would beat her up and choke her. The grandmother, who also lived in the house, took her to a shelter for abused women where she stayed for several months while waiting to get into the transitional housing facility. At the time of our project, Fannie had no contact with the father of her sons.

Fannie and Tom and Rob in Group

Fannie felt ill at ease when she first came into our group. She had just moved into the transitional housing facility, having come from a Women Against Abuse shelter, and was still adjusting to living in a shelter. She did not know any of the other women and did not try to engage with them. She was silent. I found it difficult to engage her and involve her in the group conversation. For the first few months she would silently work on her photo book, only speaking when spoken to.

As Fannie became more comfortable she began to share her own experiences with the group. She explained that nobody had taught her about how to care for a baby. When her first son was born she had to learn everything on her own. The other women in the group all seemed to have lots of experience caring for younger siblings or cousins as they were growing up, but not Fannie. She had an isolated childhood.

An uncomfortable situation arose as Fannie spoke to her children using an extremely mean tone. For the most part, all of her interactions were inappropriate to the situation. Her voice became very loud and she used a commanding rough manner. It became evident that she had no other way of being with her children in her repertoire. When this occurred, the mood was disrupted in the group and the other children became tense, looking on with concern. The other mothers did not interfere with Fannie's mothering. At first I tried modeling appropriate responses to setting limits and other interactions with her children. I hoped Fannie would follow my lead. However, a few weeks went by and when her behavior was not altered at all it became evident that a more direct intervention was needed. The quandary was how to do this without inflicting a narcissistic wound and embarrassing her in front of the other women. As it turned out, as I was wrestling with this problem, a day came when only Fannie and her boys came to group. It was the perfect opportunity to speak with Fannie alone and then to work one-on-one with Fannie with her boys during our playtime. This seemed to be a pivotal point, as Fannie became more aware of her own behavior and feelings. She would catch herself and change her tone and approach to her boys. She later shared that she struggled with her angry outbursts and knew she needed to have more patience.

Both two-year-old Tom and one-year-old Rob enjoyed the group. For several weeks they stayed very close to their mother, bringing her toys and sharing her lap. They watched the other children and soon felt comfortable enough to venture away from their mother. Tom became attached to an intern who was observing the group and began to sit on her lap and bring her toys. Rob began to walk backward and fall into my lap. Both children participated in the singing and movement, and snack time became a favorite.

As Tom adjusted to both his new living arrangements and participating in the group, he also exhibited angry episodes. His facial expression would darken as his eyebrows knitted together and he would kick and pinch not only other children, but me as well. When I spoke with Fannie about her angry tone, she was able to connect it to Tom's angry behaviors, which were meaningful to Fannie.

There were incidents when Fannie would tease Tom by holding him down with one hand and holding a toy just out of his reach. Tom would become

enraged, crying and frustrated, while Fannie seemed to sadistically enjoy his pain. I made use of the videotape to help Fannie see how teasing her child caused him to not only feel pain but to then attack back in a violent way.

The group experience was valuable to Fannie and her children; however, Fannie needed ongoing interventions to help her understand the emotional and developmental needs of her boys.

Chapter Seven

Understanding the Findings

CONTROL GROUP PARTICIPANTS

Susan and Karen and Karina

Susan was a 28-year-old African American single mother of a nine-year-old daughter and twin girls, age 32 months old. Susan had no relationship with her daughter's fathers. A drug-addicted and alcoholic mother raised Susan. Her father, who was also an alcoholic, died when she was two years old. Susan's mother would put her to bed at night and then go to the neighborhood bar for the rest of the night. Susan spoke about how frightened she was to be left alone at night and how she remembered crying herself to sleep every night. There were several incidents when drunken men found their way into her bed and various family members sexually molested her throughout her childhood until her teenage years.

Susan was fortunate in that she spent her summers with her maternal grandparents in another state. She also spent her third grade year living with her grandparents. Her memories of these times are of loving, caring support. She felt it was her grandparents who have helped her to survive. However, Susan's grandmother died when Susan was eight years old and that was a devastating loss. Susan stated that because of her own sexual abuse history she was extremely vigilant and protective of her daughters. She does not allow men to be around her children. However, her older daughter was molested on the school bus. This was terrible for Susan, as she has tried hard to protect her daughter from experiencing the horrors of her own abuse.

Susan suffered from major depression and had recently been diagnosed with bipolar disorder. She found it difficult to motivate herself but did her best to be emotionally available to her three daughters. Susan was unable to participate in the mom/baby group because of work-related time conflicts.

Robin and Linda

Robin was a 32-year-old African American, single mother of six children. Her two adolescent children lived with their father in another state. Her four youngest children, ages three, four, five, and six, lived with her. Robin was raised by a drug-addicted mother and became a drug addict herself at age 14. At the time of our project, Robin had been clean for several months and hoped to get a job in the near future.

Robin was interested in participating in the project as a Control subject but did not wish to commit the time to the twice-weekly mom/baby group, even though she was available.

Rose and Abby

Rose was a 20-year-old African American mother of a four-year-old daughter. An aunt and uncle raised Rose when she was very young and she lived with her grandparents from age five until she moved into the homeless shelter eight months before the project began. Rose felt rejected by her mother and remained very angry with her. She had difficulties controlling her impulsive angry outbursts and was asked to leave her grandparents' house because Rose and her grandmother were unable to get along. Rose was hospitalized several times, all related to her angry outbursts.

Rose completed the equivalent of two years of college and placed a heavy emphasis on academic accomplishments for her daughter. She expressed an interest in participating in the mom/baby group but her full-time job made it impossible. Rose was saving her money to buy her own home so that she may become a homeowner when she leaves the shelter system.

Diana and Mindy

Diana was a 20-year-old African American single mother with three children ages four, two, and one. At the time of our project, the father of her three children was incarcerated and will remain incarcerated for the next 20 years. Her paternal grandparents raised Diana. Her older brother was raised by an aunt; she has not seen him since she was two years old and has no memory of him. Her younger brother was raised by other relatives in another state. Diana stated that her grandparents would only raise one child and they chose her because she was a girl. Diana's mother remarried and had four more children that remained in her care.

Diana spoke of memories where her mother disappointed her. Her mother would often promise to visit and not show up. She would claim that she was robbed, or make up some other wild excuse that kept her from visiting her daughter. When Diana was 14 years old she came home from her last day of school to find her grandparent's car packed with all of her belongings. She was told that from that point on she would live with her mother. Diana was devastated and the next four years were filled with angry outbursts and interactions between Diana and her mother.

Diana was working on obtaining her GED and hoped to go to nursing school in the future. She hoped that her own three children would finish school and find professions where they could experience independence and not have to depend on others. Diana was unable to be a part of the mom/baby group because her GED preparation classes conflicted.

Helen and Erin

Helen was a 25-year-old African American, single mother to three daughters, ages four, three, and one. Helen and her two youngest daughters lived at the transitional housing facility. Helen had lost custody of her oldest daughter two years earlier when the child was two years old and had only seen her daughter twice in the past two years. Helen would like to regain custody of her daughter but was aware that it would be difficult for both of them. Helen expressed concern that her daughter would no longer know her and would be frightened if removed from her father's home. Helen has no relationship with either the father of her oldest daughter or the father of her two youngest daughters.

Helen was the youngest (along with her twin brother) of seven children. She grew up in a home with her mother as her primary caretaker until the age of 13, when her mother left and moved to another state with her boyfriend. Helen was left in the care of her older brother, whom she described as a bully and a tyrant. Her father died when she was five years old but she has fond memories of him even though he often became enraged and beat her and her siblings. Helen was devastated by her mother's abandonment and when she was 14 she went to live with her mother and her boyfriend. At this time her mother told her she had moved to get away from her children. Her mother's boyfriend molested Helen, and when she reported the abuse to her school she was removed from the home. Helen's mother did not believe her daughter and Helen spent her next four years in several different foster homes. Helen remains furious with her mother and stated that her mother *"is still with my molester to this day!"*

Helen had severe learning problems and was placed in a special education class in elementary school. She did not finish high school. She felt she was not given an adequate education and hoped that her children would not experience similar difficulties. At the time of our project, Helen had recently been diagnosed with bipolar disorder and was taking a mood stabilizer and an antidepressant. She felt the medication was helping her and she hoped to find a job and a house.

Helen had agreed to participate in the intervention group but was unable to follow through on her commitment. When it was clear that she was not going to be a part of the mom/baby group she became a participant in the control group.

DATA FROM THE AAI AND STRANGE SITUATION

The following Tables display the findings of the AAI and the Strange Situation for the Intervention and Control Groups (refer to appendix K for complete descriptions of each category for each participant). Numbers 1–5 shows the names of each mother/child dyad and their pre- and post-test classifications. The first attachment classification for an individual is predominant. In cases where there is more than one classification, they are scored in descending order. For example, several of the women were assigned as many as four classifications. These should be understood as the first being the most likely score.

HYPOTHESES: PROOF AND DISPROOF

H_1: *Adult attachment style will remain the same in both the Intervention and Control Groups.*

In the original research design I hypothesized that the attachment style of the women in both the Intervention and Control Groups would remain the same. In the Intervention Group, only two of the women scored the same in both the pre- and post- AAI. For the remaining three women, the scores were not what attachment theory would predict. For example, Lena went from *unresolved/preoccupied* to *unresolved/secure*. Christa was not *unresolved* in her pre-test, but was *unresolved* in her post-test, and Fannie was not *unresolved* in her pre-test but was in her post-test.

In the Control Group the AAI categories remained the same in the pre-and post-test for four out of the five women. Because this study had an N of 5, the results of the AAI and Strange Situation measures cannot be viewed as statistically significant. However, it is striking that there was movement in the AAI scores of the women in the Intervention Group but not in the women who participated in the Control Group. This result begs a more dynamic understanding of the results.

Table 7.1. Intervention Group

Case	Pre		Post	
	AAI	SS	AAI	SS
1. Christa & Iris	Dismissive-restricted in feeling (Ds3)	Disorganized/Secure (D/B3)	Unresolved for loss and trauma/devaluing of attachment/angry secure (U/d/D2/F5)	Disorganized/Anxiously Secure (D/B4)
2. Nina & Karl	Unresolved for loss and trauma/preoccupied by trauma/passive/dismissive-restricted in feeling (U/d/E3/E1/Ds3)	Secure-Feisty (B4)	Unresolved for loss and trauma/preoccupied by trauma/passive/dismissive-restricted in feeling (U/d/E3a/E1/Ds3)	Avoidant-ignoring/Ambivalent-resistant (A1/C1)
3. Lena & Noel	Unresolved for loss and trauma/preoccupied-angry/conflicted-passive (U/d/E2/E1)	Secure-preoccupied (B4/B3)	Unresolved for loss and trauma/Secure-autonomous/some setting aside of attachment (U/d/F1a)	Very secure (B3)
4. Zoe & Melody	Unresolved for loss and trauma/preoccupied-angry-conflicted-passive-confused (U/d/E2/E1/E3a)	infant	Unresolved for loss and trauma/cannot classify/preoccupied-angry-conflicted/dismissive-devaluing of attachment/restricted in feeling (U/d/CC/E2/Ds2/Ds3)	infant
5. Fannie & Tom & Rob	Dismissing of attachment (Ds1)	Tom: Resistant-passive (C2) & Rob: Disorganized/cannot classify/secure-preoccupied/avoidant (D/cc/B4/A1)	Unresolved for loss and trauma/dismissive-normalizing (Ds3a/U/d)	Tom: Disorganized/avoidant-ignoring/ambivalent-resistant (D/A1/C1) &Rob: Disorganized/very secure (D/B3)

Table 7.2. Control Group

Case	Pre		Post	
	AAI	SS	AAI	SS
1. Susan & Karen & Karina	Unresolved for loss and trauma/secure-autonomous/some setting aside of attachment (U/d/F1a)	Both children are secure (B3&B3)	Earned Secure (F3b)	Karen: Disorganized/ambivalent/resistant/avoidant (D/C1/A1) &Karina: Secure-ambivalent/disorganized (B4/D)
2. Robin & Linda	Cannot classify/fearfully preoccupied/passive/dismissive-restricted in feeling/unresolved for loss and trauma (CC/E3/E1/Ds3/U/d)	Secure (B3)	Unresolved for loss and trauma/dismissive-normalizing (U/d/Ds3a)	Secure-reserved (B1)
3. Rose & Abby	Unresolved for loss and trauma/cannot classify/dismissive-restricted in feeling/preoccupied-angry-conflicted (U/d/CC/D3/E2)	Resistant (C1)	Unresolved for loss and trauma/preoccupied-angry-conflicted (U/d/E2)	Resistant (C1)
4. Diana & Mindy	Preoccupied-angry-conflicted (E2)	Secure/secure-ambivalent (B3/B4)	Preoccupied-passive/secure-somewhat dismissive of attachment (E1/F2)	Disorganized/cannot classify/avoidant/secure (D/CC/A2/B2)
5. Helen & Erin	Unresolved for loss and trauma/preoccupied-angry-conflicted/preoccupied by trauma-passive (U/d/E2/E3a/E1)	xxxxx	Unresolved for loss and trauma/preoccupied-angry-conflicted (U/d/E2)	Secure-reserved (B1)

Table 7.3. Bayley Infant Assessment Scores Intervention Group Pre-Test

Case	Child	Mental	Motor	Behavioral
1	Iris	Could not be scored (refused items)	Significant delays	Non-optimal
2	Karl	Outside of age range; no scores	No scores	No scores
3	Noel	Within normal limits	Significant delays	Non-optimal
4	Melody	Not tested	Not tested	Not tested
5	Tom	Significant delays	Within normal limits	Non-optimal
6	Rob	Significant delays	Within normal limits	Within normal limits

Table 7.4. Bayley Infant Assessment Scores Intervention Group Post-Test

Case	Child	Mental	Motor	Behavioral
1	Iris	Within normal limits	Accelerated performance	Within normal limits
2	Karl	Outside of age range	No scores	No scores
3	Noel	Accelerated performance	Accelerated performance	Within normal limits
4	Melody	Not tested	Not tested	Not tested
5	Tom	Could not score (refused)	Within normal limits	Non-optimal
6	Rob	Mildly delayed	Within normal limits	Within normal limits

Table 7.5. Bayley Infant Assessment Scores Control Group Pre-Test

Case	Child	Mental	Motor	Behavioral
1	Karen	Could not score (refused)	Could not score (refused)	Non-optimal
2	Karina	Significant delays	Significant delays	Non-optimal
3	Linda	Not tested	Not tested	Not tested
4	Abby	Beyond age range	No scores	No scores
5	Mindy	Mildly delayed	Within normal limits	Within normal limits
6	Erin	Not tested	Not tested	Not tested

Table 7.6. Bayley Infant Assessment Scores Control Group Post-Test

Case	Child	Mental	Motor	Behavioral
1	Karen	Significant delays	Within normal limits	Non-optimal
2	Katrina	Mildly delayed	Within normal limits	Non-optimal
3	Linda	Not tested	Not tested	Not tested
4	Abby	Outside of age range	No scores	No scores
5	Mindy	Significantly delayed	Within normal limits	Within normal limits
6	Erin	Not tested	Not tested	Not tested

A Psychodynamic Understanding

Christa showed improvement in several AAI subscales. Most significant is the increase in her *loving scale, coherence of transcript*, and *coherence of mind*. Her scores demonstrated movement away from her *dismissive* attachment style toward a more *secure* (F4) category. Christa remained somewhat angry and rejecting yet she was better able to coherently tell her story and make use of humor after the six-month intervention. Her pre-test category of *Ds3* is more dismissive than her post-test category of *D2*. It is striking that Christa scored *unresolved* in her post-test but not in her pre-test. During the six months when we met twice per week in the mom/baby group, Christa was able to begin to reflect on her past traumas and losses as she came to trust me and as the group became a safe place to share personal feelings and experiences. It is possible that as this occurred, Christa became more reflective and she was able to tell her story in a more coherent fashion. However, because her traumas and losses were brought to the forefront she became unresolved and disoriented when speaking about loss and trauma.

Nina was one of the two women whose AAI scores stayed the same. However, there were slight improvements in several of her AAI subscales. There were decreases in her *rejecting* and *involving/reversing* experience scales, which could be considered a positive movement. Her scores for *unresolved loss* and *unresolved trauma* increased; this could be understood as a reaction to the therapeutic intervention where she was able to speak about some of her past sexual abuse. There was a slight increase in her *coherence of transcript,* which could also be understood as an outcome of the trusting relationship that developed between Nina and myself.

Lena made significant positive movement from a *disorganized preoccupied* attachment style to a *secure* pattern of attachment *(F1)*. Most notable was her increase in both her *coherence of transcript* and *coherence of mind.* Before the intervention, Lena was not able to tell her story in a coherent way. After six months of the intervention she was able to tell her story, (the same story that she previously related) but in a coherent fashion. All of these positive movements are directly attributed to the therapeutic intervention.

Fannie moved from a *Dismissive Ds1*, which is defined as restricting in feeling, to a more expressive *Ds3a/u/d.* Fannie was better able to recognize rejection and discuss it. In addition there was an increase in her *Coherence of Transcript* and *Coherence of Mind* scales. Not unlike Christa, Fannie was also scored *disorganized* in her post-test but not in her Pre-AAI. As with Christa this could be attributed to her traumas coming to the forefront through a trusting, caring relationship with me and the cohesiveness of the group. I attribute Fannie's ability to express her feelings to the therapeutic intervention.

Zoe is the second of the two women whose category remained essentially the same, with very little movement from an *unresolved preoccupied* category toward a somewhat *dismissive* category. If understood psychodynamically, this would mean that Zoe actually became more defensive and was less able to feel and experience her emotions.

H$_2$: *The Intervention Group children's attachment style will change from disorganized to insecure/organized.*

In the second hypothesis, I speculated that the children who participated in the Intervention Group would move from a *disorganized* pattern of attachment to an *insecure* but organized pattern of attachment. This did not occur. In the Control Group, two out of the six children were scored *disorganized* and remained *disorganized*. In the Control Group none of the six children were *disorganized* in their pre-test of the Strange Situation but three of the children were *disorganized* in their post-test.

Psychodynamic Understanding of the Strange Situation Results

Table 7.1 demonstrates that Iris moved from a *disorganized secure* pattern to a much angrier *disorganized/anxiously secure* pattern. The B4 child is much more expressive and becomes very distressed upon separation. This could be understood as a reaction to her mother's movement during the project. As her mother began to experience her own traumas and reflect on them, her child became more distressed and disorganized.

Karl's pre-test of *secure* but angry is difficult to understand. It seems that his post-test category is more correct as he appeared to me as an avoidant/ ambivalently resistant child. It is difficult to understand why he did not score as a *disorganized* child since his mother was scored *unresolved* in both her pre- and post-tests and had suffered severe multiple traumas.

Noel's scores moved from an *angry secure category* to a *very secure* pattern of attachment. Again, like Karl, Noel is not scored as *disorganized*. This cannot be explained given her mother's *unresolved* category and history of trauma.

Tom's pre-test result of *C2* was totally unexpected. The literature would have predicted that he would be *disorganized* and *avoidant*. His post-test category seems more accurate. It is interesting to note that as the mother scored *unresolved* (perhaps due to being more capable of expressing and reflecting on her feelings), both of her children scored *Disorganized*.

Rob's attachment pattern improved from *disorganized angry/secure/ avoidant* to *disorganized/very secure*. This may be a result of his mother's slight positive movement and his being put into daycare during our project.

Until this time he had been with his mother full-time. She was extremely overwhelmed with two little boys and recently becoming homeless. It is important to note that it has been determined that the "quality of nonfamilial care during early childhood can affect attachment quality" (Brisch, 2002, p. 40).

H_3: *There will be an increase in cognitive function in the intervention group children. There will be less of an increase in cognitive function in the Control Group.*

The third hypothesis that I postulated was there would be an increase in cognitive function in the Intervention Group children, with less increase in cognitive function in the Control Group. Overall, the children in the Intervention Group had improved cognitive function, while the children in the Control Group did not improve as much. In the Control Group there was slight improvement in two children while one child demonstrated a decrease in cognitive function. In the Intervention Group all of the children that were tested demonstrated improved cognitive abilities.

H_4: *Experience Scores will improve in the AAI for the women in the Intervention Group but not for the women in the Control Group.*

H_5: *State of Mind Scales will improve on the AAI for the women in the Intervention Group but not for the women in the Control Group.*

H_6: *Scales for Overall States of Mind will improve on the AAI for women in the Intervention Group but not for the women in the Control Group.*

Hypotheses 4–6 predicted that the subscales involving *Experience, State of Mind,* and *Overall states of mind* would improve in the women who participate in the Intervention Group but would not show improvement in the women who participated in the Control Group. In all of these subscales there was more movement (positive and negative) in the Intervention Group than the Control Group. When viewed through a psychodynamic lens, these positive and negative movements could be ascribed to what took place interpersonally within the relationships that developed with myself and with each other. Christa's AAI exhibited movement (both positive and negative) in several of the subscales. For example her *idealizing, involving anger,* and *derogation* subscales were much higher in her pre-test than in her post-test (see appendix K for exact scores), which could be viewed as Christa beginning to modulate her rage/anger. Especially striking is the movement within the subscales *coherence of transcript* and *coherence of mind.* In both of these subscales, Christa moved from a score of 3 to a score of 5, which pushed her into a more *secure* category. Similar movement in all of the women is apparent.

Understanding the AAI and Strange Situation Results

The attachment research and literature states that there is a high correlation between the mother's attachment category and that of her child. In fact the mother's AAI category is extremely predictive of her child's attachment category. Ainsworth and her colleagues (1978) reported "highly significant correlations between the sensitivity of a mother's care and the attachment quality of children in the pioneering Baltimore study; this finding has been weaker in subsequent studies. The current state of research assumes that only 12% of the variance in children's attachment patterns is explained by material sensitivity" (Brisch, 2002, p. 29).

For close to three decades research on maternal distress on the mother-child relationship has shown that infant development is at risk when the parent is distraught. "Research on depressed mothers and their infants shows that these infants are at risk for insecure attachments and compromised cognitive outcomes" (Beebe, 2007, p. 8).

In my study there was very little correlation between the mother's AAI category and that of her child. In fact the results of my study were, in many cases, completely opposite to what the attachment research literature predicts. There were several cases where the mother was unresolved for loss and trauma, which is predictive of a disorganized insecure child. Within the attachment literature "maternal unresolved mourning has been specifically linked to infant and childhood disorganized attachment, a form of insecure attachment that predicts childhood psychotherapy" (Beebe, 2007, p. 8).

However, in my study the child was not deemed disorganized or insecure but was scored in a secure category. There are several possible reasons for this outcome. For example it is possible that the AAI and the Strange Situation are not sensitive enough instruments in picking up the cultural differences in parenting in this minority population. Perhaps using these measures as repeat instruments to measure change is not useful in a population where there is severe trauma. The Strange Situation has been criticized that it "captures only one specific aspect of mother-child interaction—that it constituted a snapshot—and that its evaluation is specifically geared to the behavior of the child while ignoring maternal reactions" (Brisch, 2002, p. 25).

Another valid and important factor in understanding the correlation between the mother's AAI score and the attachment style of her child is the child's genetic disposition and its contribution to the maternal/child interaction. It is interesting to note that children "characterized by higher irritability in early infancy and weaker orientation reactions in the first few weeks after birth were more frequently evaluated as insecurely attached in the Strange Situation" (Brisch, 2002, p. 29). This was true even when the mother was considered to be secure in her own attachment style.

As stated earlier, there were several variables that I was unable to control for. For example: *1*. The study population was too small. *2*. Age of the children ranged from birth to almost four years old. *3*. I was unable to use random selection, but the study participants were self-selected. This swayed the study, as women who were interested in getting help joined the Intervention Group, where women who wanted to make a little money and had no interest in improving their relationship with their child joined the Control Group. *4*. It was necessary that I perform multiple functions in the study. All of these reasons could have invalidated the results of the AAI and Strange Situation.

It is important to emphasize that an individual's attachment style in the AAI is evaluated not by what they say but instead by how they say it. What is assessed is how the individual tells her story, and the coherence of the narrative is analyzed. The AAI refers to Grice (1975), who states: "coherent discourse must meet the criteria of quality (be honest and provide evidence for your statements), of quantity (be brief but complete of relevance (stay on topic and don't stray from it), and structural comprehensibility (order your ideas and make them understandable)" (Brisch, 2002, p. 31).

In both the Intervention and Control Groups, all of the women had experienced some level of trauma and loss. It was not their painful experiences that predicted their attachment style but how they were able to process their experiences and speak about them. I was surprised to see two of the women in the Intervention Group move from insecure attachments toward more secure patterns of attachment. In both of these cases, after developing a trusting relationship with the therapist and making use of their group experience to begin to come to terms with their past traumatic experiences, these women were able to tell their stories in a much more coherent fashion than when we began.

Christa moved from a *dismissive-restricted* in feeling *(Ds3)* to *unresolved* for loss and trauma/*dismissive-devaluing* of attachment/*secure-resentful-conflicted (u/d/D2/F5)*, while her two-year-old daughter, Iris, remained *disorganized* (which is expected and predicted), but was *very secure* in her pre-test and ended up in the *angry, secure* category. It is interesting that Christa did not score *unresolved* in her pre-test. The *dismissive* category is a category where the individual is restrictive in expressing feelings, and it is predicted that her child would be *avoidant*. I understand Christa's movement into *unresolved* for loss and trauma as a positive move. Through her participation in the mom/baby group and her relationship with me, she began to think more self-reflectively and began to speak about her past traumatic history. As she experienced memories and tearfully spoke about her most difficult experiences, she began to move out of being *dismissive* of her feelings and those of others. Christa became confused and disorganized in her thoughts of her past. Moving into the *earned* secure *(F5)* category may demonstrate that the mother's "report of adverse childhood experiences per se does not predict his or her infant's Strange Situation classification. What matters is how that adverse childhood is processed and talked about" (Brisch, 2002, p. 32).

One significant limitation of my project was that we ended after six months. Certainly years of therapeutic intervention are needed in order for women who have experienced a lifetime of neglect and abuse to begin to resolve their losses. It is also understandable that as Christa began to feel and experience her trauma, her daughter remained *disorganized* and became somewhat less *secure* but became more expressive of her angry feelings.

In the second example, Lena was *unresolved for loss and trauma/preoccupied-angry-conflicted/preoccupied-passive (u/d/E2/E1)* in her pre-test and *unresolved for loss and trauma/secure-autonomous-some setting aside of attachment (u/d/F1a)*, in her post-test, while her two-year-old daughter Noel was scored *secure-feisty/very secure (B4/B3)* and *very secure (B3)* respectively. Notice that Lena remained *unresolved for loss and trauma* but moved from *preoccupied* to *secure* and her child moved from an *angry secure* to a *very secure* category.

The following vignette is an example of subtle differences in child rearing in this population, which may serve as an explanation of attachment scores. This interaction occurred in one of our last mom/baby group sessions:

All of the mothers were sitting on the floor on our quilt while the children played with the toys. The children occasionally interacted with one another, frequently returning to their mothers to show them a toy or sit on their lap. Lena was chatting with another mother when Noel threw a toy across the room, perhaps to regain her mother's undivided attention, and the toy accidentally hit another little girl on the back of her head. The other child was not hurt and hardly even noticed the offense other than to turn around to see what hit her. Noel made a beeline across the room, keeping her back turned toward her mother. Lena became harsh and in a somewhat loud and mean-sounding tone insisted that her daughter apologize to the other little girl. Noel continued to completely ignore her mother, refusing to acknowledge her demand, pretending that she did not even hear her mother calling to her.

I was sitting next to Lena and had observed the whole thing. I suggested to Lena that Noel had not meant to hurt the other child and the whole incident had been an accident. In my mind, I was thinking that Noel need not be disciplined since she obviously had hit the other child inadvertently. Lena turned to me and explained: "I know she didn't do it on purpose and it doesn't matter that Iris wasn't hurt, but out there she could get killed. People don't care if you didn't mean it. She has to say she's sorry." At that moment I knew that Lena's harsh tone demanding that her child apologize was not mean, but was urgently teaching her child how to survive in their world. Five minutes later Noel came skipping over to her mother, sat on her lap with her nose touching her mother's nose and exclaimed in the most innocent of voices: "Were you calling me? Did you call me?" Lena just laughed exclaiming: "Yes I called you! I called you five minutes ago! I sure did call you!" And the incident was forgotten.

To my ear, Lena sounded overly harsh, unnecessarily mean. Perhaps what I misinterpreted was an alarming urgency to teach her child to keep herself safe in a very hard, harsh world. I would further speculate that Noel interpreted her mother's words as loving even though she was somewhat afraid of getting into trouble, which is probably why she avoided her mother's demand to apologize. However, she knew that she would be accepted lovingly back into her mother's arms, which is exactly what happened.

The preceding two examples of unexpected results on the AAI and Strange Situation are only two of other unexpected results in this study. Even though there were a multitude of design flaws in this study, these examples raise the question of the validity of these attachment instruments with African American homeless mothers and children. As stated above, perhaps these measurements do not pick up subtleties in cultural differences, such as bringing up your child so they will develop survival techniques for life on the inner-city streets while making it clear to the child that she is loved and respected. Certainly this study consisted of far too small of a population sample to make any generalizations, yet the results do raise questions as to the usefulness of the measures, as both the AAI and the Strange Situation measurements were standardized on white middle-class families.

All of the women in the Intervention Group possessed wishes and dreams for their children. All of the mothers hoped to perpetuate the best qualities in themselves in their children. From their interviews on both the AAI and for the documentary, when asked about the future, they all wanted their children to fulfill what has been unrealized in their own lives. However, children may also be the "recipients of what is most painfully secret in the parent's psyches. When this happens, [children] become the carriers of the parents' unconscious fears, impulses, and other repressed or disowned parts of themselves" (Lieberman, 1999, p. 737).

Attachment patterns during the first few years of life are not the exclusive determinant of future development, "nor do infancy attachment classifications allow one to make absolute predictions" (Brisch, 2002, p. 38). There are several other factors that influence development. "The socioemotional development of attachment quality as assessed in the Strange Situation is only one aspect, albeit an important one, of the entire developmental spectrum of the parent-child relationship" (Brisch, 2002, p. 39). It should be noted that a great deal depends on other attachment figures in the child's life. A secondary or even tertiary person may be extremely valuable during a crisis or stressful life experience. "Many studies of emotional stability and resilience in children conclude that the presence of at least one available attachment figure constitutes a protective factor and can prevent the child from decompensating in the face of stress and developing further symptoms. Under these conditions, the child's psyche may remain relatively healthy even in the face of great stress (Brisch, 2002, p. 40).

BAYLEY INFANT ASSESSMENT RESULTS

There was a significant difference in cognitive development between the Intervention and Control group children. These results point to the value of the mom/baby group and the relationships that developed between myself and the families, which facilitated changes in the relationships of the mothers with their children. In the Intervention Group, four of the six children received scores from the Bayley. Iris and Noel demonstrated significant progress. Iris's scores moved from non-optimal to normal and even accelerated in one area of development. Likewise, Noel showed similar changes. Noel's mental and motor scores moved from showing significant delays to accelerated development, while her behavior score moved from non-optimal to normal. Tom demonstrated no changes in cognitive development. However, his little brother Rob made slight improvements in his mental development. Rob scored in the significant delays range in mental development in his pretest and mildly delayed in his post-test. Fannie had the most difficulties in parenting and understanding her children's behaviors, so these scores are not unexpected.

Three of the children from the Control Group received Bayley scores. Only one child demonstrated slight improvement. Karina moved from the significant delayed range to mildly delayed in mental abilities and moved from significant delays to normal in her motor capabilities. Mindy demonstrated a decrease in her mental abilities, moving from mildly delayed to significantly delayed in her mental capacities.

Chapter Eight

Where Do We Go from Here?

INTERVENTIONS

All five women and their children benefited from this project in a multitude of ways. One of the most valued interventions for all the mothers was the photo books we made together. The women looked forward to our hour, when we would talk as they worked on their books. They eagerly anticipated the new batch of photos each week and shared them around the table, making jokes and admiring each other's children. In addition to the cameras they were given to take pictures at home, they also brought in newborn photos and photographs of their other children. One mother added photos of her baby's father. All of the women asked me for extra books to take home after our project was over so they could begin books for their other children. On the last day, the women took home their books and additional supplies so they could continue the book for a long time to come.

Not only were the books a great source of pride as the women took care in decorating each page, requesting that I bring bows and ribbons and glitter, but the books and the activity served as a needed affect regulator as we spoke about worries about their children, their relationships, and their futures. It was not unusual for past abuse stories to resurface, and the women seemed to take refuge in making their books when anxiety was heightened.

It was striking to see the differences in the books. For example, Lena carefully matched colors of her pages with what her little girl was wearing in the photo. She often called her child a "movie star" and a "beauty." It was Lena who insisted that I bring glitter. Zoe's book demonstrated beautifully what she took in from me and from our group experience. One important goal of the group was to begin to help the women to see their children as separate individuals with feelings and thoughts of their own, to be mindful and to begin to mentalize. Zoe wrote above a photo of her infant: "I wonder what little Melody is thinking? I wonder what is on her mind?" And on another page where she is kissing and kissing her tiny infant's face she writes: "Too many kisses! I think Melody thinks too many kisses!" I feel that those two pages in Zoe's photo book made the whole project a huge success!

Yet another example of the use of the books was Nina's book. Nina had suffered severe abuse throughout her childhood, which began was she was born to a drug-addicted 14-year-old mother. She had multiple unresolved traumas and losses, and now as a young adult suffered from vast mood swings where she was sometimes manic but most often severely depressed. It was difficult for Nina to make pages for her book although she was artistically inclined. Her photos were painful to look at, as they depicted a very sad mother and son. Nina asked me to bring in brightly colored glass jewels. She spent hours and hours in session after session completely covering the front of her book with brightly covered beads. As she did this sometimes she was silent, listening to the others, at times she was silly and loud verging on being disruptive. One time she came in crying and told how that past weekend she had attended a party at her grandmother's house and her childhood rapist had been invited. That morning, Nina added one jewel to her book and went home to bed. That was a sad morning when even smiling babies and glittering jewels could not brighten spirits.

GROUP DISCUSSION

The group discussions during our first hour of group were also highly valued by the women. I wanted to make sure that I presented ample information about child development and parenting education, yet I knew that if I approached the group with a prepared lecture or outline for each session it would fail. I decided that since we were making a parenting film I would elicit from the women what they thought other women needed to know about becoming mothers. This worked very well, as I was able to give important information in connection with what the women wanted to tell others in similar situations.

The women came up with the following topics, which were discussed in multiple sessions as they worked on their photo books:

1. Pregnancy!?
2. Is This My Baby?
3. Difficult Nights!
4. Growth Spurts

5. A Safe Place to Crawl
6. NO! NO! NO!
7. Potty Time
8. Temper Tantrums
9. Fathers

There were two sessions when only one woman showed up. In the first, Fannie came alone. This gave me the opportunity to have a full two hours alone with Fannie and her sons. Fannie had some cognitive/developmental limitations and would speak in a very harsh, mean tone of voice to her children. At first I attempted to model appropriate behavior but that did not work. Her overly harsh and mean behavior toward her children became very uncomfortable for the other participants in the group. When only Fannie came to session it was an ideal time to work with her on this without causing her embarrassment. It turned out to be beneficial as Fannie was able to speak about her short temper as I told her my concerns for her children. I explained to her that I thought that Tom was a very angry little boy, and I was concerned about how he was going to deal with so many angry feelings. Already he was hitting and biting and making angry facial expressions. Fannie shared my concerns stating that she was worried that he was "just like his father." I feel I made some headway in helping Fannie to begin to understand how her behaviors affected her children, and our two hours alone together helped her to focus on thinking about what her children might be feeling and thinking.

In the second session where only one person attended, I was able to focus all of my attention on Nina and her little boy Karl. Nina suffered from major depression and PTSD and often was unable to relate to and address her son's emotional needs. In this session we built a fort using chairs and our quilt, and they had a wonderful time "living" and playing in the makeshift home.

PLAYTIME

All of the women and children enjoyed our playtime. Both the women and the children found safety and consistency in our routine. The children interacted with their mothers, bringing them toys from the toy box and sitting on their laps. The children seemed to insist on physical contact with their mothers. At first the women reluctantly sat on the floor with their children but quickly came to know that it was expected of them, and even though they often moaned and groaned they seemed to enjoy sitting on our quilt during this playtime.

When cleanup time was announced, there was a flurry of excitement as the children eagerly gathered up the toys and returned them to the toy box, anticipating our singing and movement time. The two little girls in the group especially enjoyed the singing and dancing, learning the words to the songs and imitating my movements. This was a lively fun time that we all enjoyed.

Next came a slowing down time. Cookies and juice were distributed to all of the mothers and children and story time began. I read the same three or four stories each week, all relating to separation, object constancy, and mother/child interactions about feelings. For example a favorite was *The Runaway Bunny*; another favorite was *The Kissing Hand*. The children and women came to know the books very well and never tired of them. The mothers craned their necks to see the pictures, and the children liked to choose which book I would read next. By the end of the project I noticed that several of the women had memorized the stories, and as I read their lips moved in time to my words.

At the very end of each session, the children helped to throw away all the garbage and fold up our quilt. We often had a child or two who wanted to be folded up inside the quilt, which gave me the opportunity to put words to the feelings that go along with endings and leavings, in addition to modeling patience for the mothers.

DOCUMENTARY AND PARENTING FILMS

All of the women were intrigued by the idea of making a documentary from the very beginning of the project. During our discussion time it was brought up as they questioned what the goal of the film was. They felt it was important to tell their stories, but also felt limits and boundaries needed to be maintained. I was simultaneously formulating the film with my videographer (Dom) as I processed with the women what it means to tell one's story. The women felt it was important to show the world that they had hopes and dreams just as everyone else, and that homelessness was never in any of their plans. All five of the women were shocked to find themselves living in a shelter, and were grappling with trying to get themselves back on their feet. Shelter living made all of the women feel infantilized; and even though the shelter provided safety and a caring "holding environment" they also felt angry that their independence and autonomy was being violated. The women were clear that they wanted to come across as strong women who loved their children and who were working toward a better life.

Dom and I agreed that we did not want the film to sensationalize the women's lives but at the same time wanted to be truthful to the hardships they have endured. We decided to make use of actors in the very beginning of the film. This prologue was filmed in an abandoned building with a voice-over depicting the racism, oppression, and abject poverty that is instrumental in the cause of drug and alcohol addiction, domestic violence, and child abuse.

The women were very excited about their part in the documentary. They were given a set of questions they would be asked in a formal interview one week before shooting. A professional makeup artist did their makeup and hair and a food table was set up. Each woman was given a two-hour time slot for the preparation and filming to take place. We did this in two days. All of the women were asked the following questions:

1. What brought you to the transitional housing facility?
2. What is it like for you to live here?
3. In what way is the mom/baby group helpful to you?
4. What do you wish for yourself for the future?
5. What do you wish for your children for the future?

In addition to a feeling of wonder and excitement about the filming process, all of the women described a sense of pride and empowerment to be able to tell their story and perhaps make a difference for others.

PARENTING FILM

As a group, we worked on the parenting film for many months. In our sessions we would chose a topic and talk about it. In choosing the topics I asked the women to think about what they believed other young women who find themselves single, pregnant, and possibly homeless would need to know about being a mom. They were extremely thoughtful and we agreed upon the following topics: Pregnancy!?, Is This My Baby?, Difficult Nights!, Needy Not Greedy, A Safe Place to Crawl, NO! NO! NO!, Potty Time, Temper Tantrums, and Fathers.

I had some preconceived ideas of what I wanted to show in this parenting video, and was surprised at some of the topics the women thought of. With the help of Spiral Q Puppet Theater, a non-profit organization that helps the disadvantaged tell their stories through the use of handmade puppets, the women put on a puppet show. They made all of their own puppets and the stage. One woman sat in front of the stage and told her story, as the other women took turns being the puppeteers.

Pregnancy

I suggested that we start at the beginning and talk about pregnancy. What the women had to say was unexpected. Their message to other young mothers was "Do not hide your pregnancy!" They told their stories sharing their fear and humiliation.

Is This My Baby?

All of the women had the experience of being very surprised by the light skin tone of their newborns. This caused much concern, and one mother told the nurse that this infant could not possibly be her baby because the infant's skin tone was so light and she and the baby's father were dark skinned. Another woman had the experience that the father asked: "Do you have something to tell me?" This father was concerned that this was not his child. Imagine how disruptive these feelings, thoughts, and worries are to welcoming your newborn infant into the world. Doubting that your baby is yours is not a good way to begin.

Difficult Nights

In this segment, Nina describes how she was alone with no help from anyone and her newborn baby could not be comforted. She tried everything but nothing she did could stop his piercing cries. "I didn't even want to be the mom. I just wanted to throw him out the window." I asked how she stopped herself from doing just that. She replied: "I went in the other room and put my music on and then I went back in and began all over again. I rocked him and he finally fell asleep." This is an important lesson for other young mothers who find themselves alone in the middle of the night with no one to take over the childcare. A colicky baby can tax any mother's patience.

Needy Not Greedy!

In this segment, after I speak briefly about growth spurts and the importance of holding your baby, the women tell their experiences and advise other young mothers to feed their babies on demand and to assure them that their baby cannot be spoiled by holding him and loving him.

A Safe Place to Crawl

Many of the women know what it is like to live in an unsafe home with a small child. They wanted other young mothers to know that crawling is an important phase of development. They understood that their baby needed to explore and that this helps cognitive development and helps the baby to grow up and be a separate person. Christa demonstrated with the puppet theater how to cover up splintered floorboards and how to make a safe place for your baby to crawl and learn about the world.

NO! NO! NO!

I spoke with the women about how the word "NO" becomes the most important word a child learns to say around two years old. I told them that it is a normal part of their child's development, emphasizing separation-individuation and the development of independence and autonomy. Many parents do not understand the importance of this developmental phase and may think that their child is being disrespectful or mean. The women did a wonderful job acting this out with puppets and describing how they have learned to interpret what their child really means when they say "no."

Potty Time

During our six months together, Lena's two-year-old Noel was toilet trained, and Lena told their story. Earlier in the project we discussed toilet training in our group, as two of the women were in the middle of toilet training with their two-year old daughters. At one point I turned to Fannie, whose three-year-old son was toilet trained, and I asked: "How did you toilet train Tom?" Fannie replied: "I beat him." A silence fell over the room for what felt like several minutes but was probably only several seconds. Lena spoke up: "Well, you can beat him but my brother was beat and he's in jail now so. . . ." Lena broke the ice and the group was then able to address this issue.

Temper Tantrums

This was a topic that was difficult for the women to understand. They all felt strongly that when children had temper tantrums they were misbehaving and were in need of punishment. No matter how I attempted to explain what happens when a child becomes overwhelmed with negative feelings, they did not agree. I spoke about how we all have temper tantrums even as adults; we are often able to control ourselves and calm down, but a two-year-old is unable to do this and is actually in pain. The women had nothing positive to say and were unable to problem solve when it came to temper tantrums. I wonder if this would have changed with more time together; or perhaps there is another way to impart the information that would be more agreeable.

I did not have any film footage of the women on this topic but I felt it was too important to leave out of the film so I spoke briefly about temper tantrums and we moved on to the important topic of "Fathers."

Fathers

This subject always elicited lively and affect-laden conversations. All of the women had difficult experiences with the fathers of their children. Two of the fathers either were in jail or had been incarcerated in the recent past. Zoe's four children each had a different father. She told of experiences where the father stole money from her for his drugs and took the money that was meant for the baby's formula. Three of the fathers are involved in their children's lives but the father of her second child has no relationship with his son. This is a sad situation, as this boy asks his mother if his father does not love him, and he feels left out when the other children visit their father's families. Zoe told how she will try to give him extra time or do something special with him when the other children are away. The fathers of their children had abused both Lena and Fannie, and both women sought refuge in a "Women Against Abuse" shelter.

WHERE TO GO FROM HERE?

The famous African proverb "It takes a village to raise a child" has signifi-cant meaning within the African American culture. In the African American community, child rearing is often viewed as a communal process. Extended families are valued, and often children grow up in multi-generational homes where disciplining and the socialization of children are distributed among all the adult members of the household. Chronic stress due to abject poverty and homelessness may cause the young single mother to feel overwhelmed by anger, resentment, and frustration, all of which combine to make her feel powerless and inadequate.

Studies have shown that mothers who have more peers in their support net-work are more competent parents. Mothers who receive greater support from family and friends "tend to be more emotionally responsive to their children" (MacPhee et al., 1996, p. 3279). Most of the women in shelters experience multiple forms of racism and oppression. As African American women they face racism on a daily basis. As poor, homeless women they experience chronic stress due to their marginalized status in society. Many of the women also live with the deeply personal wound of being rejected by their own fami-lies, left to care for their children alone and without support. Many homeless women with children expend all of their energy trying to meet their own and their children's basic needs. If a woman is worried about food and shelter she will often not have the energy (or the wherewithal) to interact with her children in a loving way, or be able to provide interesting activities for her children. The majority of homeless women have not had their own emotional needs met (in the past or present) and thus are more likely to be critical and irritable with their own children (MacPhee et al., 1996).

It seems obvious that homelessness would impair a mother's ability to parent her children effectively, yet there is little empirical research on the parenting and attachment styles of the homeless. By capitalizing on the strengths of the African American family, and providing interventions that assist the homeless mother in providing greater support and control and nurturing, agencies can help high-risk families function more effectively in society. Mental health practitioners must appreciate ethnic and racial differences so they may facilitate ethnic pride within the families with whom they work. This in turn will help families be more receptive to formal supports with more positive outcomes.

PRACTICE IMPLICATIONS AND FUTURE RESEARCH

The stories of the women and children illustrate several areas where mental health workers need to focus. Professionals working with children who have experienced chronic trauma such as homelessness, profound poverty, physical and sexual abuses, and physical and emotional neglect often become overwhelmed. Many times only a specific maladaptive behavior is focused on and treatment is analogous to a bandage on a hemorrhage. In our future work with these families early attachment relationships must come into clear focus, and a combined treatment with both the child and the parent may be optimal. The parent's own attachment past must be acknowledged and dealt with.

Psychoanalytic leaders such as Anna Freud, Mahler et al., Parens, Greenspan, and others, valued the vital importance of intervention in the first years of life. Mother-infant therapy has been spearheaded by Fraiberg, Adelson & Shapiro (1975); Call (1963); Fraiberg (1971, 1980); Greenacre (1971); Greenspan (1981); Spitz (1965); and Liberman & Pawl (1993). The last decade "has shown great progress in conceptualizing methods of intervention with parents and infants. Both psychodynamic approaches aimed at the mother's representations and interactional approaches attempting to intervene into specific behavioral transactions are effective (see for example Brazelton, 1994; Fraiberg 1980; Field et al., 1996; Hofacker & Papousek, 1998; Hopkins, 1992; McDonough, 1993; Marvin, Cooper, Hoffman, & Powell, 2002; Malphurs et al., 1996; Seligman, 1994; Stern, 1995; Van den Boom, 1995)" (Beebe, 2007, p. 9). Several mother-infant interventions have demonstrated positive outcomes and improvements in the mother-infant relationship (Cramer et al., 1990). However it is important to note that mother-infant intervention and treatment continues to be unavailable to underserved populations such as homeless mothers and children.

Another important area that needs to be addressed is providing culturally appropriate parenting classes and properly facilitated mom/baby groups that teach child development and help young mothers begin to recognize attachment behaviors in their babies. Those of us who have had the opportunity to work with parent/child dyads have observed how exquisitely sensitive these relationships are. A small change in the parent can make all the difference. As Daniel Stern describes in his book *The Motherhood Constellation*, the ultimate goal of parent/child therapy is to "free infants from the distortions and displaced affects engulfing them in parental conflict and to change the parent's internal representations of himself or herself and of the child" (Stern, 1995).

In my earlier exploratory work conducting parenting groups for homeless women, I searched for parenting films to show in class. Most studies examining parenting (and videos that teach parenting) have been conducted with Caucasian and African American middle-class families. Several of the films depicted single mothers who experienced poverty; however all of the families shown in these films had a home to go to after their baby was born. These teaching materials proved to be ineffective and even detrimental to the very poor families I worked with. Not only are the women unable to relate to the families shown on the films, but these films added to the sense of worthlessness and poor self-esteem that these families already bear.

This project has produced a parenting video that homeless women and teenage single mothers will be able to identify with and learn from. The parenting video may be used in inner-city high school programs, foster care agencies, and the Department of Human Services as an aid in working with young girls/women who become pregnant.

The documentary film gives voice to the otherwise silenced homeless women. In this film the women raise their voices and speak out. These five courageous women have chosen to no longer remain silently invisible to a society that would like them to disappear.

WHAT WORKED AND WHY

Because of the work of Selma Fraiberg (1980) and her colleagues, psychoanalytically informed clinicians have been working with mothers and babies for over 40 years. Within the psychoanalytic community, working with the mother-infant dyad is highly valued. In our work with high-risk mothers and children who have experienced trauma, the environment is not easily controlled or modified. While these circumstances may be viewed as unconventional and challenging, it is also becoming clear that these difficult populations benefit from psychoanalytically informed interventions.

We know that in mother-infant dyads that are troubled, the mother's "representation of the baby has been distorted by unmetabolized and undifferentiated affects stemming from her own early and usually traumatic relationship experiences. The goal of infant-parent psychotherapy is to disentangle these affects from the relationship with the baby" (Slade et al., 2006, p. 79). It is in the relationship between the mother and the therapist that change occurs and representations begin to shift. The ultimate goal is that the child will no longer be the recipient of the mother's traumatic projections (Slade et al., 2006).

All of us who participated in this research project benefited. It is clear that the results of the quantitative measurements, the AAI, the Strange Situation, and the Bayley Infant Assessment, did not and could not tell our story—the story of our group. The stories unfold in the matrix of the trusting, caring relationships that developed between myself, the women, and their children. The AAI elicited facts, and the Strange Situation measured a moment in time when the children were made to experience heightened anxiety as their mothers left them alone in a University laboratory "playroom;" but it was within the transferences that new relationships unfolded. In this study I provided an essential transforming substitute to the women's earlier relationships with their mothers. Most valuable was the experience of being heard and seen and feeling valued by me. This in itself can be instrumental in freeing the mother and baby from earlier neglectful and harmful relationships (Slade et al., 2006). However, it is not always easy to gain the trust and respect of women who have been abandoned and abused their whole lives. I feel the alliances that I was able to develop with the women were often disrupted by "transferential reactions on the part of mothers who had been betrayed and hurt by those who cared for them" (Slade et al., 2006, p. 83). This was acted out by the women missing sessions or making me pursue them. I often found myself coaxing a mother to attend and giving frequent reminders of when we met. While this was frustrating and exhausting, I understood the multitude of internal conflicts that were stirred up as our relationship deepened. Becoming close was frightening to most of these women, and the fear and resulting defenses needed to be respected and understood.

Change and growth could be observed as the women gathered around the table where they worked on their photo books and shared glorious and painful experiences of what it means to be homeless and to be a mother. It was rare that all five women attended a given session; yet they always knew I would be there, session after session, week after week. I was consistent and dependable, something they had never experienced before in an important relationship. As we spoke they sensed my appreciation of what they could teach me, and developed a powerful sense of pride that I was giving them the opportunity to help others. As they came to see me as dependable and caring they began to integrate bits and pieces of information I offered them. A couple of the women identified with me and took my words as their own when making the films and writing in their photo books. Because I showed them that I appreciated and valued their minds (their thoughts and feelings) they in turn, began to notice and value the minds of their children.

I demonstrated a commitment and dedication to their well-being that they, as a group, came to value. Over the course of this six-month project we weathered many storms, both intrapsychic and environmental. We cried together and listened to painful stories but we also laughed and played. I became their playmate, a playful, loving mother, bringing glitter and shiny stones, singing songs and dancing to childhood lyrics. I read them bedtime stories while I fed them cookies and juice. Our group provided a safe "holding environment," a place and time that was always the same. Within this sameness trust developed and healing could begin. They shared childhood memories and disappointments and began to ask for certain childhood stories and songs. As I demonstrated flexibility and creative processes, they too were able to become more flexible and creative. In the beginning, all five of the women had difficulties playing with their children. As the months wore on, all of the participants were more comfortable playing, not only with me, but also with their own children.

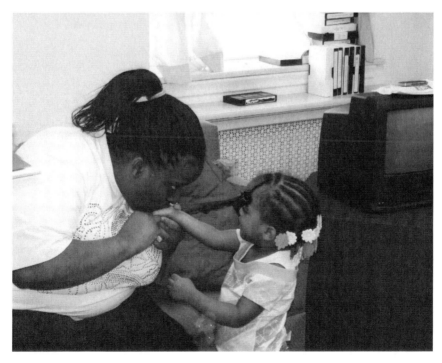

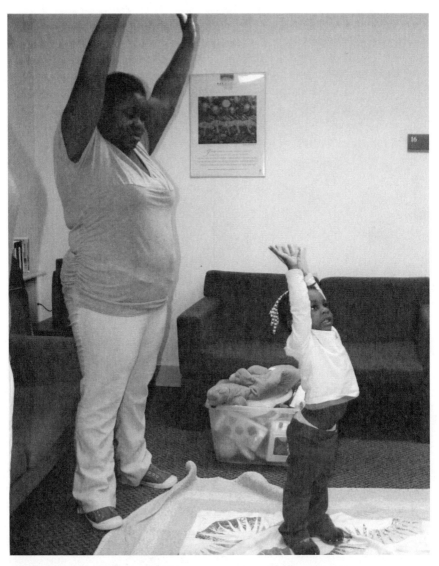

The stories of all of the women and children in this study may demonstrate weaknesses in our society and in our social service systems, but these stories also show the remarkable strength and resiliency that so many of these vulnerable families possess.

I am honored to have had the opportunity to work with and get to know all of the families. I leave them humbled by their strength and courage and proud of their ability to continue to dream for a better future for themselves and their children.

Chapter Nine

Comments on
Mothering without a Home

Alexandra Murray Harrison

This remarkable book—though it was designed as an empirical study—reads like a narrative. The story is that of five homeless families—five single mothers and their young children—and how they used a psychoanalytically informed intervention to find hope and a vision for the future. The author, Ann Smolen, began with the intention of identifying a helpful intervention for homeless families with young children and testing its effectiveness. She chose three measures to create a baseline and determine whether the mothers and children improved in important domains related to the attachment system. The measures were the AAI, to test the mother's attachment status; the Strange Situation, to test the child's attachment status; and the Bayley, to test the child's cognitive developmental status. What she found was either no significant difference between before and after, or confusing results. What she also found was objective observational and subjective perceptual signs of positive growth.

Smolen began with the hypotheses (1) that the adult attachment style would remain the same in the five mothers in the intervention group and in the five mothers in the control group; (2) the intervention group children's attachment style would change from disorganized to insecure/organized; (3) there would be a greater increase in cognitive function in the intervention group children compared with the control group; (4) the experience scores would improve in the AAI for the women in the intervention group but not for those in the control group; (5) that state of mind scales would improve on the AAI for women in the intervention group but not for those in the control group; and (6) that the scales for overall states of mind would improve on the AAI for women in the intervention group but not for those in the control group. These changes were predicated on the assumption that improvement in "mentalization" in both the mothers and the babies would be reflected in these scores.

143

The study design focused on building mentalization skills through therapeutic interventions that aimed to help the mothers imagine the mind of their
babies while also learning to reflect on their own inner worlds and their own
traumatic past histories. This work was done in the therapeutic groups and in
viewing videotapes of the mothers interacting with their children.The project
included two, two-hour groups per week and the production of two films, the
first a documentary and the second a parenting video, both films featuring
the women in the study. Another goal of the study was the development of
an intervention tool—the therapeutic groups. The groups were designed to
attend to the needs of the mothers without the interruption of their children,
and also to include the children so that the mother-child interaction could be
observed, filmed, and discussed. The first hour of the group time was with
just the mothers and Dr. Smolen, while the children played with a clinician
supervised by Dr. Smolen. The second hour included the children in a playgroup with their mothers.

These groups were rich and full of creative activities. The mothers'
group included a wonderful activity of creating a baby book of photos and
writings for each mother's baby. This seemed to offer these mothers a rare
opportunity to celebrate the birth of their babies, to document their babies'
developmental accomplishments, to recognize their babies' unique person-
alities, and finally, to acknowledge their positive role as a mother. In the
playgroup that included mothers and children, there was a free play period
and structured activities—singing and dancing, mothers reading books to
the children, cleanup, and snack. The playgroup introduced the reading of
books into the lives of these families, particularly books that could be read
in the ritual of bedtime stories. The singing and dancing could be seen as
contributing to the mothers' repertoires of regulating behaviors to help their
children calm when dysregulated (Perry). The regular sequence of activities
served as an organizing routine for the families to anticipate and incorporate,
offering them an alternative to the chaotic lives of the mothers' childhoods
and their recent homeless past.

Throughout the activities of the intervention—the groups; the testing situations of the AAI, Strange Situation, and Bayley; and the film productions—is
the theme of the steady, nurturing, and organizing therapist, Dr. Smolen. In
part transference, in part "corrective emotional experience" or "new object,"
she—as she says—provided a "holding environment" for the homeless
mothers and their families. In her multiple roles—therapist, photographer,
principal investigator, clinical supervisor, organizer of ancillary personnel,
carpooler—Dr. Smolen brought together great resources for these families
and held them together in a coherent program. Included in these resources
were puppeteers, filmmakers, a lab for conducting the Strange Situation test,

and trained coders for coding the tests, AAI coders, a clinician to run the child group, and more.

Dr. Smolen is well aware of the study difficulties, and there were many. The intervention and control groups were self-selected in ways that biased the intervention group toward a positive result. The time of the groups (mornings) meant that women with full-time jobs could not participate. The tests were very hard to schedule and accomplish, and there were also many no-shows for the groups; occasionally Dr. Smolen ran the group with one woman and her children. In addition to these complications, the women in the study were cared for in many other ways by the residence in which they lived at the time. The shelter provided them with security, comfort, and an opportunity to take charge of their lives in a way that must have been a new experience for most if not all of them. The shelter had its own living unit for each family that included a kitchen, bathroom, and up to three bedrooms. The families had intensive case management, as well as subsidized daycare, therapists, and many other services. Yet, the description of the groups is compelling, and the reader cannot but believe that they provided something not just additional but also special and unique to these homeless families.

The book is also rich in its literature review. Smolen summarizes Spitz, Mahler, Parens, Greenspan, Tronick, Beebe, Harrison, and the relevant literature on attachment theory, neurobiology and attachment, trauma, and homeless families.

Although the quantitative part of the study could not be used to demonstrate change, Smolen did see change in the families in the intervention group. All the women in the study group showed some improvement in their ability to tell their personal stories in a coherent fashion. Two improved to the point where they moved from an insecure to a more secure category. One interesting aspect of the book is the movement the reader perceives in Smolen from a rather definitive belief in the value of the AAI and Strange Situation measures to a more nuanced and relativist sense of their value, and a parallel movement toward a belief in the value of her own psychoanalytically informed observations of the individuals in her study. Smolen says, "In my study there was very little correlation between the mother's AAI category and that of her child. In fact the results of my study were, in many cases, completely opposite to what the attachment research literature predicts" (p. 110). Smolen wonders why this was true. Was it because the AAI and Strange Situation are not sensitive enough to cultural differences in this minority population? She notes, "subtle differences in child rearing" (p. 111) in this population that might be related to attachment scores and gives a good example of Lena and Noel. She concludes that this study raises the question of the validity of these attachment instruments with African American homeless mothers and children. She also notes two other important complicating factors—the socio-economic realities of the families and the presence of other helpful caregiving figures in the child's life—both actual and potential influences on the child's development. Smolen also asks whether these tests can reliably be used as repeat instruments to measure change where there is severe trauma. There is also the issue of the child's genetic disposition. Smolen notes again the problems in her study design, including the small n, the self-selection of the study participants, the age range of children from birth to almost four, and the fact that the study stopped after six months. Maybe another reason the results are confusing is that this study includes much more data on each individual participant than these measures can make sense of. In order to organize these data in a meaningful way you can benefit from a psychoanalytic perspective that is designed to deal with complexity.

The two films were another piece of this enormously ambitious study. The documentary turned these women's negative identity of single mothers and homeless people into the positive one of film stars and also helpers of a prospective audience. In a similar way, the parenting film gave the women an opportunity to occupy the self-enhancing role of mothers who had wisdom to offer to other women in their life situation. In the process of making the film, unexpected information was brought up, for example, the women's distress over the light skin of their newborns, leading to the section of the film entitled "Is This My Baby?" The mothers identified the confusion about parentage as the stressor, a confusion shared by the fathers of their babies. This universal theme is represented in fairy tales such as "The Ugly Duckling" and the contemporary children's book *Are You My Mother?* But I also wondered about another stressor. Perhaps in addition to the concern that the babies looked different from their mothers, the light skin at birth represented to them "something good emerging from something bad," the bad being the mothers' negative self-images. Perhaps they worried that they would not be capable of maintaining the good in their babies, of helping these precious light children survive and grow.

Dr. Smolen asks the important question, "Where to go from here?" She notes correctly that mother-infant intervention and treatment continues to be unavailable to underserved populations such as homeless mothers and children. The existing parenting films just made these women feel worse. The new parenting film they made can be distributed. That is good. She continues, "It was clear that the results of the quantitative measurements, the AAI, the Strange Situation, and the Baylet Infant Assessment did not and could not tell our story—the story of our group" (p. 136). The AAI elicited facts and the Strange Situation measured a moment in time, "but it was within the transferences that new relationships unfolded" (p. 136). "Most valuable was being heard and seen and feeling by me" (p. 136). She points out though that negative transferential reactions generated by the old experiences of abandonment and abuse figured into the missed sessions, or making her pursue them. The group provided a safe "holding environment" (p. 138). I would add that here the term "transference" must be used in the most generous sense in that the enormous effort Dr. Smolen put into the project must have been clear to all the participants. She not only provided a "holding environment", she provided concrete resources, exciting activities, and new opportunities for learning and self-enhancement.

As I read the book, I asked myself what I would do differently. First of all, I doubt I would dare to undertake such a wonderful and ambitious project in the first place. However, I would definitely want to run parents' groups. One thing I would do differently in the parents' groups is to make the video observation into an essential ritual that occurred every group session. I would focus on positive interactions and show them again and again.* Just as I am sure Smolen did, I would ask the participants to identify what was good about these interactions and help them understand the developmentally facilitating features of the caregiver's behavior. In my experience running parents' groups with video, the members of the group rapidly learn how to analyze videotapes, how to recognize repeating patterns of interaction, and how to call attention to them in empathic ways, including challenging a parent about a problem pattern, much like Smolen's example of teasing in her mothers' group.

In addition to the parents' groups, I would hold parents' workshops, to which I would invite a larger audience, for example, other residents of the shelter or of other programs. I would structure the workshops around questions the mothers' group participants generated about parenting, much as Smolen did in her writing of the parenting film. In these workshops I would teach simple lessons about child development, illustrated by positive interactions of the mothers and children in the groups. This is a method I developed in working with the caregiving staff of a children's home in El Salvador. The caregivers were highly responsive to the developmental teaching and found the video illustrations very helpful.

CONCLUSION

The book as a narrative of this brave and generous study offers those of us concerned about this population valuable knowledge—not only about how

---

* The theory is that in a family, a nonlinear system, building the strength of positive interactional patterns through repetition causes the negative patterns to come apart and weaken (Granic et al.).

the study succeeded, but also about how it did not succeed. I am reminded
of what Louis Sander said about the longitudinal study in which the results
were less than chance. Instead of becoming discouraged, he said, "We should
have been happy."* He meant that having your expectations contradicted was
an opportunity to look at the world through a new lens. You were forced to
find a new meaning.

* Louis W. Sander, Personal Communication.

Epilogue

Our project ended in 2008. All five families had moved from the shelter into their own homes within 18 months after the end of our work together.

Christa became pregnant shortly after moving into her own home. She was overwhelmed by this pregnancy and was unable to care for her newborn son. Because of the bond that developed through our group, Lena came to Christa's aid and took over the care of the baby. Lena is bringing him up as her own, but remains close to Christa.

Nina was raped by a boyfriend of another resident at the shelter and became pregnant. She became profoundly depressed and was hospitalized for a short period of time. Nina's mother is raising that baby. Nina is realizing her dream and is currently enrolled in community college with the goal of completing a four-year program.

Fannie and Lena each had another child. Lena is working toward being credentialed as a childcare worker.

Zoe has been gainfully employed for the last three and a half years. She works long hours and struggles to keep her family together but remains determined to do so.

All of the women reported that their children are doing well in school.

Acknowledgments

Thank you to Drueding Center, Project Rainbow, for supporting my work through the years and for providing a wonderful "home" for families in need. I am grateful to Anita Bryce, PhD; Carolyn Gruber, PhD; Aimee Nover, PhD; and Irv Dubinsky, PhD, for supporting and guiding me through this research project.

A special thank-you to Hossein Etezady, MD, and Mary Davis, MD, for making this book a reality. I am also grateful to Mary for her superb editing skills and advice.

I especially wish to thank Jennifer Bonovitz, PhD, my supervisor, mentor and friend, who suggested I make a parenting film, and provided clinical supervision for all of my work with homeless mothers and children. Jennifer patiently showed me how to bear the unbearable, for this I am forever grateful.

Finally, I thank all of the women and children who generously shared their stories.

Funding for the research project, *Mothering without a Home*, was provided by The Foundation of the Psychoanalytic Center of Philadelphia, The International Psychoanalytic Association, and First Center Trust.

Appendix A

The Strange Situation

SUMMARY OF EIGHT
EPISODES OF THE STRANGE SITUATION

1. Mother, Child & Principal Investigator 30 seconds: Principal Investigator introduces mother and child to playroom.
2. Mother & Child 3 minutes: Child is led into the room and allowed to approach toys. Mother sits in her chair. Child explores.
3. Stranger enters, 1 minute sits in silence; 2nd minute talks with mother, 3rd minute sits next to child. Mother leaves room unobtrusively.
4. Stranger and child 3 minutes or less: First separation episode. Stranger's behavior is geared to that of child.
5. Mother & Child 3 minutes or more: First reunion episode. Mother greets child and/or comforts child, then tries to settle him/her again in play. Returns to her chair. Stranger leaves after child is playing. Mother leaves after 3 minutes (knock on window) saying "bye-bye."
6. Child alone in room 3 minutes or less: second separation episode.
7. Stranger & child 3 minutes or less: Continuation of second separation. Stranger enters and gears her behaviors to that of child.
8. Mother & Child 3 minutes: Second reunion episode. Mother enters, greets child, then picks him/her up. Meanwhile Stranger leaves unobtrusively. Mother eventually returns to chair.

Episode is curtailed if the baby is unduly distressed. Episode is prolonged if more time is required for the baby to become reinvolved in play (Ainsworth et al., 1978).

Appendix B

Adult Attachment Interview

Sample questions:

1. Introduce the interview explaining that we will be mostly speaking about her childhood and her relationships with her parents. Then we will speak about her adolescence and end up in the present.
2. Could you start by helping me get oriented to your early family situation, and where you lived and so on? If you could tell me where you were born, whether you moved around much, what your family did at various times for a living? Who raised you? Did you see much of your grandparents when you were little?
3. I'd like you to try to describe your relationship with your parents as a young child . . . if you could start as far back as you can remember?
4. I would like you to choose five adjectives, words, or phrases that reflect your relationship with your mother starting from as far back as you can remember, say age 5 to 12. This may take some time. Take a few seconds to think. I'll write each one down as you think of them. (Interviewer asks for specific examples/memories from each word)
5. Now we will do the same with your father. (In my study I sometimes asked about a grandparent or aunt depending on the relationship).
6. Which parent did you feel closest to and why? Why isn't there this feeling with the other parent?
7. When you were upset as a child what would you do? When you were emotionally upset? When you were hurt physically? When you were ill? I was wondering, do you remember being held by either of your parents at any of these times? I mean when you were upset, hurt, or ill?

8. What is the first time you remember being separated from your parents? How did you respond? Do you remember how your parents responded? Are there any other separations that come to mind?

9. Did you ever feel rejected as a young child? How old were you when you felt this way? Why do you think your parents did those things? Do you think they realized he/she was rejecting you? Did you ever feel pushed away or ignored? Were you ever frightened as a child?

10. Were your parents ever threatening with you in any way—maybe for discipline or even joking? Some people have told us that their parents use the silent treatment—did that ever happen to you? Some people have memories of some kind of behavior that was abusive. Did anything like that ever happen in your family? How old were you at the time? Did it happen frequently? Do you feel this experience affects you now as an adult? Does it influence your approach to your own child? Did you have any such experiences involving people outside your family?

11. In general, how do you think your overall experiences with your parents have affected your adult personality? Are there any aspects to your early experiences that you feel were a setback to your development?

12. Why do you think your parents behaved as they did during your childhood?

13. Were there any other adults with whom you were close, like parents, as a child? Or any other adults who were especially important to you?

14. Did you experience the loss of a parent or other close loved one while you were a young child—for example, a sibling or close family member? Could you tell me what happened? How did you respond at the time? Was this death sudden or was it expected? Can you recall your feelings at that time? Have your feelings regarding this death changed much over time? Did you attend the funeral? What would you say the effect on your family was? Would you say this loss has had an effect on your adult personality? How does this affect your approach to your own child?

15. Did you lose any other important persons during your childhood? Have you lost other close persons in adult years? (same questions as above).

16. Other than any difficult experiences you've already described, have you had any other experiences which you regard as potentially traumatic? Were there any experiences which were overwhelmingly and immediately terrifying?

17. Now I'd like to ask you a few more questions about your relationship with your parents. Were there many changes in your relationship with your parents after childhood? Changes between childhood and adulthood.

18. What is your relationship with your parents like now?

19. Now for a different sort of question. How do you feel now when you separate from your child? Do you ever feel worried about your child?
20. If you had three wishes for your children for 20 years from now what would they be?
21. Is there any particular thing, which you feel you learned above all from your own childhood experiences? I'm thinking here of something you feel you might have gained from the kind of childhood you had.
22. We've been focusing a lot on the past, but now I would like to end up looking into the future. I'd like to end by asking you what would you hope your child might have learned from his/her experiences of being parented by you (Geroge, Kaplan & Main, 1996)?

Appendix C

Participant Survey

SURVEY

Which of the following did you feel was the most helpful and useful to you? Please rate from 1–10.

Photo Book
Adult Interview
Strange Situation
Bayley Infant Assessment
Group Discussions (adults only)
Group Play with your child
Singing and movement in Group
Stories at end of Group
Participating in the Parenting Film
Participating in the Documentary

SURVEY RESULTS

All of the women in the Intervention Group completed a simple survey at the last group meeting. They were asked to rate ten different components of the project on a scale of 1–10. One being the least useful on up to ten being the most valuable and useful part of their experience in the project.

The following are the 10 items on the survey and a summary of what they meant to the women.

1. *Photo Book:* All of the women gave this activity a 10 except for Nina, who rated it a 7. Nina was never able to work on her photo pages. She spent the first three months gluing bright stones onto her cover until it was completely covered except for a small space for their names.
2. *AAI:* This was the least useful of all of the components. Lena gave this a low rating of 6, while the other women rated this experience as 8 or 9 on usefulness to them.
3. *Strange Situation:* Only one woman found this to be a useful experience. Several women stated that it was interesting to watch their child react to separation from behind the one-way mirror, most felt this to be a source of anxiety and discomfort.
4. *Bayley Infant Assessment:* None of the women gave a rating because the results had not been discussed with them at this time.
5. *Group Discussions (Adults Only):* This seemed to be the most important element of the project. All of the women rated this with a 10. Group discussions were extremely valuable as we grew cohesive as a group, building trust and confidence in one another. There was often humor and silliness as well as many moments of profound sadness. Above all there was a camaraderie that evolved that drew us close and made our sessions enjoyable and enriching.
6. *Group Play with Your Child:* This also received all 10s from the women. At times playtime was a little wild and there were incidents where a child would get very upset and the mother would react harshly. But for the most part, our playtimes were fun and lively.
7. *Singing and Movement in the Group:* All but one woman (Nina) found this to be an enjoyable and useful activity. The children learned the words to many of the songs and many of the women asked for written copies so they could sing them at home.
8. *Stories at End of Group:* All but Nina found this to be enjoyable and useful. The Principal Investigator found it interesting that even when the children were unable to sit still for a story the women were focused. At times she noticed that a few of the women would read along and would crane their necks to see if a child got in the way. The Principal Investigator often felt as if the stories were more important to the mothers then to their children.
9. *Participating in the Parenting Film:* All of the women found this to be a useful experience and gave a 10 rating.
10. *Participating in the Documentary:* This was also perceived as a useful experience and received all 10s.

Appendix D

AAI Classification System

All of the following AAI scales come from Main & Hesse, Adult Attachment Scoring and Classification Systems, 2002.

LOVING

The loving scale assesses the extent to which the interviewee has experienced loving or unloving behaviors from their parents. The interviewee will receive a low score if there is only indirect evidence of loving behaviors or if there is a lack of loving behaviors. Individuals who receive a low score for loving often use positive adjectives to describe their relationship, such as "loving" and "caring" yet are unable to provide any examples.

A score of 5 (on a scale of 1–9), is judged as having a "good-enough" experience of loving behaviors. This parent's unloving behaviors are balanced by affectionate aspects in his/her behavior. A score of 7–9 is given when a parent is described as actively loving and accepting (p. 15)

Loving Scores (pp. 18–19)

1 = Lacking in love
3 = Attention and assistance are provided throughout childhood; or mixed experiences with unloving behavior outweighing loving behavior.
5 = Mild indices of active loving are present, but without indications of special attention to the child.
7 = The parent is loving and accepting
9 = Very loving. This parent is dedicated to their child's development. The interviewee has strong loving memories.

Rejecting Scores (pp. 22–23)

1 = Not at all rejecting of attachment
3 = Mildly rejecting of attachment
5 = Moderately rejecting of attachment
7 = Rejecting
9 = Extremely rejecting

Involving/Role-Reversing/Preoccupying (pp. 99–100)

1 = Parent's well-being was not made a concern to the child
3 = Slight concern about or excessive attention to the parent at times, but parent did not need child and was not the child's responsibility.
5 = Parent implicitly or explicitly seeks attention from the child, and/or child is repeatedly persuaded to attempt to "please" the parent.
7 = Beginning of real role reversal, spousification, or parent strongly depending upon child's company/attention for feelings of safety.
9 = Role reversal; spousification; or extreme need for the child's company and attention due to emotional needs.

Neglecting Scores (pp. 33–34)

1 = Not inattentive
3 = Mildly inattentive
5 = Inattentive
7 = Neglecting
9 = Strongly Neglecting

Pressure to Achieve (pp. 37–38)

1 = Interviewee may or may not have been encouraged to achieve, but was definitely not pushed or pressured toward achievement
3 = Slight pressure to achieve
5 = Moderate pressure to achieve
7 = Pressure to achieve
9 = Extreme pressure to achieve

AAI STATES OF MIND (P. 39)

Coherence (pp. 42–53)

Overall coherence of transcript is the strongest correlate of infant security of attachment. This scale quantifies the interviewee's capability to present the past and its influences in a way that makes it understandable to the listener. In other words, this scale is judged on how well the interviewee tells her story (p. 42).

1 = Not coherent
3 = Low coherence
5 = Moderate coherence
7 = Coherent
9 = Highly coherent

Metacognitive Monitoring (pp. 55–64)

Metacognitive monitoring is when the interviewee is able to monitor and report on her thought processes. This is a high-level awareness of one's own thought processes. Individuals who score high on this scale are usually scored within the secure/autonomous and can reflect on their own attachment process. They also demonstrate a high level of autonomy of the self (pp. 55).

1 = No evidence of metacognitive monitoring.
3 = Two instances of metacognitive monitoring
5 = Two or three instances
7 = Several instances. At least one is in depth.
9 = Metacognitive monitoring is present in several places throughout the interview.

Overall Coherence of Mind (p. 64)

Coherence of mind is the overall score for the most accurate indication of the interviewee's "state of mind" with respect to attachment. This subscale is the best predictor of the infant's overall security of attachment to his/her mother (the interviewee). In addition it is also the best predictor of the interviewee's overall functioning as it is related to attachment (pp. 62).

1 = Striking absence of coherence of mind
3 = Only slight coherence of mind
5 = Moderate coherence of mind

7 = Marked coherence of mind
9 = Strong coherence of mind

SCALES ASSOCIATED WITH DISMISSING STATES OF MIND
(PP. 65–84)

Idealization

This scale assesses the extent to which the interviewee speaks of her parent as "excellent" which is different from the account of the actual experiences.

1 = No idealization
3 = Slight idealization of parent
5 = Moderate idealization of parent
7 = Marked idealization of the parent
9 = Very strong idealization of the parent

Inability to Recall Childhood

This scale refers exclusively to lack of memory. The frequency with which the interviewee claims they do not remember and the strength of this insistence is looked at.

1 = Virtually no insistence upon inability to recall childhood
3 = Infrequent, or soon belied, insistence upon inability to recall childhood
5 = Some insistence upon inability to recall childhood
7 = Frequent or strong insistence upon inability to recall childhood
9 = Very frequent or very strong insistence upon inability to recall childhood

Active, Derogating Dismissal of Attachment

A high score on this subscale is given when the interviewee does not disguise their dislike of the person and speak of their major attachment figure as foolish, laughable, or not worth their time. Derogation here is defines as someone who is dismissed as beneath consideration. In addition the interviewee does not take responsibility for their attitude, but blames the person that is disliked.

1 = No dismissing derogation of attachment
3 = Minor, actively defensive or else humorous use of dismissing derogation
5 = Some dismissing derogation

7 = Marked, active dismissing derogation of attachment-related experiences
9 = Strong, active dismissing derogation appearing in more than one place within the interview.

Fear of Loss of the Child through Death

This scale is based on the interviewee's narrative about their own child, rather than their past relationships with their parents. This scale captures the fears of interviewees who are unable to connect them with their source.

1 = No fear of loss of child is expressed.
3 = Fear that the child might be lost is convincingly described as being confined to the past, or is connected to the source.
5 = The interviewee expressed fear of loss and is unable to identify the source.
7 = Fear of loss of the child through death is unidentified as to the source but affects behavior only mildly.
9 = Fear of loss of child through death is unidentified as to source and is directive of the interviewee's behavior in general regarding the child.

SCALES ASSOCIATED WITH PREOCCUPIED STATES (PP. 85–114)

Involving/Preoccupying Anger

This scale focuses on language used by the interviewee that is considered indicative of involving/preoccupied anger. These expressions are not limited to childhood experiences but may appear in the telling of the present.

1 = No direct expressions of involving/preoccupied anger.
3 = Slightly involving/preoccupying anger
5 = Moderately involving/preoccupying anger
7 = Strongly involving/preoccupying anger
9 = Extremely involving/preoccupying anger

Passivity or Vagueness in Discourse

Passivity must be distinguished from dysfluency. When an individual is dysfluent they may re-start a sentence and may change direction in mid-sentence but they do complete the sentence. When one is passive they often do not complete their thoughts. Passivity is scored across the transcript as a whole.

1 = No evidence for passivity or vagueness
3 = Slight passivity or vagueness
5 = Moderate passivity or vagueness
7 = Definite passivity or vagueness
9 = Extreme passivity or vagueness

Appendix E

Strange Situation Coding

The Ainsworth Strange Situation classifications (Ainsworth, Blehar & Wall, 1978) are based on the interactions with the mother in the two reunion episodes. There are four 7-point scales: proximity seeking, contact maintaining, avoidance of proximity and contact, and resistance to contact and comforting.

PROXIMITY AND CONTACT SEEKING BEHAVIOR

7 = Very Active Effort and Initiative in Achieving Physical Contact
    The child approaches the mother. He goes the whole way and achieves contact through his own efforts. The cooperation of the mother is not required.
6 = Active Effort and Initiative in Achieving Physical Contact

a. The child goes to the mother but requires her cooperation.
b. The child goes to the adult and asks to be picked up but the mother does not pick him up.
c. The approach to the mother would have been scored a 7 but it was delayed.
d. The child's stay with the mother is too brief.
e. The child approaches the mother by way of exploration, but completes his approach purposefully.

5 = Some Active Effort to Achieve Physical Contact.

a. The child approaches the mother purposefully but does not ask to be picked up.
b. The child is being held by the stranger but strains toward the mother.

c. He delays making contact with the mother but asks to be picked up.
d. Same as c but needs the mother's cooperation in order to be picked up.
e. The child makes three active bids for contact but the mother does not respond.

4 = Obvious Desire to Achieve Physical Contact, but with Ineffective or Lack of Initiative OR Active Effort to Gain Proximity Without Persisting Toward Contact.

This score is for children who desire contact but show little initiative in getting it. They are content with minimal contact.

a. The child signals his desire for contact by a reach, lean, or directed cry as though he expected the adult to pick him up.
b. The child approaches the adult but only goes halfway and waits for the adult to come to him.
c. The child makes repeated approaches either without completing contact or with only momentary contact.
d. The child makes a full approach, obviously wanting contact, but the adult does not cooperate and does not pick him up.
e. The child makes a full approach that ends up in contact but only after he is invited to do so.

3 = Weak Effort to Achieve Physical Contact OR Moderately Strong Effort to Gain Proximity.

The child may show a desire to gain contact but is ineffective in his effort. The child does not achieve contact because he does not especially seek it.

a. The child is distressed and stops crying when given contact, but does not give any specific signal that he wants contact.
b. The child is distressed and does reach, lean or slightly crawl indicating his wish for contact, but only after the adult has offered hands or after a long delay.
c. The child makes a spontaneous full approach but does not make contact nor does he seem to want to.
d. The child makes a full approach but merely touches the adult.
e. The child signals for contact with a reach (no cry) but if the adult does not respond he does not persist.
f. The child, having been invited by the adult, makes a full approach but there is no contact and no wish for contact.

2 = Minimal Effort to Achieve Physical Contact or Proximity.

a. The child begins to approach but stops and does not follow up with further signals of desire for contact.
b. The child seems to be making a full approach but changes direction without interaction with the adult.
c. After the adult offers a hand, the desire for contact is weak and underlined by the fact that the child is not even crying when the invitation is offered.

1 = No Effort to Achieve Physical Contact or Proximity

a. The child merely looks, or smiles and interacts from a distance. No contact is desired.
b. The child accepts contact, even being picked up, but merely accepts it.
c. The child approaches accidentally in the course of exploration or pursuing a toy, no contact is made.

CONTACT-MAINTAINING BEHAVIOR

This score deals with the persistence of the child to maintain contact once it is gained.

7 = Very Active and Persistent Effort to Maintain Physical Contact.

a. The child shows at least two instances of active resistance to release. This includes clinging or turning toward the adult to gain closer contact.
b. The adult holds the child for 2 minutes or more, but does not attempt to release him. The child embraces the adult in a relaxed manner.
c. The child initiates contact and remains in contact for over 2 minutes.

6 = Active and fairly Persistent Effort to Maintain Physical Contact.

a. The child shows at least one instance of active resistance to release. Shows desire for contact by holding on, sinking in, or reclining against the adult.
b. The child, having spontaneously approached the adult, sustains contact for longer than 1 minute, and shows at least one active clambering or resisting cessation of contact after the initial behavior.
c. The child, in the course of contact lasting longer than 2 minutes, clings or actively resists being put down. But when he is put down he makes no effort to regain contact.

5 = Some Active Effort to Maintain Physical Contact.

a. The child, in the course of contact lasting for less than a minute, shows one instance of resistance to release which results in maintaining contact.
b. Or, he shows two instances of active behavior, neither of which results in contact.
c. Or, having actively initiated contact, he resists release once even though this may not be a marked instance of resistance.
d. The child is held by the mother for more than a minute; the child makes no effort to resist release. The child shows his desire for contact but the adult's response to his behavior gives him no opportunity to demonstrate more active behavior in maintaining contact.
e. Or, the child is held for less than a minute, clinging, and protests strongly when put down.

4 = Obvious Desire to Maintain Physical Contact but Relatively Little Active Effort to Do So.

a. The child has been held, maybe clinging, diminished crying when picked up; when put down, he protests.
b. Child was picked up when distressed, was not truly comforted by the contact, nevertheless he shows his desire to maintain contact by clinging.
c. The baby quiets when picked up with some clinging; after less than a minute he is put down and makes no protest.
d. The child, having been held, is released, he resists briefly by attempting to hold on briefly but when ineffective he accepts the release without protest.

3 = Some Apparent Desire to Maintain Physical Contact but Relatively Little Effort to Do So.

a. The child initiates contact twice or more times by touching or being held only briefly, when contact is broken there is no resistance from the child.
b. The child initiates contact once and shows other attachment behaviors but does not persist in the contact for more than a few moments and spontaneously breaks away.
c. The adult initiates contact, child accepts the contact but does not cling, when put down he protests briefly.
d. The adult initiates all contact, which persists for a minute, the child accepts the contact passively and gives the impression of liking it but when put down he does not protest.

2 = Physical Contact, but Apparently Little Effort or Desire to Maintain It.

  a. Child initiates contact no more than once and either breaks it off or if the adult breaks it off the child does not protest.
  b. The adult initiates contact and the child accepts it briefly and makes a minimal protest.
  c. The adult picks the child up who is very distressed, the child accepts contact but he is not comforted. When put down he cries more intensely. Even though he is very distressed, he seems somewhat less distressed when in contact with the adult than when he is not.

1 = Either No Physical Contact or No Effort to maintain it.

  a. The child is not held or touched.
  b. Or, if picked up, he neither clings nor holds on, and when put down, does not protest.

RESISTANT BEHAVIOR

This scale relates to the intensity and frequency of resistant behavior evoked by the adult who comes into contact with the child. The child's mood is angry-pouting, cranky fussing, angry distress, or temper tantrums. The behaviors are: pushing away, throwing away, dropping, batting away, hitting, kicking, squirming to be put down, jerking away, stepping angrily, and resistant to be picked up. These behaviors alternate with active efforts to achieve or maintain contact with the person who is being rejected.

7 = Very Intense and Persistent Resistance.

  a. Repeated hitting of the person, or other aggressive behavior.
  b. Strong resistance to being held, shown by strongly pushing away or struggling to be put down.
  c. A full-blown temper tantrum, with angry screaming.
  d. Angry resistance to attempts of the adult to control the child's posture, location, or action.
  e. Strong and repeated pushing away, throwing down, or hitting at toys offered.

6 = Intense and/or Persistent Resistance

a. Repeated or persistent temper tantrums.
b. Very strong/persistent struggle against being held.
c. Definite and repeated rejection of the adult.
d. Repeated, strong rejection of toys-pushing away, throwing.
e. A combination of less intense manifestations of resistance, including squirming to be put down, resistance to interference, refusal of contact, rejection of toys, and petulance.

5 = Some Resistance, Either Less Intense, or, If Intense, More Isolated and Less Persistent than the above.

a. Repeated rejection of toys but with no strong pushing away or batting away.
b. Persistent resistance to the adult when she seeks interaction, but without the intensity of struggling, pushing away, hitting, and so on.
c. Resistance to being held by the mother, shown by squirming immediately to be put down, but without an intense struggle.
d. Persistent low-intensity pouting or cranky fussing.

4 = Isolated but Definite Instances of Resistance in the Absence of a Pervasive Angry Mood.

a. Refusal of contact with stranger.
b. Two refusals of toy, kicking and crying.
c. One strong but isolated behavior with a cry.
d. One manifestation of resistance to being held by the mother.

3 = Slight Resistance

a. Two instances of resistance behavior that is neither strong nor intense, no crying.
b. One instance of resistant behavior with a pout or protest.
c. A marked pout

2 = Very Slight Resistance

a. One isolated instance of non-intense resistance, like a little kick of the leg when being picked up.
b. One brief, slight protest noise when the adult enters

1 = No Resistance

None of the above behaviors. The child accepts proximity or is unresponsive. He may be occupied with other things.

AVOIDANT BEHAVIOR

This deals with the intensity, persistence, duration, and promptness of the baby's avoidance of proximity and of interaction even across a distance.

7 = Very Marked and persistent Avoidance
Of Mother: The child does not greet the mother upon her return in a reunion episode.
Of Stranger: The child repeatedly and persistently avoids the stranger by some kind of strong behavior.

6 = Marked and Persistent Avoidance
Of Mother: The child behaves as above, giving the mother no greeting except a look.
Of Stranger: This score is reserved for an episode in which the end of the episode comes before it is confirmed that the child's avoidance would have been repeated and persistent.

5 = Clear-Cut Avoidance But Less Persistent
Of mother:

a. The child may look, but gives the mother no greeting, then looks away, or turns away and ignores the mother for 30 seconds, during which time the mother makes no effort to gain his attention; then he looks again and seems more responsive to her, but he does not seek contact and may even avoid it if it is offered.
b. The child gives the mother no greeting; the mother strives to gain his attention, after 15 seconds he gives her his attention but he is fairly unresponsive even then.
c. The child greets his mother or starts to approach her, but then he either turns away or goes past her. He ignores her efforts to gain his attention.

Of Stranger: The child avoids the stranger, but without intensity.

4 = Brief but Clear-Cut Avoidance OR Persistent Low-Keyed Avoidance
Of Mother:

a. The child greets the mother but turns away. The mother goes to her chair and sits without making an effort to approach her child. The child goes on playing. He is not ignoring his mother but would approach her if given the cue.
b. The child snubs the mother by failing to greet her, by being slow to look at her, or by looking away, but then responds to the mother as she reaches out for him.
c. The child fails to greet the mother and ignores her for a time and then takes the initiative in making contact or undertaking interaction, even though the mother has not sought his attention.

Of Stranger: The child shows avoidance but looks at the stranger.

3 = Slight, Isolated Avoidance Behavior
Of Mother:

a. The child is distressed and is slow either in looking at his mother or in responding to her overtures, but then he does.
b. The child is not distressed; he looks up at his mother when she arrives, perhaps greeting her, and then looks away briefly; then he is responsive. He does not initiate contact.

Of Stranger:

a. The child retreats from the stranger to the mother but without anxiety. He does not approach the stranger but does not avoid the stranger's advances.
b. One avoidance of the stranger by twisting away, turning away, or moving back a little but could be friendly.

2 = Very Slight Avoidance
Of Mother: The child may delay very briefly in responding to his mother's return or may give her a brief snub by looking away, but seeks proximity to her.
Of Stranger: One slight instance of avoidance.

1 = No Avoidance
Of Mother: The child responds appropriately to his mother and her behavior, neither avoiding her overtures nor ignoring her return after an absence.

Of Stranger: The child may be friendly with the stranger and does not avoid the stranger.

CRITERIA FOR CLASSIFICATION
IN TERMS OF ATTACHMENT SECURITY

Secure (Group B)

The child actively seeks proximity and/or interaction with the mother. When he obtains contact he seeks to maintain it and will resist being put down. He has little tendency to resist contact with the mother. He responds to his mother in the return episodes with more than a casual greeting. He does not avoid the mother in reunion episodes. He may or may not be friendly with the stranger, but is clearly more interested in contact and interaction with the mother. He may or may not be distressed at separation episodes, but if distressed it is clearly connected to his mother's absence, not merely being alone. He may be comforted by the stranger, but it is clear he wants his mother.

Insecure Avoidant (Group A)

Conspicuous avoidance of proximity to or interaction with the mother in the reunion episodes. The child may ignore his mother. He may greet her but mingles his welcome with avoidance responses such as turning away, moving past, and averting his gaze. Little or no tendency to seek proximity or interaction with the mother, even in the reunion episodes. If picked up, there is little or no tendency to cling or to resist being released. On the other hand, there is little or no tendency toward active resistance to contact or interaction with the mother. There is a tendency to treat the stranger as he does the mother, but with less avoidance. If the child is distressed during separation it is because he has been left alone rather than the mother's absence.

Insecure Resistant (Group C)

The child displays conspicuous contact and interaction resisting behavior. He shows moderate to strong seeking of proximity and contact and seeking to maintain contact once gained, so that he gives the impression of being ambivalent to his mother. He shows little or no tendency to ignore his mother in the reunion episode, or to turn away or avert his gaze. He may display generally maladaptive behavior. Either he tends to be more angry or more passive than other children.

Insecure Disorganized (Group D)

A key to the Disorganized classification is that the behaviors are limited to the reunion episodes. However, it is not totally clear whether this behavior reflects (a) primarily an attachment problem or (b) a developmental problem that leads to difficult interactions and thus to an attachment problem, or (c) odd behavior that is evident in the stress of the Strange Situation but not necessarily associated with secure base behavior at home.

Appendix F

AAI Data Analysis Intervention Group

Case #1 CHRISTA Pre-Test

Experience Scales	M	F	Other
Loving	3	NA	
Rejecting	7	NA	
Involving/Reversing	CR	NA	
Pressured to Achieve	1	NA	
Neglecting	(7)	NA	

States of Mind Respecting the Parents (or other persons)

Idealizing	6	NA	
Involving Anger	4	NA	

Overall States of Mind

Overall Derogation of Attachment	1
Insistence on Lack of Recall	1
Metacognitive Processes	1
Passivity of Thought Processes	3
Fear of Loss	1
Highest Score for Unresolved Loss	1
Highest Score for Unresolved Trauma	NA
Coherence of Transcript	3
Coherence of Mind	3

Classification: Ds3
Ds3: Restricted in feeling

Transcripts are placed in this category when the interviewee describes experiences of hurt feelings and resentments but they are taken back, minimized, downplayed, or are followed by a positive wrap-up. There is evidence of rejection, lack of closeness to parents, or conflict with parents. However the interviewee does not feel that these experiences have had any effect upon her adult personality (Main, Goldwyn, & Hesse, 2002).

Child: Iris Pre-Test Classification D/B3
Disorganized in behavior
Subgroup B3

The child actively seeks physical contact with the mother and resists her release of him. Occasionally, a child who seems especially secure in his relationship with his mother will be content with mere interaction with a proximity to her, without seeking to be held. There is little or no sign of either avoiding or resisting proximity with the mother. If he shows distress he is clearly more active in seeking contact and in resisting release than B1 or B2 children. Although his attachment behavior is heightened in the reunion episodes, he does not seem wholly preoccupied with his mother in the preseparation episodes.

Case #1 CHRISTA Post-Test

Experience Scales	M	GM	GF
Loving	2	6	5
Rejecting	4	2	3
Involving/Reversing	5	1	1

States of Mind Respecting the Parents (or other persons)			
Idealizing	1	4	2.5
Involving Anger	1	4	2.5
Derogation	4	1	1

Overall States of Mind	
Overall Derogation of Attachment	1
Insistence on Lack of Recall	1
Metacognitive Processes	1
Passivity of Thought Processes	3
Fear of Loss	1
Highest Score for Unresolved Loss	1
Highest Score for Unresolved Trauma	NA
Coherence of Transcript	3
Coherence of Mind	3

Classification
D2/F5 (Borderline U/d)
D2. Devaluing of Attachment

There is a devaluing of attachment when speaking of parents. These individuals may emphasize personal strength and materialism, craftiness or manipulativeness with respect to relationships may be expressed. However, in spite of an overriding coolness toward attachment figures they may make passionate remarks about individuals from their childhood (Main, Goldwyn & Hesse, 2002)

F5. Somewhat resentful/conflicted while accepting of continuing involvement.

These individuals may be angrily preoccupied with attachment figures but their text is coherent, contained, and sometimes humorous. Parents may be described as rejecting or role/reversing. These individuals will often indicate that they are still caught up in the relationship via active complaints (Main, Goldwyn, & Hesse, 2002).

Child: Iris Post-Test Classification D/B4 Disorganized/Forced Secure-Ambivalent
Disorganized in behavior

Subgroup B4

The child wants contact and seeks it. He seems wholly preoccupied with his mother throughout the strange situation. He gives the impression of feeling anxious throughout, with much crying. In the second separation he seems very distressed. He may show resistance to his mother, and indeed he may avoid her by drawing back from her or averting his face when held by her. The impression is of some ambivalence, although not as much as is shown by Group-C children (Ainsworth, Bleher, Waters & Wall, 1978).

Case #2 NINA Pre-Test

Experience Scales	M	F	Other
Loving	1	1	(1)
Rejecting	9	9	(5)
Involving/Reversing	9	CR	CR
Pressured to Achieve	CR	CR	CR
Neglecting	9	CR	CR

States of Mind Respecting the Parents (or other persons)

Idealizing	3	3	CR
Involving Anger	4	1	CR
Derogation	1	1	CR

Overall States of Mind

Overall Derogation of Attachment	1
Insistence on Lack of Recall	3
Metacognitive Processes	1
Passivity of Thought Processes	4
Fear of Loss	1
Highest Score for Unresolved Loss	7.5
Highest Score for Unresolved Trauma	8.5
Coherence of Transcript	1
Coherence of Mind	1

Classification
U/d/E3/E1/Ds3
Nina has been classified as Unresolved with respect to trauma. The adult who receives this classification will also be assigned a second, best-fitting classification. NINA received three such classifications.
E3. Fearfully preoccupied by traumatic events.
   This attachment style is found in individuals who have had fearful experiences related to attachment and these experiences are presently preoccupying or even unpredictably controlling mental processes.
E1. Passive
   There is an implied passivity or vagueness of thought processes regarding experiences of childhood. There is a weak, vague, or incomplete presentation of self or personal identity and a tendency to remain unfocused.
Ds3. Restricted in feeling
   Transcripts are placed in this category when the interviewee describes experiences of hurt feelings and resentments but they are taken back, minimized, downplayed or are followed by a positive wrap-up. There is evidence of rejection, lack of closeness to parents, or conflict with parents. However

the interviewee does not feel that these experiences have had any effect upon her adult personality (Main, Goldwyn, & Hesse, 2002).

Child Pre-Test: Karl age 36 months, Male, Pre-Test Classification: Secure-feisty (B4-feisty)

Subgroup B4

The child wants contact and seeks it. He seems wholly preoccupied with his mother throughout the strange situation. He gives the impression of feeling anxious throughout, with much crying. In the second separation he seems very distressed. He may show resistance to his mother, and indeed he may avoid her by drawing back from her or averting his face when held by her. The impression is of some ambivalence, although not as much as is shown by Group-C children.

Secure-Feisty

These children show a confident bossiness. They may show playful scorn or mocking of the parent. These children can be considered "full of themselves," "cocky," "sassy," or "high-spirited." This attitude may be affectionate in nature (Cassidy & Marvin. 1992).

Case #2 NINA Post-Test

Experience Scales	M	F	GM
Loving	1	3	2
Rejecting	6	4	7
Involving/Reversing	8	1	1
Pressured to Achieve	3	1	1
Neglecting	9	1	3

States of Mind Respecting the Parents (or other persons)			
Idealizing	1	4	4
Involving Anger	6	1	3
Derogation	1	1	1

Overall States of Mind	
Overall Derogation of Attachment	1
Insistence on Lack of Recall	5
Metacognitive Processes	1
Passivity of Thought Processes	6
Fear of Loss	1
Highest Score for Unresolved Loss	9
Highest Score for Unresolved Trauma	9
Coherence of Transcript	1.5
Coherence of Mind	1

Classification
U/d/E3a/E1/Ds3
U/d. Unresolved for Trauma.
E3a. Fearfully preoccupied by traumatic events.

Confused, fearful and overwhelmed by traumatic/frightening experiences. Reference to trauma is predominant yet incoherent. This kind of overwhelming preoccupation appears to invade discourse, giving the impression that the speaker cannot control, focus, or shift attention away from traumatic/frightening events in favor of the continued discussion of relationships.

E1. Passive

There is an implied passivity or vagueness of thought processes regarding experiences of childhood. There is a weak, vague, or incomplete presentation of self or personal identity and a tendency to remain unfocused.

Ds3. Restricted in feeling

Transcripts are placed in this category when the interviewee describes experiences of hurt feelings and resentments but they are taken back, minimized, downplayed, or are followed by a positive wrap-up. There is evidence of rejection, lack of closeness to parents, or conflict with parents. However the interviewee does not feel that these experiences have had any effect upon her adult personality (Main, Goldwyn, & Hesse, 2002).

Child Post-Test: Karl 42-month-old male
A1/C1
Subgroup A1. Avoidant-ignoring

This child ignores the parent as much as possible. The child may show strong physical and conversational avoidance. The child may never even turn to look at the parent. These children tend not to initiate conversation and respond only minimally.

Subgroup C1. Ambivalent-resistant

These children may show direct, angry, whiney resistance. These children are distressed by separation and it may take longer for them to calm down and return to play. These children may struggle with their parent. This often takes the form of the child wanting to engage in some activity while the parent discourages him through reasoning and distracting. These children show anger directly to the parent, but without the aim of trying to control the parent. Ambivalence to physical proximity may be a strong. The child may hang on the parent or show loving behaviors such as hugging or sitting on the parent's lap. However, these behaviors will be mixed with signs of ambivalence, such as intentions of moving away, slapping the parent and arguing (Cassidy & Marvin, 1992).

Case #3 LENA Pre-Test

Case #3 LENA Pre-Test

Experience Scales	*M*	*F*	*GM*
Loving	3		CR
Rejecting	CR		CR
Involving/Reversing	8		CR
Pressured to Achieve	CR		CR
Neglecting	CR		CR

States of Mind Respecting the Parents (or other persons)

Idealizing	3		CR(1)
Involving Anger	9		CR(1)
Derogation	1		CR(1)

Overall States of Mind

Overall Derogation of Attachment	1
Insistence on Lack of Recall	2
Metacognitive Processes	1
Passivity of Thought Processes	9
Fear of Loss	1
Highest Score for Unresolved Loss	9
Highest Score for Unresolved Trauma	5
Coherence of Transcript	2
Coherence of Mind	1

Classification
U/d/E2/E1
Unresolved with respect to trauma
E2. Angry/conflicted
High scores for involving/preoccupying anger with respect to at least one parent with excessive blaming.
E1. Passive
There is an implied passivity or vagueness of thought processes regarding experiences of childhood. There is a weak, vague, or incomplete presentation of self or personal identity and a tendency to remain unfocused (Main, Goldwyn, & Hesse, 2002).
Child: Noel 26-month-old Female, Pre-Test Classification: B4/B3
Subgroup B3
The child actively seeks physical contact with the mother and resists her release of him. Occasionally, a child who seems especially secure in his relationship with his mother will be content with mere interaction with a proximity to her, without seeking to be held. There is little or no sign of

either avoiding or resisting proximity with the mother. If he shows distress he is clearly more active in seeking contact and in resisting release than B1 or B2 children. Although his attachment behavior is heightened in the reunion episodes, he does not seem wholly preoccupied with his mother in the preseparation episodes.

Subgroup B4

The child wants contact and seeks it. He seems wholly preoccupied with his mother throughout the strange situation. He gives the impression of feeling anxious throughout, with much crying. In the second separation he seems very distressed. He may show resistance to his mother, and indeed he may avoid her by drawing back from her or averting his face when held by her. The impression is of some ambivalence, although not as much as is shown by Group-C children (Ainsworth, Bleher, Waters & Wall, 1978).

Case #3 LENA Post-Test

Case #3 LENA Post-Test

Experience Scales	M	F	GM
Loving	3.6		1
Rejecting	1		CR
Involving/Reversing	5		CR
Pressured to Achieve	1		9
Neglecting	7		CR

States of Mind Respecting the Parents (or other persons)			
Idealizing	3		1
Involving Anger	1		1
Derogation	1		1

Overall States of Mind	
Overall Derogation of Attachment	1
Insistence on Lack of Recall	1
Metacognitive Processes	1
Passivity of Thought Processes	2
Fear of Loss	1
Highest Score for Unresolved Loss	7
Highest Score for Unresolved Trauma	3
Coherence of Transcript	6
Coherence of Mind	4

Classification
U/d/F1a
U/d. Unresolved for trauma
F1a. Secure-autonomous attachment/some setting aside of attachment.
An individual with this classification has redirected their personal life after experiencing a difficult childhood. These interviewees tend to have had harsh experiences with attachment figures but have reevaluated and redirected their lives in terms of relationships (Main, Goldwyn, & Hesse, 2002).
Child Post-Test: Noel 32-month old female. classification: B3
Subgroup 3. Very secure
These children show calm, comfortable enjoyment of the parent with virtually no avoidance, disorganization, or controlling behaviors. Interaction with the parent begins almost immediately upon reunion. They may greet the parent directly or plunge right into conversation. Casual and comfortable contact may occur. The child may put her face close to the parent's face in an intimate way or there may be full, lingering eye contact. These children may be very distressed by separation but upon reunion are calmed easily (Cassidy & Marvin, 1992)
Case #4 ZOE Pre-Test

Case #4 ZOE Pre-Test

Experience Scales	M	F	GM
Loving	1.5	2	
Rejecting	6	4	
Involving/Reversing	5	(1)	
Pressured to Achieve	2	1	
Neglecting	7	CR	

States of Mind Respecting the Parents (or other persons)		
Idealizing	2	4
Involving Anger	5	1
Derogation	3	1

Overall States of Mind	
Overall Derogation of Attachment	3
Insistence on Lack of Recall	2
Metacognitive Processes	1
Passivity of Thought Processes	5
Fear of Loss	4
Highest Score for Unresolved Loss	5
Highest Score for Unresolved Trauma	4
Coherence of Transcript	2
Coherence of Mind	1

Classification
U/d/E2/E1/E3a
Unresolved for trauma
E2. Angry/conflicted
  High scores for involving/preoccupying anger with respect to at least one parent with excessive blaming.
E1. Passive
  There is an implied passivity or vagueness of thought processes regarding experiences of childhood. There is a weak, vague, or incomplete presentation of self or personal identity and a tendency to remain unfocused.
  E3a. Confused, fearful and overwhelmed by traumatic/frightening experiences. When the individual speaks about her traumatic experiences they are incoherent (Main, Goldwyn, & Hesse, 2002).
Child: Melody Newborn female. Classification: Too young for testing.
Case #4 ZOE Post-Test

Case #4 ZOE Post-Test

Experience Scales	M	F	GM
Loving	1.5	1	1.5
Rejecting	6	4	5
Involving/Reversing	5	1	1
Pressured to Achieve	1	1	1
Neglecting	7	7	1

States of Mind Respecting the Parents (or other persons)			
Idealizing	3	3	1
Involving Anger	5	1	1
Derogation	5	3	1

Overall States of Mind	
Overall Derogation of Attachment	5
Insistence on Lack of Recall	5
Metacognitive Processes	1
Passivity of Thought Processes	4.5
Fear of Loss	1
Highest Score for Unresolved Loss	6
Highest Score for Unresolved Trauma	6
Coherence of Transcript	2
Coherence of Mind	1.5

Classification
U/d/CC/E2/Ds2/Ds3
U/d. Unresolved for trauma
CC. Cannot classify
E2. Angry/conflicted
High scores for involving/preoccupying anger with respect to at least one parent with excessive blaming.
D2. Devaluing of Attachment
There is a devaluing of attachment when speaking of parents. These individuals may emphasize personal strength and materialism, craftiness or manipulativeness with respect to relationships may be expressed. However, in spite of an overriding coolness toward attachment figures they may make passionate remarks about individuals from their childhood.
Ds3. Restricted in feeling
Transcripts are placed in this category when the interviewee describes experiences of hurt feelings and resentments but they are taken back, minimized, downplayed, or are followed by a positive wrap-up. There is evidence of rejection, lack of closeness to parents, or conflict with parents. However the interviewee does not feel that these experiences have had any effect upon her adult personality (Main, Goldwyn, & Hesse, 2002).
Case #5 FANNIE Pre-Test

Case #5 FANNIE Pre-Test

Experience Scales	M	F	Other
Loving	(5)	(5)	
Rejecting	CR	CR	
Involving/Reversing	CR	CR	
Pressured to Achieve	CR	(5)	
Neglecting	2	1	

States of Mind Respecting the Parents (or other persons)		
Idealizing	6	8
Involving Anger	1	1
Derogation	1	1

Overall States of Mind	
Overall Derogation of Attachment	1
Insistence on Lack of Recall	7
Metacognitive Processes	1
Passivity of Thought Processes	2
Fear of Loss	1
Highest Score for Unresolved Loss	5
Highest Score for Unresolved Trauma	NA
Coherence of Transcript	1
Coherence of Mind	1

Classification
Ds1
Dismissing of attachment.

In this category idealization of at least one parent is strong. There is also a marked discrepancy between the generalized picture of the parent as warm loving, etc., and episodes from childhood that fail to support this picture of parenting (Main, Goldwyn, & Hesse, 2002).

Child #1: Tom 30 months old, Male. Pre-Test Classification: C2
Subgroup C2

The C2 child is very passive. Their exploratory behavior is limited and their interactive behaviors are lacking. In the reunion episode they want proximity to and contact with their mothers, even though they tend to use signaling behavior rather than active approach, and protest against being put down rather than actively resist release. Resistant behavior tends to be strong. (Cassidy & Marvin, 1992).

Child #2: Rob 19-months-old male. Pre-Test Classification: D/CC/B4/A1 D = 3.5
Subgroup D. Disorganized

These children show a disordering of expected temporal sequences, in-complete or undirected movements and expressions, direct indices of confu-sion and apprehension, dazed and disoriented expressions, and indices of depressed affect.

Subgroup CC. Cannot classify

This means cannot classify. A coder will give this score when they are unsure of the appropriate classification.

Subgroup B4.

The child wants contact and seeks it. He seems wholly preoccupied with his mother throughout the strange situation. He gives the impression of feeling anxious throughout, with much crying. In the second separation he seems very distressed. He may show resistance to his mother, and indeed he may avoid her by drawing back from her or averting his face when held by her. The impression is of some ambivalence, although not as much as is shown by Group-C children.

Subgroup A1.

Conspicuous avoidance of the mother in reunion episodes, which is likely to consist of ignoring her altogether. There may be some looking away, turn-ing away, or moving away. If there is a greeting when the mother returns, it tends to be a mere smile or look. Either the child does not approach the mother on reunion, or the approach is aborted with the child going past the mother, or it tends to occur after much coaxing. If picked up, the child shows little or no contact-maintaining behavior. He tends not to cuddle, he looks away, and may squirm to get down (Ainsworth, Blehar, Waters, & Wall, 1978).

Case #5 FANNIE Post-Test

Case #5 FANNIE Post-Test

Experience Scales	M	F	Other
Loving	3.5	3	
Rejecting	5	1	
Involving/Reversing	1	1	
Pressured to Achieve	3	1	
Neglecting	3	3	

States of Mind Respecting the Parents (or other persons)		
Idealizing	5.5	3
Involving Anger	2	1
Derogation	1	1

Overall States of Mind	
Overall Derogation of Attachment	1
Insistence on Lack of Recall	5
Metacognitive Processes	1
Passivity of Thought Processes	2
Fear of Loss	2
Highest Score for Unresolved Loss	5
Highest Score for Unresolved Trauma	NA
Coherence of Transcript	3
Coherence of Mind	3

Classification
Ds3a/U/d
Ds3a.
 The individual appears to recognize aspects of rejection and can discuss them with some resentment, however, these accounts of negative experiences are succeeded by "normalizing," with claims that these were good for them, gave them strength and was not adversely affected.
U/d. Unresolved for trauma (Main, Goldwyn, & Hesse, 2002).
Child #1: Tom 36-month-old male. Post-Test Classification: D/A1/C1
Disorganized/Avoidant-Ignoring/Ambivalent-Resistant
Subgroup D. Disorganized
 These children show a disordering of expected temporal sequences, incomplete or undirected movements and expressions, direct indices of confusion and apprehension, dazed and disoriented expressions, and indices of depressed affect.
Subgroup A1. Avoidant-ignoring
 This child ignores the parent as much as possible. The child may show strong physical and conversational avoidance. The child may never even turn

to look at the parent. These children tend not to initiate conversation and respond only minimally.

Subgroup C1. Ambivalent-resistant

These children may show direct, angry, whiney resistance. These children are distressed by separation and it may take longer for them to calm down and return to play. These children may struggle with their parent. This often takes the form of the child wanting to engage in some activity while the parent discourages him through reasoning and distracting. These children show anger directly to the parent, but without the aim of trying to control the parent. Ambivalence to physical proximity may be strong. The child may hang on the parent or show loving behaviors such as hugging or sitting on the parent's lap. However, these behaviors will be mixed with signs of ambivalence, such as intentions of moving away, slapping the parent, and arguing (Cassidy & Marvin, 1992).

Child #2: Rob 25-month-old male. Post-Test Classification: D/B3
Subgroup D. Disorganized

These children show a disordering of expected temporal sequences, incomplete or undirected movements and expressions, direct indices of confusion and apprehension, dazed and disoriented expressions, and indices of depressed affect.

Subgroup 3. Very secure

These children show calm, comfortable enjoyment of the parent with virtually no avoidance, disorganization, or controlling behaviors. Interaction with the parent begins almost immediately upon reunion. They may greet the parent directly or plunge right into conversation. Casual and comfortable contact may occur. The child may put her face close to the parent's face in an intimate way or there may be full, lingering eye-contact. These children may be very distressed by separation but upon reunion are calmed easily (Cassidy & Marvin, 1992).

AAI Data Analysis Control Group
Case #1 SUSAN Pre-Test

Case #1 SUSAN Pre-Test

Experience Scales	M	F	Other
Loving	8	2	
Rejecting	1	1	
Involving/Reversing	1	1	
Pressured to Achieve	9	(1)	
Neglecting	1	3	

States of Mind Respecting the Parents (or other persons)

Idealizing	1	3	
Involving Anger	1	1	
Derogation	1	1	

Overall States of Mind

Overall Derogation of Attachment	1
Insistence on Lack of Recall	4
Metacognitive Processes	1
Passivity of Thought Processes	3
Fear of Loss	1
Highest Score for Unresolved Loss	5
Highest Score for Unresolved Trauma	NA
Coherence of Transcript	7
Coherence of Mind	5

Classification
U/d/F1a
U/d. Unresolved for trauma.
F1a. Secure-autonomous attachment/some setting aside of attachment.
   An individual with this classification has redirected their personal life after experiencing a difficult childhood. These interviewees tend to have had harsh experiences with attachment figures but have reevaluated and redirected their lives in terms of relationships (Main, Goldwyn, & Hesse, 2002).
Child #1: Karen 27-month-old female (twin). Pre-Test Classification: B3 D = 1
Subgroup B3
   The child actively seeks physical contact with the mother and resists her release of him. Occasionally, a child who seems especially secure in his relationship with his mother will be content with mere interaction with a proximity to her, without seeking to be held. There is little or no sign of either avoiding or resisting proximity with the mother. If he shows distress he is clearly more active in seeking contact and in resisting release than B1 or B2 children. Although his attachment behavior is heightened in the reunion

episodes, he does not seem wholly preoccupied with his mother in the preseparation episodes (Ainsworth, Blehar, Waters, & Wall, 1978).
*Child #2: Karina 27-month old female (twin) Pre-Test Classification: B3 D
= 2*
Subgroup B3
   The child actively seeks physical contact with the mother and resists her
release of him. Occasionally, a child who seems especially secure in his
relationship with his mother will be content with mere interaction with a
proximity to her, without seeking to be held. There is little or no sign of either avoiding or resisting proximity with the mother. If he shows distress he
is clearly more active in seeking contact and in resisting release than B1 or
B2 children. Although his attachment behavior is heightened in the reunion
episodes, he does not seem wholly preoccupied with his mother in the pre-
separation episodes (Ainsworth, Blehar, Waters, & Wall, 1978).
Case #1 SUSAN Post-Test

Case #1 SUSAN Post-Test

Experience Scales	M	F	Other
Loving	8	2	
Rejecting	1	1	
Involving/Reversing	1	1	
Pressured to Achieve	9	(1)	
Neglecting	1	3	

States of Mind Respecting the Parents (or other persons)		
Idealizing	1	3
Involving Anger	1	1
Derogation	1	1

Overall States of Mind	
Overall Derogation of Attachment	1
Insistence on Lack of Recall	4
Metacognitive Processes	1
Passivity of Thought Processes	3
Fear of Loss	1
Highest Score for Unresolved Loss	3.5
Highest Score for Unresolved Trauma	3
Coherence of Transcript	7
Coherence of Mind	7

Classification
F3b
F3b. Earned secure
The mark of these interviews is clarity and objectivity. These individuals give the impression of being highly developed with a strong sense of self. The interview task is often met with exceptional thoughtfulness or reflectiveness. Unfavorable experiences with attachment figures are recounted with forgiveness, balance, or humor (Main, Goldwyn, & Hesse, 2002).
Child #1: Karen 33-month-old female Post-Test Classification: D/C1/A1
Disorganized/Ambivalent-Resistant/Avoidant-Ignoring
Subgroup D. Disorganized
These children show a disordering of expected temporal sequences, incomplete or undirected movements and expressions, direct indices of confusion and apprehension, dazed and disoriented expressions, and indices of depressed affect.
Subgroup C1. Ambivalent-resistant
These children may show direct, angry, whiney resistance. These children are distressed by separation and it may take longer for them to calm down and return to play. These children may struggle with their parent. This often takes the form of the child wanting to engage in some activity while the parent discourages him through reasoning and distracting. These children show anger directly to the parent, but without the aim of trying to control the parent. Ambivalence to physical proximity may be strong. The child may hang on the parent or show loving behaviors such as hugging or sitting on the parent's lap. However, these behaviors will be mixed with signs of ambivalence, such as intentions of moving away, slapping the parent, and arguing.
Subgroup A1. Avoidant-ignoring
This child ignores the parent as much as possible. The child may show strong physical and conversational avoidance. The child may never even turn to look at the parent. These children tend not to initiate conversation and respond only minimally (Cassidy & Marvin, 1992).
Child #2: Karina 33-month-old female Post-Test Classification: B4/D
Secure-Ambivalent/Disorganized
Subgroup B4. Secure-ambivalent
These children are generally secure with elements of immature, dependent, ambivalent, or resistant behaviors.
Subgroup D. Disorganized
These children show a disordering of expected temporal sequences, incomplete or undirected movements and expressions, direct indices of confusion and apprehension, dazed and disoriented expressions, and indices of depressed affect (Cassidy & Marvin, 1992).
Case #2 ROBIN Pre-Test

Case #2 ROBIN Pre-Test

Experience Scales	M	F	Other
Loving	2		
Rejecting	(1)		
Involving/Reversing	8		
Pressured to Achieve	1		
Neglecting	7		

States of Mind Respecting the Parents (or other persons)

Idealizing	3		
Involving Anger	1		
Derogation	1		

Overall States of Mind

Overall Derogation of Attachment	1		
Insistence on Lack of Recall	5		
Metacognitive Processes	1		
Passivity of Thought Processes	6		
Fear of Loss	1		
Highest Score for Unresolved Loss	(3)		
Highest Score for Unresolved Trauma	(CR)		
Coherence of Transcript	2		
Coherence of Mind	2		

Classification
CC/E3/E1/Ds3/u/d
CC. Cannot classify.

When a transcript is assigned CC alternative organized categories must also be considered. In some cases several subcategories may be deemed applicable and should be listed in order of descending fit.

E3. Fearfully preoccupied by traumatic events.

This attachment style is found in individuals who have had fearful experiences related to attachment and these experiences are presently preoccupying or even unpredictably controlling mental processes.

E1. Passive

There is an implied passivity or vagueness of thought processes regarding experiences of childhood. There is a weak, vague, or incomplete presentation of self or personal identity and a tendency to remain unfocused.

Ds3: Restricted in feeling

Transcripts are placed in this category when the interviewee describes experiences of hurt feelings and resentments but they are taken back, minimized, downplayed, or are followed by a positive wrap-up. There is evidence of rejection, lack of closeness to parents, or conflict with parents. However the interviewee does not feel that these experiences have had any effect upon her adult personality.

U/d. Unresolved for trauma (Main, Goldwyn, & Hesse, 2002).

Child: Linda 36-month-old female. Pre-Test Classification:B3
Subgroup B3.

The child actively seeks physical contact with the mother and resists her release of him. Occasionally, a child who seems especially secure in his relationship with his mother will be content with mere interaction with a proximity to her, without seeking to be held. There is little or no sign of either avoiding or resisting proximity with the mother. If he shows distress he is clearly more active in seeking contact and in resisting release than B1 or B2 children. Although his attachment behavior is heightened in the reunion episodes, he does not seem wholly preoccupied with his mother in the preseparation episodes (Cassidy & Marvin, 1992).

Case #2 ROBIN Post-Test

Case #2 ROBIN Post-Test

Experience Scales	M	F	GM
Loving	2	1	4
Rejecting	5	CR	1
Involving/Reversing	1	CR	1
Pressured to Achieve	1	CR	
Neglecting	7	CR	CR

States of Mind Respecting the Parents (or other persons)			
Idealizing	7	1	4
Involving Anger	1	1	1
Derogation	1	1	1

Overall States of Mind	
Overall Derogation of Attachment	1
Insistence on Lack of Recall	5
Metacognitive Processes	1
Passivity of Thought Processes	2
Fear of Loss	1
Highest Score for Unresolved Loss	6
Highest Score for Unresolved Trauma	1
Coherence of Transcript	3
Coherence of Mind	2

Classification
U/d/Ds3a
U/d. Unresolved for trauma
Ds3a.

The individual appears to recognize aspects of rejection and can discuss them with some resentment, however, these accounts of negative experiences are succeeded by "normalizing," with claims that these were good for them or gave them strength and they were not adversely affected (Main, Goldwyn, & Hesse, 2002).

Child: Linda 42-month-old female Post-Test Classification: B1
Secure-Reserved
B1. Secure-reserved

This child may appear slow to warm up with minimal response at first and long periods of not looking or orienting. Soon, however the child warms up, and behaves toward the parent in a secure manner. Initial avoidance lasts 15–30 seconds (Cassidy & Marvin, 1992).

Case #3 ROSE Pre-Test

Case #3 ROSE Pre-Test

Experience Scales	M	F	Other
Loving	2	3	4 2
Rejecting	4	1	CR 1
Involving/Reversing	(3)	2	1 1
Pressured to Achieve	1	1	1 1
Neglecting	1	1	1 1

States of Mind Respecting the Parents (or other persons)		
Idealizing	3	4(gm) 5(gf) 5(a) 2(u)
Involving Anger	4	5(gm) 4(gf) 1(a) 1(u)
Derogation	1	1(gm) 1(gf) 1(a) a(u)

Overall States of Mind	
Overall Derogation of Attachment	1
Insistence on Lack of Recall	5
Metacognitive Processes	1
Passivity of Thought Processes	2
Fear of Loss	1
Highest Score for Unresolved Loss	5
Highest Score for Unresolved Trauma	CR
Coherence of Transcript	3
Coherence of Mind	3

Classification
U/d/CC/D3/E2
U/d. Unresolved for trauma
CC. Cannot classify
Ds3: Restricted in feeling
   Transcripts are placed in this category when the interviewee describes experiences of hurt feelings and resentments but they are taken back, minimized, downplayed, or are followed by a positive wrap-up. There is evidence of rejection, lack of closeness to parents, or conflict with parents. However the interviewee does not feel that these experiences have had any effect upon her adult personality.
E2. Angry/conflicted
   High scores for involving/preoccupying anger with respect to at least one parent with excessive blaming Main, Goldwyn, & hesse, 2002).
Child: Abby 40-month-old female. Pre-Test Classification: C1
Subgroup C1.
   Proximity seeking and contact maintaining are strong in the reunion episodes, and are also more likely to occur in the pre-separation episodes. Resistant behavior is particularly conspicuous. The mixture of seeking and yet resisting contact and interaction has an unmistakably angry quality and indeed an angry tone may characterize behavior even in the pre-separation episodes (Cassidy & Marvin, 1992).
Case #3 ROSE Post-Test

Case #3 ROSE Post-Test

Experience Scales	M	F	GM
Loving	1	3	1
Rejecting	8	1	CR
Involving/Reversing	1	3	CR
Pressured to Achieve	9	1	CR
Neglecting	9	1	CR

States of Mind Respecting the Parents (or other persons)			
Idealizing	3	4	1
Involving Anger	6	1	8
Derogation	1	1	1

Overall States of Mind	
Overall Derogation of Attachment	1
Insistence on Lack of Recall	2
Metacognitive Processes	1
Passivity of Thought Processes	3.5
Fear of Loss	1
Highest Score for Unresolved Loss	5
Highest Score for Unresolved Trauma	6
Coherence of Transcript	3
Coherence of Mind	3

Classification
U/d/E2
U/d. Unresolved for trauma
E2. Angry/conflicted
　　High scores for involving/preoccupying anger with respect to at least one parent with excessive blaming (Main, Goldwyn, & Hesse, 2002).
Child: Abby 45-month-old female Post-Test Classification: C1
Ambivalent-Resistant
Subgroup C1. Ambivalent-resistant
　　Proximity seeking and contact maintaining are strong in the reunion episodes, and are also more likely to occur in the pre-separation episodes. Resistant behavior is particularly conspicuous. The mixture of seeking and yet resisting contact and interaction has an unmistakably angry quality and indeed an angry tone may characterize behavior even in the pre-separation episodes (Cassidy & Marvin, 1992).
Case #4 Diana Pre-Test

Case #4 Diana Pre-Test

Experience Scales	M	F	GM
Loving	5	2.5	1
Rejecting	3	3	CR
Involving/Reversing	4	1	CR
Pressured to Achieve	1	1	1
Neglecting	2	2	CR

States of Mind Respecting the Parents (or other persons)

Idealizing	1	4	4
Involving Anger	3	1	8
Derogation	1	1	1

Overall States of Mind

Overall Derogation of Attachment	1
Insistence on Lack of Recall	2
Metacognitive Processes	1
Passivity of Thought Processes	5
Fear of Loss	1
Highest Score for Unresolved Loss	3
Highest Score for Unresolved Trauma	CR
Coherence of Transcript	3
Coherence of Mind	3

Classification E2

E2. Angry/conflicted

High scores for involving/preoccupying anger with respect to at least one parent with excessive blaming (Main, Goldwyn, & Hesse, 2002).

Child: Mindy 19-month-old female. Pre-Test Classification: B3/B4

Subgroup B3.

The child actively seeks physical contact with the mother and resists her release of him. Occasionally, a child who seems especially secure in his relationship with his mother will be content with mere interaction with a proximity to her, without seeking to be held. There is little or no sign of either avoiding or resisting proximity with the mother. If he shows distress he is clearly more active in seeking contact and in resisting release than B1 or B2 children. Although his attachment behavior is heightened in the reunion episodes, he does not seem wholly preoccupied with his mother in the pre-separation episodes.

Subgroup B4. Secure-ambivalent

These children are generally secure with elements of immature, dependent, ambivalent, or resistant behaviors (Ainsworth, Blehar, Waters, & Wall, 1978).

Case #4 Diana Post-Test

Case #4 Diana Post-Test

Experience Scales	M	GM	GF	GGM	SF
Loving	2	5	3	3	3
Rejecting	9	1	CR	CR	CR
Involving/Reversing	1	1	CR	CR	1
Pressured to Achieve	1	1	CR	CR	1
Neglecting	CR	CR	CR	CR	1

States of Mind Respecting the Parents (or other persons)

Idealizing	3	1	3	1	3
Involving Anger	1	3	1	1	1
Derogation	1	1	1	1	1

Overall States of Mind

Overall Derogation of Attachment	1
Insistence on Lack of Recall	3
Metacognitive Processes	1
Passivity of Thought Processes	2
Fear of Loss	1
Highest Score for Unresolved Loss	2
Highest Score for Unresolved Trauma	NA
Coherence of Transcript	6
Coherence of Mind	6

Classification: E1/F2

E1. Passive

There is an implied passivity or vagueness of thought processes regarding experiences of childhood. There is a weak, vague, or incomplete presentation of self or personal identity and a tendency to remain unfocused.

F2. Somewhat dismissive or restricting of attachment (Main, Goldwyn, & Hesse, 2002).

Child: Mindy 25-month-old female Post-Test Classification: D/CC/A2/B2

Subgroup D. Disorganized

These children show a disordering of expected temporal sequences, incomplete or undirected movements and expressions, direct indices of confusion and apprehension, dazed and disoriented expressions, and indices of depressed affect.

CC: Cannot classify

Subgroup A2

This child demonstrates a mixed response to his mother on reunion. He both attempts to greet her and turns away from her. He may move past her and avert his gaze from her or even ignore her. There is proximity seeking and avoidance simultaneously.

Subgroup B2

The child greets the mother and tends to approach her and seems to want contact with her but not to the extent of a B3 child. He tends to show little distress during separation episodes.

Case #5 HELEN Pre-Test

Case #5 HELEN Pre-Test

Experience Scales	M	F	Other (brother)
Loving	1	(CR)	1
Rejecting	9	(5)	CR
Involving/Reversing	1	(CR)	(CR)
Pressured to Achieve	1	(CR)	(CR)
Neglecting	9	(CR)	(CR)

States of Mind Respecting the Parents (or other persons)

Idealizing	3	3	CR
Involving Anger	5	1	9
Derogation	1	1	1

Overall States of Mind

Overall Derogation of Attachment	1
Insistence on Lack of Recall	2
Metacognitive Processes	1
Passivity of Thought Processes	CR
Fear of Loss	1
Highest Score for Unresolved Loss	1
Highest Score for Unresolved Trauma	7
Coherence of Transcript	1
Coherence of Mind	1

Classification
U/d/E2/E3a/E1
U/d. Unresolved for trauma
E2. Angry/conflicted

High scores for involving/preoccupying anger with respect to at least one parent with excessive blaming.

E3a. Fearfully preoccupied by traumatic events

Confused, fearful and overwhelmed by traumatic/frightening experiences. When the individual speaks about her traumatic experiences they are incoherent.

E1. Passive

There is an implied passivity or vagueness of thought processes regarding experiences of childhood. There is a weak, vague, or incomplete presentation of self or personal identity and a tendency to remain unfocused (Main, Goldwyn, & Hesse, 2002).

Child: (this child did not receive a pre-test because of unforeseen complications with the mother's situation)

Case #5 HELEN Post-Test

Case #5 HELEN Post-Test

Experience Scales	M	F	Other (brother)
Loving	1	3	1
Rejecting	8	1	CR
Involving/Reversing	1	3	CR
Pressured to Achieve	9	1	CR
Neglecting	9	1	CR

States of Mind Respecting the Parents (or other persons)			
Idealizing	3	4	1
Involving Anger	6	1	8
Derogation	1	1	1

Overall States of Mind	
Overall Derogation of Attachment	1
Insistence on Lack of Recall	2
Metacognitive Processes	1
Passivity of Thought Processes	3.5
Fear of Loss	1
Highest Score for Unresolved Loss	5
Highest Score for Unresolved Trauma	6
Coherence of Transcript	3
Coherence of Mind	3

Classification
U/d/E2
U/d. Unresolved for trauma
E2. Angry/conflicted
High scores for involving/preoccupying anger with respect to at least one parent with excessive blaming (Main, Goldwyn, & Hesse, 2002).
Child: Erin Post-Test Classification: B1
B1. Secure-reserved
This child may appear slow to warm up with minimal response at first and long periods of not looking or orienting. Soon, however the child warms up, and behaves toward the parent in a secure manner. Initial avoidance lasts 15–30 seconds (Cassidy & Marvin, 1992).

References

Ainsworth, M., Blehar, M., Waters, E., & Wall, S. (1978). *Patterns of attachment*. Hillsdale, NJ: Lawrence Erlbaum.

Bacon, H., & Richardson, S. (2001). Attachment theory and child abuse: An overview of the literature for practitioners. *Child Abuse Review, 10*, 377–397.

Bakermans-Kranenburg, M., Van Ijzendoorn, M., Juffer, F. (2003). Less is more: Meta-analyses of sensitivity and attachment interventions in early childhood. *Psychological Bulletin, 129*(2), 195–215.

Bassuk, E. L., Weinreb, L. F., Dawson, R., Perloff, J. N., & Buckner, J. C. (1997). Determinants of behavior in homeless and low-income housed preschool children. *Pediatrics, 100*(1), 92–100.

Bassuk, E. L., Rubin, L. & Lauriat, A. S. (1986). Characteristics of sheltered homeless families. *American Journal of Public Health, 76*(9), 1097–1101.

Bassuk E., & Rubin, L. (1987). Homeless children: A neglected population. *American Journal of Orthopsychiatry, 57*(2), 279–286.

Baumohl, J. (Ed.) (1996). *Homelessness in America.* Arizona: The Oryx Press.

Bayley, N. (1993). *Bayley scales of infant development-II.* New York: Psychological Corporation.

Becker, S. K. (1994). *Relationship patterns among homeless and housed African American single mothers: A study of adult attachment and social support.* Unpublished manuscript, University of Miami.

Beebe, B., Lachmann, F., & Jaffe, J. (1997). Mother-infant interaction structures and presymbolic self and object representations. *Psychoanalytic Dialogues, 7*, 133–182.

Beebe, B., & Sloate, P. (1982). Assessment and treatment of difficulties in mother-infant attunement in the first three years of life: A case history. *Psychoanalytic Inquiry, 1*(4), 601–623.

Beebe, B. (1985). Interpersonal timing: The application of an adult dialogue model to mother-infant vocal and kinesic interactions. In T. Field & N. A. Fox (Eds.), *Social perceptions in infants.* Ablex Pub. Corp.

Beebe, B. (2000). Co-constructing mother-infant distress. *Psychoanalytic Inquiry, 20*, 421–440.

Beebe, B. (2003). Brief mother-infant treatment using psychoanalytically informed video microanalysis. *Infant Mental Health Journal, 24*(1), 24–52.

Beebe, B. (2006). Co-constructing mother-infant distress in face-to-face interactions: Contributions of microanalysis. *Infant Observation, 9*(2), 151–164.

Beebe, B., (2007). Mother-infant research informs mother-infant treatment. *Psychoanalytic Study of the Child, 60*, 7–46.

Beebe, B., Rustin, J., Sorter, D., Knoblauch, S. (2003). *Psychoanalytic Dialogues, 13*(6), 805–841.

Beebe, B., & Lachmann, F. M. (1994). Representations and internalizations in infancy: Three principles of salience. *Psychoanalytic Psychology, 11*, 127–165.

Beebe, B., & Lachmann, F. M. (1988). The contribution of mother-infant influences to the origins of self- and object representations. *Psychoanalytic Psychology, 6*, 305–337.

Beebe, B. & Lachmann, F. M. (1998). Co-constructing inner and relational processes: Self- and mutual regulation in infant research and adult treatment. *Psychoanalytic Psychology, 15*, 480–516.

Bowlby, J. (1960). Grief and mourning in infancy and early childhood. *Psychoanalytic Study of the Child, 15*, 9–52.

Bowlby, J. (1969). *Attachment and loss. Vol. 1, Attachment.* New York: Basic Books.

Bowlby, J. (1973). *Attachment and loss. Vol. 2: Separation, anxiety and anger.* New York: Basic Books.

Bowlby, J. (1979). *The making and breaking of affectional bonds.* London: Tavistock.

Bowlby, J. (1982). *Attachment: Attachment and loss Vol. I, 2nd ed.* London: The Hogarth Press.

Bowlby, J. (1988). *A secure base: Parent-child attachment and healthy human development.* New York: Basic Books.

Brazelton, T. B. (1994). Touchpoints: Opportunities for preventing problems in the parent-child relationship. *Acta Paediatrica, 394*(Suppl.), 35–39.

Brazelton, T., & Tronick, E. (1980). Preverbal communication between mothers and infants. In D. R. Olson (Ed.), *The social foundations of language and thought* (pp. 299–315). New York: Norton.

Brinich, P. M. (1982). Rituals and meanings—The emergence of mother-child communication. *The Psychoanalytic Study of the Child, 37*, 3–14.

Brisch K. H. (2002). *Treating attachment disorders from theory to therapy.* London: The Guilford Press.

Call, J. (1963). Prevention of autism in a young infant in a well-child conference. *Journal of the American Academy of Child Psychiatry, 2*, 451–459.

Cassidy, J., & Marvin, R. S. (1992). *Attachment organization in preschool children: Procedures and coding manual.* Unpublished manuscript.

Castelnuovo-Tedesco, P. (1994). The "widening scope" reconsidered: Where do psychoanalysis and psychoanalytic psychotherapy meet? *The Psychoanalytic Study of the Child, 49*, 159–174.

Cicchetti, D., Toth, S. L., & Rogosch, F. A. (1999). Toddler-parent psychotherapy as a preventive intervention to alter attachment organization in offspring of depressed mothers. *Attachment and Human Development, 1*, 34–66.

Coen, S. J. (1997). How to help patients (and analysts) bear the unbearable. *Journal of the American Psychoanalytic Association, 45*(4), 1183–1207.

Coen, S. J. (2001). How much does the analyst at work need to feel? Unpublished paper.

Cohen, N. J., Lojkasek, M., Muir, R., & Parker, C. J. (2002). Six-month follow-up of two mother-infant psychotherapies: Convergence of therapeutic outcomes. *Infant Mental Health Journal, 23*, 361–380.

Connell, J. P., & Goldsmith, H. H. (1982). A structural modeling approach to the study of attachment and strange situation behaviors. In R. N. Emde & R. J. Harmon (Eds.), *The development of attachment and affiliative Systems* (pp. 213–243). New York: Plenum.

Cramer, B., Robert-Tissot, C., Stern, D., Serpa-Rusconi, S., De Muralt, M., Besson, G. (1990). Outcome evaluation in brief mother-infant psychotherapy: A preliminary report. *Infant Mental Health Journal, 11*(3), 278–300.

Eagle, M. (1995). The developmental perspectives of attachment and psychoanalytic theory. In S. Goldberg, R. Muir, & J. Kerr (Eds.), *Attachment theory social, developmental, and clinical perspectives.* Hillsdale, NJ: The Analytic Press.

Emde, R. N. (1985). Maternal emotional signaling: Its effect on visual cliff behavior of 1-year-olds. *Developmental Psychology, 21*, 195–200.

Erikson, E. (1950). *Childhood and society.* New York: Norton.

Erle, J. B., and Goldberg, D. A. (1984). Observations on assessment of analyzability by experienced analysts. *Journal of the American Psychoanalytic Association, 32*(4), 715–737.

Field, T., Healy, B., Goldstein, S., Perry, D., Bendell, D., Schanberg S. (1988). Infants of depressed mothers show "depressed" behavior even with nondepressed adults. *Child Development, 59*, 1569–1579.

Fonagy, P., Steele, H., Steele, M. (1991). Maternal representations of attachment during pregnancy predict the organization of infant-mother attachment at one year of age. *Child Development, 62*, 891–905.

Fonagy, P., & Target, M. (1997). Attachment and reflective function: Their role in self-organization. *Development and Psychopathology, 9*, 679–700.

Fonagy, P., & Target, M. (1998). Mentalization and the changing aims of child psychoanalysis. *Psychoanalytic Dialogues, 8*, 87–114.

Fonagy, P., Gergely, G., Jurist, E., & Target, M. (2002). *Affect regulation, mentalization, and the development of the self.* New York: Other Books.

Fonagy, P., Steele, M., Steele, H., Leigh, T., Kennedy, R., Mattoon, G., & Target, M. (1995). Attachment, the reflective self, and borderline states: The predictive specificity of the adult attachment interview and pathological emotional development. In S. Goldberg, R., Muir, & J. Kerr (Eds.) *Attachment theory: Social, developmental and clinical perspectives* (pp. 223–279). Hillsdale, NJ: Analytic Press.

Fonagy, P., Target, M., Gergely, G., Allen, J. G., Bateman, A. W. (2003). The developmental roots of borderline personality disorder in early attachment relationships. *Psychoanalytic Inquiry, 23*(3), 412–459.

Fonagy, P. (2001). In F. A. Henn, N. Sartorius, H. Helmchen, & H. Lauter (Eds.), *Contemporary psychiatry*. Berlin: Springer.

Fraiberg, S. (1959). *The magic years*. New York: Simon & Schuster.

Fraiberg, S. (1971). Intervention in infancy: A program for blind infants. *Journal of the American Academy of Child Psychiatry, 10*(3), 381–405.

Fraiberg, S. (1980). *Clinical studies in infant mental health: The first year of life*. New York: Basic Books.

Fraiberg, S. (1982). Pathological defenses in infancy. *Psychoanalytic Quarterly, LI*, 612–635.

Fraiberg, S., Adelson, E., & Shapiro, V. (1975). Ghosts in the nursery: A psychoanalytic approach to the problem of impaired infant-mother relationships. *Journal of the American Academy of Child Psychiatry, 14*(3), 387–421.

Freud, S. (1923). *The ego and the id*. S.E., v. XIX, p. 26.

Freud, A. (1965). *Normality and pathology in childhood*. New York: International Universities Press.

George, C., & Solomon, J. (1999). Attachment and caregiving: The caregiving behavioral system. In J. Cassidy & P. H. Shaver (Eds.), *Handbook of attachment theory, research, and clinical applications* (pp. 649–670). New York: The Guilford Press.

George, C., Kaplan, N., & Main, M. (1996). *Adult attachment interview*. Department of Psychology, University of California, Berkeley, California.

Gianino, A., & Tronick, E. Z. (Eds.) (1988). The mutual regulation model: The infant's self and interactive regulation and coping and defensive capacities. Hillsdale, NJ: Lawrence Erlbaum.

Greenacre, P. (1971). *Emotional growth*. New York: International Universities Press.

Greenspan, S. (1981). *Psychopathology and adaptation in infancy and early childhood: Principals of clinical diagnosis and preventive intervention*. New York: International Universities Press.

Greenspan, S. (1990). Comprehensive clinical approaches to infants and families. In S. Meisels & J. Shonkoff (Eds.), *Handbook of early interventions*. New York: Cambridge University Press.

Greenspan, S. I. (1981). *Psychopathology and adaptation in infancy and early childhood. Principles of clinical diagnosis and preventive intervention*. International Universities Press.

Grice, H. (1975). Logic and conversation. In P. Cole & J. L. Moran (Eds.), *Syntax and semantics* (pp. 41–58). New York: Academic Press.

Gross, D., & Grady, J. (2002) Group-based parent training for preventing mental health disorders in children. *Issues in Mental Health Nursing*.

Gossett, O. M. (2004). *Maternal attachment, depression, and caregiving: Relationships with child behavior in homeless mothers of toddlers*. Unpublished manuscript, University of South Carolina.

Hardy, L. T. (2007). Attachment theory and reactive attachment disorder: Theoretical perspectives and treatment implications. *Journal of Child and Adolescent Psychiatric Nursing, 20*(1), 27–39.

Harrison, A. M. (2005). Herding the animals into the barn: A parent consultation model. *The Psychoanalytic Study of the Child, 60*, 128–153.

Harrison, A. M., & Tronick, E. Z. (2011). "The noise monitor": A developmental perspective on verbal and nonverbal meaning-making in psychoanalysis. *Journal of the American Psychoanalytic Association, 59*(5), 961–982.

Harwood, I. (2006). Head start is too late: Integrating and applying infant observation studies, and attachment, trauma, and neurobiological research to groups with pregnant and new mothers. *International Journal of Group Psychotherapy, 56*(1), 5–15.

Heinicke, C., Fineman, N., Ruth, G., Recchia, L., Guthrie, D., & Rodning, C. (1999). Relationship-based intervention with at-risk first time mothers: Outcome in the first year of life. *Infant Mental Health Journal, 20*, 349–374.

Heinicke, C., Fineman, N., Ponce, V. A., &Guthrie, D. (2001). Relation-based intervention with at-risk mothers: Outcomes in the second year of life. *Infant Mental Health Journal, 22*, 431–462.

Hesse, E., (1999). The adult attachment interview historical and current perspectives. J. Cassidy & P. R. Shaver (Eds.), *Handbook of attachment theory, research, and clinical applications* (pp. 395–433). New York: The Guilford Press.

Hesse, E., & Main, M. (2000). Disorganized infant, child, and adult attachment: Collapse in behavioral and attentional strategies. *Journal of the American Psychoanalytic Association, 48*(4), 1017–1127.

Hesse, E., & Main, M. (2006). Frightened, threatening, and dissociative parental behavior in low-risk samples: Description, discussion, and interpretations. *Development and Psychopathology, 18*, 309–343.

Hodnicki, D. R., & Horner, S. D. (1993). Homeless mothers' caring for children in a shelter. *Issues Mental Health Nursing, 14*(4), 349–356.

Hofacker, N., & Papousek, M. (1998). Disorders of excessive crying, feeding, and sleeping: The Munich interdisciplinary research and intervention program. *Infant Mental Health Journal, 19*(2), 180–201.

Hopkins, J. (1992). Infant and parent psychotherapy. *Journal of Child Psychotherapy, 18*(1), 5–19.

Hughes, D.A. (1997). *Facilitating developmental attachment*. Northvale, NJ: Jason Aronson.

Jaffe, J., Beebe, B., Feldstein, S., Crown, C. L. & Jasnow, M. D. (2001). Rhythms of dialogue in infancy. *Monogr. Soc. Res. Child Dev., 66*(2).

Kachele, H., Buchheim, A., Schmucker, G., Brisch, K. H. (2001). Development, attachment and relationship: New psychoanalytic concepts: In F. A. Henn, N. Sartorius, H. Helmchen, & H. Lauter (Eds.), *Contemporary psychiatry*. Berlin: Springer.

Karen, R. (1998). *Becoming attached: First relationships and how they shape our capacity to love.* New York: Warner Books.

Kennedy, H., & Moran, G. (1991). Reflections on the aim of child analysis. *The Psychoanalytic Study of the Child, 46*, 181–198.

Kohut, H. (1971). *The analysis of the self.* New York: International Universities Press.

Koplow, L. (Ed.). (1996). *Unsmiling faces.* New York: Teachers College Press.

Kris, A. O. (1956). The recovery of childhood memories in psychoanalysis. *The Psychoanalytic Study of the Child, 11*, 54–88.

Krystal, H. (1978). Trauma and affects. *Psychoanalytic Study of the Child, 33*, 81–116.

Lieberman, A. F. (1997). Toddlers' internalizations of maternal attributions as a factor in quality of attachment. In K. Zucker & L. Atkinson (Eds.), *Attachment and psychopathology* (pp. 277–290). New York: Guilford Press.

Lieberman, A. F. (1999). Negative maternal attributions: Effects on toddlers' sense of self. *Psychoanalytic Inquiry, 19*, 737–765.

Lieberman, A. F., Weston, D., & Pawl, J. (1991). Preventive intervention and outcome with anxiously attached dyads. *Child Development, 62*, 199–209.

Lieberman, A., & Pawl, J. (1993). Infant-parent psychotherapy. In C. Zeanah (Ed.), *Handbook of infant mental health* (pp. 427–442). New York: Guilford Press.

Lieberman, A. F., Silverman, R., & Pawl, J. (1999). Infant-parent psychotherapy: Core concepts and current approaches. In C. Zeanah (Ed.), *Handbook of infant mental health* (pp. 472–485). New York: Guilford Press.

Lyons-Ruth, K., Connell, D. B., & Grunebaum, H. U. (1990). Infants at social risk: Maternal depression and family support services as mediators of infant development and security of attachment. *Child Development, 61*, 85–98.

Lyons-Ruth, K. (1998). Attachment disorganization: Unresolved loss, relational violence, and lapses in behavioral and attentional strategies. In J. Cassidy & P. Shaver (Eds.), *Handbook of attachment theory and research* (pp. 520–554). New York: Guilford Press.

MacPhee, D., Fritz, J., & Miller-Heyl, J. (1996). Ethnic variations in personal social networks and parenting. *Child Development, 67*, 3278–3295.

Mahler, M. S. (1952). On child psychosis and schizophrenia. *The Psychoanalytic Study of the Child, 7,* 286–305.

Mahler, M. S. (1963). Thoughts about development and individuation. *The Psychoanalytic Study of the Child, 18*, 307–324.

Mahler, M. S. (1968). *On human symbiosis and the vicissitudes of individuation.* New York: International University Press.

Mahler, M., Pine, F., Bergman, A. (1975). *The psychological birth of the human infant.* New York: Basic Books.

Main, M. (1991). Metacognitive knowledge, metacognitive monitoring, and singular (coherent) vs. multiple (incoherent) model of attachment: Findings and directions for future research. In C. M. Parkes, J. Stevenson-Hinde, P. Marris (Eds.), *Attachment across the life cycle* (pp. 127–159). London: Routledge.

Main, M. (1995). Recent studies in attachment: Overview with selected implications for clinical work. In S. Goldberg , R. Muir, J. Kerr (Eds), *Attachment theory: Social development and clinical perspectives.* Hillsdale, NJ: Lawrence Erlbaum.

Main, M. (1996). Introduction to the special section on attachment and psychopathology: 2. Overview of the field of attachment. *Journal of Consulting and Clinical Psychology, 64*, 237–243.

Main, M. (2000). The organized categories of infant, child, and adult attachment: Flexible vs. inflexible attention under attachment-related stress. *Journal of the American Psychoanalytic Association, 48*(4), 1055–1096.

Malphurs, J., Field, T., Larraine, C., Pickens, J., Pelaez-Noguras, M., Yando, R. (1996). Altering withdrawn and intrusive interaction behaviors in depressed mothers. *Infant Mental Health Journal, 17*(2), 152–160.

Marvin, R. S., & Whelan, W. F. (2003). Disordered attachments: Toward evidence-based clinical practice. *Attachment & Human Development, 5*, 283–288.

Marvin, R., Cooper, G., Hoffman, K., Powell, B. (2002). The circle of security project: Attachment-based intervention with caregiver-pre-school dyads. *Attachment & Human Development, 4*(1), 107–124.

McDonough, S. (1993). Interaction guidance. In C. Zeanah (Ed.), *Handbook of infant mental health* (pp. 414–426). New York: Guilford Press.

Meadows, O. M. (2003). Mothering in public: A meta-synthesis of homeless women with children living in shelters. *J Spec Pediatr Nurs, 8*(4), 130–136.

Meltzoff, A. N. (1990). Foundations for developing a concept of self: The role of imitation in relating self to other and the value of social mirroring, social modeling and self-practice in infancy. In D. Cicchetti & M. Beeghly (Eds.), *The self in transition.* Chicago, IL: University of Chicago Press.

Meltzoff, A. N., & Moore, M. K. (1977). Imitation of facial and manual gestures by human neonates. *Science, 198*, 75–78.

Meltzoff, A. N., & Moore, M. K. (1989). Imitation in newborn infants: Exploring the range of gestures imitated and the underlying mechanisms. *Developmental Psychology, 25*, 954–962.

Meltzoff, A. N., & Moore, M. K. (1998). Object representation, identity, and the paradox of early permanence: Steps toward a new framework. *Infant Behavior and Development, 21*(2), 201–235.

Menke, E. M., & Wagner, J. D. (1997). A comparative study of homeless, previously homeless, and never homeless school-aged children's health. *Comprehensive Pediatric Nursing, 20*, 153–173.

Minde, K. (2003). Assessment and treatment of attachment disorders. *Current Opinion in Psychiatry, 16*, 377–381.

Moran, G., Neufeld Bailey, H., Gleason, K., DeOliveira, C. A., & Pererson, D. R. (2007). Exploring the mind behind unresolved attachment: Lessons from and for attachment-based interventions with infants and their traumatized mothers. In H. Steele & M. Steele (Eds.), *Clinical applications of the adult attachment interview* (pp. 371–398). New York: Guilford Press.

Morton, J., & Johnson, M. H. (1991). Conspec and Conlearn: A two-process theory of infant face recognition. *Psychological Review, 98*(2), 164–181.

Murphy, L. B., Mintzer, D., and Lipsitt, L. L. (1989). Psychoanalytic views of infancy. In S. I. Greenspan and G. H. Pollock (Eds.), *The Course of Life, Vol. I: Infancy* (pp. 561–641).

Nylan, K. J, Moran, T. E., Franklin, C. L., O'Hara, M. (2006). Maternal depression: A review of relevant treatment approaches for mothers and infants. *Infant Mental Health Journal, 27*(4), 327–343.

Parens, H. (1979). *The development of aggression in early childhood.* Northvale, NJ: Jason Aronson.

Parens, H., Pollock, L., Stern, J. & Kramer, S. (1976). On the girl's entry into the Oedipus complex. *Journal of the American Psychoanalytic Association, 27*(suppl.), 79–107.

Paret, I. H., Shapiro, V. B. (1998). The splintered holding environment and the vulnerable ego. *The Psychoanalytic Study of the Child, 53*, 300–324.

Peters, R. D., Petrunka, K., Arnold, R. (2003). The better beginnings, better futures project: A Universal, comprehensive, community-based prevention approach for primary school children and their families. *Journal of Clinical Child and Adolescent Psychology, 32*(2), 215–227.

Pinderhughes, E. (1995). Empowering diverse populations: Family practice in the 21st century. *Families in Society, 76*(3), 131–140.

Pine, F. (1992). Some refinements of the separation-individuation concept in light of research on infants. *The Psychoanalytic Study of the Child, 47,* 103–116.

Pine, F., & Furer, M. (1963). Studies of the separation-individuation phase: A methodological overview. *The Psychoanalytic Study of the Child, 18,* 325–342.

Provence, S. (Ed.) (1983). Infants and parents: Clinical case reports. *Clinical Infant Reports: The National Center for Clinical Infant Programs.* New York: International Universities Press.

Schechter, D. (2004). How post-traumatic stress affects mothers' perceptions of their babies: A brief video feedback intervention makes a difference. *Zero to Three,* 43–49.

Schore, A. N. (2002). Clinical implications of a psychoneurobiological model of projective identification. In S. Alhanti (Ed.), *Primitive mental states, Volume II: Psychobiological and psychoanalytic perspectives on early trauma and personality development* (pp. 1–66). New York: Karnac.

Schore, A. (1994). *Affect regulation and the origin of the self: The neurobiology of emotional development.* Hillsdale, NJ: Lawrence Erlbaum.

Schore, A. (2002). Advances in neuropsychoanalysis, attachment theory, and trauma research: Implications for self-psychology. *Psychoanalytic Inquiry, 22,* 433–484.

Seligman, S. (1994). Applying psychoanalysis in an unconventional context: Adapting infant-parent psychotherapy to a changing population. *Psychoanalytic Study of the Child, 49,* 481–510.

Shaver, P. R., & Cassidy, J. (Eds.) (1999). *Handbook of attachment: Theory, research, and clinical applications.* New York: Guilford.

Shopper, M. (1984). Psychopathology and adaptation in infancy and early childhood. Principles of clinical diagnosis and preventive intervention (review). *The Psychoanalytic Quarterly, 53,* 122–127.

Slade, A. (1998). Representation, symbolization, and affect regulation in the concomitant treatment of a mother and child: Attachment theory and child psychotherapy. *Psychoanalytic Dialogues, 8,* 797–830.

Slade, A. (2002). Keeping the baby in mind: A critical factor in perinatal mental. *Zero to Three* June/July.

Slade, A., Sadler, L., De Dios-Kenn, C., Webb, D., Currier-Ezepchick, J., & Mayes, L. (2006). *The Psychoanalytic Study of the Child, 60,* 74–100.

Spitz, R. A. (1945). Hospitalism. *The Psychoanalytic Study of the Child, 1,* 53–74.

Spitz, R. A. (1946). Anaclitic depression. *Psychoanalytic Study of the Child, 2,* 313–342.

Spitz, R. A., (1950). Relevancy of direct infant observation. *The Psychoanalytic Study of the Child, 5,* 66–73.

Spitz, R. A. (1965). *The first year of life. A psychoanalytic study of normal and deviant development of object relations.* New York: International Universities Press.

Spitz, R. (1983). The evolution of dialogue. In R. Emde (Ed.), *René Spitz: Dialogues from infancy, selected papers.* New York: International Universities Press.

Stern, D. (1985). *The interpersonal world of the infant.* New York: Basic Books.

Stern, D. (1995). *The motherhood constellation: A unified view of parent-infant psychotherapy.* New York: Basic Books.

Stern, D., Sander, L. W., Nahum, J. P., Harrison, A. M., Lyons-Ruth, K., Morgan, A. C., Bruschweilerstern, N., Tronick, E. Z. (1998). Non-interpretive mechanisms in psychoanalytic therapy: The "something more" than interpretation. *International Journal of Psychoanalysis, 79*, 903–921.

Stone, L. (1954). The widening scope of indications for psychoanalysis. *Journal of the American Psychoanalytic Association, 2*, 567–594.

Teicher, M. H., Anderon, S. L., Polcari, A., Anderson, C. M., Navalta, C. P., & Kim, D. M. (2003). The neurobiological consequences of early stress and childhood maltreatment. *Neuroscience & Biobehavioral Reviews, 27*, 33–44.

Thrasher, S. P., & Mowbray, C. T. (1995). A strengths perspective: An ethnographic study of homeless women with children. *Health Social Work, 20*(2), 93–101.

Trevarthen, C. (1979). Communication and cooperation in early infancy: A description of primary intersubjectivity. In M. Bullowa (Ed.), *Before speech: The beginning of interpersonal communication.* Cambridge: Cambridge University Press.

Tronick, E. Z., Als., H., Adamson, L., Wise, S., Brazelton, T. B. (1978). The infant's response to entrapment between contradictory messages in face-to-face interaction. *American Academy of Child Psychiatry, 17*, 1–13.

Tronick, E. Z. (1989). Emotions and emotional communication in infants. *Am. Psychol., 44*, 112–119.

Tronick, E. Z., and Weinberg, M. K. (1997). Depressed mothers and infants: Failure to form dyadic states of consciousness. In L. Murray and P. J. Cooper (Eds.), *Postpartum depression and child development* (pp. 54–81). New York: Guilford.

Van Den Boom, D. (1995). Do first-year intervention effects endure? Follow-up during toddlerhood of a sample of Dutch irritable infants. *Child Development, 66*, 1798–1816.

Van der Kolk, B. A., Relcovitz, D., Roth, S., Mandel, F. S. (1996). Dissociation, somatization, and affect dysregulation: The complexity of adaption to trauma. *The American Journal of Psychiatry, 153*(suppl.), 83–93.

Van Ijzendoorn, M. H. (1995). Adult attachment representations, parental responsiveness, and infant attachment: A meta-analysis on the predictive validity of the adult attachment interview. *Psychological Bulletin, 117*, 387–403.

Wagonfeld, S., & Emde, R. N. (1982). Anaclitic depression: A follow-up from infancy to puberty. *Psychoanalytic Study of the Child, 37*, 67–94.

Winnicott, D. W. (1960). The theory of the parent-infant relationship. *International Journal of Psychoanalysis, 41*, 585–595.

Winnicott, D. W.(1971). *Playing and reality.* New York: Basic Books.

Winnicott, D. W. (1974). Fear of breakdown. *International Journal of Psychoanalysis, 1*, 103–107.

Winnicott, D. W. (1987). *Babies and their mothers.* New York: Addison-Wesley.

Winnicott, D. W. (1996). *Thinking about children.* Reading, MA: Addison-Wesley.

Zeanah, C. H., Larrieu, J. A., Heller, S. S., Valliere, J. (2000). Infant-parent relationship assessment. C. H. Zeanah, Jr. (Ed.), *Handbook of infant mental health.* New York: Guilford Press.

Index

About the Author

Ann G. Smolen, PhD, is a training and supervising analyst in child, adolescent, and adult psychoanalysis and is on the faculty of The Psychoanalytic Center of Philadelphia. Dr. Smolen is the author of several articles and book chapters and has presented her clinical work both nationally and internationally. Dr. Smolen is in private practice in Ardmore, PA.

Alexandra M. Harrison, MD, is a training and supervising analyst at the Boston Psychoanalytic Society and Institute in adult and child and adolescent psychoanalysis; an assistant clinical professor of psychiatry, Harvard Medical School; and on the faculty of the Infant-Parent Mental Health Post Graduate Certificate Program at University of Massachusetts Boston. Dr. Harrison has a private practice in both adult and child psychoanalysis and psychiatry. In the context of visits to orphanages in Central America and India, Dr. Harrison has developed a model for mental health professionals in developed countries to volunteer their consultation services to caregivers of children in care in developing countries in the context of a long-term relationship with episodic visits and regular Skype and video contact.